A CONTINUATION
OF
SIR PHILIP SIDNEY'S
Arcadia

WOMEN WRITERS IN ENGLISH
1350–1850

GENERAL EDITORS
Susanne Woods and Elizabeth H. Hageman

MANAGING EDITOR
Julia Flanders

SECTION EDITORS
Patricia Caldwell
Stuart Curran
Margaret J. M. Ezell
Elizabeth H. Hageman

WOMEN WRITERS PROJECT
Brown University

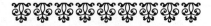

A Continuation
of
Sir Philip Sidney's
Arcadia

Anna Weamys

EDITED BY

Patrick Colborn Cullen

New York   Oxford

OXFORD UNIVERSITY PRESS

1994

OXFORD UNIVERSITY PRESS

Oxford   New York
Athens   Auckland   Bangkok   Bombay
Calcutta   Cape Town   Dar es Salaam   Delhi
Florence   Hong Kong   Istanbul   Karachi
Kuala Lumpur   Madras   Madrid   Melbourne
Mexico City   Nairobi   Paris   Singapore
Taipei   Tokyo   Toronto

and associated companies in
Berlin   Ibadan

Published by Oxford University Press, Inc.,
200 Madison Avenue, New York, New York 10016

Oxford is a registered trademark of Oxford University Press

Library of Congress Cataloging-in-Publication Data

Weamys, Anna, b. ca. 1630.
A continuation of Sir Philip Sidney's "Arcadia"/
Anna Weamys; edited by Patrick Colborn Cullen.
p.   cm. -- (Women writers in English 1350–1850)
Includes bibliographical references.
I. Cullen, Patrick, 1940–   . II. Sidney, Philip, Sir, 1554–1586. Arcadia. III. Title. IV. Series.
PR3763.W25C66   1994   823'.4—dc20   94-18534
ISBN 0-19-507884-5 (cloth)
ISBN 0-19-508719-4 (paper)

This volume was supported in part by the National Endowment
for the Humanities, an independent federal agency.

Printing (last digit): 9   8   7   6   5   4   3   2   1

Printed in the United States of America
on acid-free paper

For Hope Colborn Cullen

and

The Excellent Women of Crisfield

CONTENTS

A Continuation of Sir Philip Sidney's *Arcadia*

A map of the ancient world appears on page 213.

FOREWORD

Women Writers in English 1350–1850 presents texts of cultural and literary interest in the English-speaking tradition, often for the first time since their original publication. Most of the writers represented in the series were well known and highly regarded until the professionalization of English studies in the later nineteenth century coincided with their excision from canonical status and from the majority of literary histories.

The purpose of this series is to make available a wide range of unfamiliar texts by women, thus challenging the common assumption that women wrote little of real value before the Victorian period. While no one can doubt the relative difficulty women experienced in writing for an audience before that time, or indeed have encountered since, this series shows that women nonetheless had been writing from early on and in a variety of genres, that they maintained a clear eye to readers, and that they experimented with an interesting array of literary strategies for claiming their authorial voices. Despite the tendency to treat the powerful fictions of Virginia Woolf's *A Room of One's Own* (1928) as if they were fact, we now know, against her suggestion to the contrary, that there were many "Judith Shakespeares," and that not all of them died lamentable deaths before fulfilling their literary ambitions.

This series is unique in at least two ways. It offers, for the first time, concrete evidence of a rich and lively heritage of women writing in English before the mid-nineteenth century, and it is based on one of the most sophisticated and forward-looking electronic resources in the world: the Brown University Women Writers Project textbase (full text database) of works by early women writers. The Brown University Women Writers Project (WWP) was established in 1988 with a grant from the National Endowment for the Humanities, which continues to assist in its development.

Women Writers in English 1350–1850 is a print publication project derived from the WWP. It offers lightly annotated versions based on single good copies or, in some cases, collated versions of texts with more complex editorial histories, normally in their original spelling. The editions are aimed at a wide audience, from the informed undergraduate through professional students of literature, and they attempt to include the general reader who is interested in exploring a fuller tradition of early texts in English than has been available through the almost exclusively male canonical tradition.

SUSANNE WOODS
ELIZABETH H. HAGEMAN
General Editors

ACKNOWLEDGMENTS

The tremendous collaborative effort that is the Women Writers Project thrives on the contributions of all its members; I can hardly say enough here to acknowledge everyone who deserves thanks and recognition. In particular the students whose energy and enthusiasm have sustained the Project over the years are by now far too numerous to list by name.

Ongoing thanks are due to Brown University and to its administrators for their continued support, especially President Vartan Gregorian, Provost Frank Rothman, Dean of the Faculty Bryan Shepp, and Vice President Brian Hawkins. We are also very grateful to the Brown English Department and in particular to Elizabeth Kirk, Stephen Foley, and Marilyn Netter. In Brown's Computing and Information Services Don Wolfe and Geoffrey Bilder have helped and sustained the Project as well.

I have been delighted to work with our associates at Oxford University Press, Elizabeth Maguire, Claude Conyers, Jeff Edelstein, and Ellen Barrie, who have been so generous with their creativity and patience.

It is hard to imagine a more committed set of colleagues than the Women Writers Project staff. Carole Mah, Maria Fish, and Elizabeth Adams have been true comrades, tireless and inspiring in their efforts. Many thanks are due to Syd Bauman, who continues to guide us expertly through the intricacies of the computer. Thanks go as well to Elaine Brennan for her work in establishing this volume and the series itself, and for bringing the Women Writers Project so far. Others who have helped make this series possible include Anthony Arnove, Rebecca Bailey, Kim Bordner, Susie Castellanos, Cathleen Drake, Faye Halpern, John Marx, Jennifer Reid, Caleb Rounds, Elizabeth Terzakis, Andrea Weisman, and Kristen Whissel. Sarah Brown deserves special thanks for her help all along the way. Finally, all of us owe a great debt of affection and gratitude to our local co-director, Allen Renear, whose energy and vision inspire us all.

JULIA FLANDERS
Managing Editor

ACKNOWLEDGMENTS

This book would not be in your hands were it not for the Women Writers Project; in particular, without Julia Flanders, Elaine Brennan, Susanne Woods, Elizabeth Hageman, and Margaret Ezell, Anna Weamys would not have this opportunity to be read again. Margaret Ezell lent not only her own time and acumen to this project but also the services of her own sharp-eyed graduate assistant, Blake Bickham.

The very existence of the Society for the Study of Women in the Renaissance (New York) has been a source of encouragement, but I am especially indebted to Betty Travitsky, Joan Hartman, and Margaret Mikesell.

For access to editions of Weamys, I am grateful to the Folger Shakespeare Library, the Harvard University Library, the Beinecke Library, the Newberry Library, and the British Library. The textual introduction was aided by the insights of Nicholas Barker (the British Library), Paul W. Nash (the Bodleian Library), John Morrison (the Wing STC Revision Project), Stephen Parks (the Beinecke Library), Peter Blayney (the Folger), Georgianna Ziegler (the Folger), and W. Speed Hill (CUNY). Thanks are also due M. E. Ellis (the Royal Commission on Historical Manuscripts), Peter G. Vasey (the National Register of Archives, Scotland), M. E. Townley (the National Library of Scotland), William P. Haugaard (Seabury Western Theological Seminary), and Drew Kadel (the Burke Library, Union Theological Seminary).

The Penguin Group has generously permitted me to reproduce freely Maurice Evans's modernized edition of *The Countess of Pembroke's Arcadia;* without their generosity, the labors of clarifying the connections between Sidney and Weamys would have been greatly more burdensome for readers of this edition.

I am indebted to both the National Endowment for the Humanities and the City University of New York for the support they have given this project. At the City University I am profoundly owing to Joseph Wittreich, the executive officer of the English program at the Graduate Center, who sent my way three wonderfully bright and dedicated graduate assistants, Kathryn Coad, James Pervin, and Chris Wessman. It was he who also made possible an inter-college seminar on Renaissance women, directed by Joan Hartman and me in the Spring of 1992, which brought together students from the Graduate Center, Columbia, and Yale to study with some of the leading scholars in this field, each of whom deserves my thanks for articulating the excitement of research in the field of Renaissance women studies: Rona Goffen, Georgianna Ziegler, Rinaldina Russell, Susanne Woods, Jean Howard, Phyllis Rackin, Margaret Mikesell, Betty Travitsky, Ann Rosalind Jones, Maureen Quilligan, Lynette McGrath, Diane Wolfthal, and Lauren Silberman. At the College of Staten Island, where I do my undergraduate teaching, I owe a special debt to my chair, David Falk, and the Dean of Humanities and Social Sciences, Mirella Affron. The City University has also been the occasion, if only one, for my indebtednesses to Tom Oveis, Lynn Kadison, Margaret and Mary Ann Rorison, Elaine Baruch, Mason Cooley, Jarrod Hayes, Sharon Cumberland, Mary Murdy, Bennett Scott, Charles Riley, and Jane Collins.

At my undergraduate and graduate schools, three women were the chief inspirers and shapers of my love of literature: Christine Pabon (née Olpin), Nancy Tatum, and Barbara Lewalski.

The ultimate origins of this book are the women of my dedication. I grew up in Crisfield: a small town on Maryland's Eastern Shore, but a town unusually large in the excellence of its women. Within a strong and insistent patriarchy, women invented and, in many respects, ruled. From the home to school, from school to Sunday school, it was the women who taught us what it was to be "educated," and they were not carelessly transgressed. Most of these women are gone now, but their names still have power and authority for the generations of students who studied under them: Dorothy Kellam, Virginia Somers, Irma Riggin, Sally Sterling, LouElla Tawes, Anne Whittington, Catherine Parks, Margaret Lee Tawes, Sara Blueford, Suzanne Coons, Elizabeth Tull (née Hoagland), Tres Nelson. Tres Nelson was my godmother. I did not formally study with her, but I was never in her presence and not taught by her; she became my second mother.

The women I have mentioned were all teachers, and all members of my mother's generation and before, whose generous and powerful excellence moulded their community. That tradition of excellence continues, changed but still powerful and generous, in the women who have followed them. Those closest to me are Sylvia Cullen and Donna Ward: Sylvia, whose vigilant intelligence constantly astonishes and whose voice is steady and true; Donna, whose noble and indomitable spirit has refused to yield to the tragic and untimely death of her husband and my brother. I owe an immeasurable debt to the two women who have been Mom's daily caretakers for the greater part of her illness, Nora Evans and Stephanie Ward; perhaps only those who have known Alzheimer's can fully appreciate just how great that debt is.

Hope Colborn Cullen gave me her name and, as it turned out, her profession: English teacher. Saying anything about her is painful, for what I write here is, in effect, an obituary. This brilliant woman, word-giver to hundreds of students in her lifetime (including me), is now speechless from Alzheimer's. I ask myself how she would wish to be remembered. Certainly she would wish to be remembered as a teacher, and generations of Crisfielders valued her for that, yet this was only part of her life. She was involved in a host of organizations, and president of most of them; she served on local and state committees for various good causes, education chiefly, and frequently found herself taking on the males who were inclined to tell her and other women teachers how and what to teach. She was also a gardener and a traveller; it is difficult to say which gave her more pleasure, her roses at home or the Yugoslavian coast. However, what mattered most to Mom, and it disfigures her praise not to remember this, were the traditional roles of her womanhood. For her those roles were difficult but not problematic, and they were at the core of her being: she was wife of her husband, mother of her children, and a lady to everyone. It goes without saying that I was, and continue to be, the beneficiary of her being my mother. Another of her beneficiaries is Anna Weamys. For if it had not been for Mom's loving cultivation of me as her son and student, if she had not provided me with a lifelong model for women's capability and grace, this edition of Anna Weamys would never have been born.

It grieves me deeply that Mom will not speak again, for I remember her chiefly through her voice: its agile colors, the warm vibrato of its Southernness, the rich play of its coherence. Underlying my editing of Anna Weamys was, I think, a hope to resist the dying of the voice, to give Mom a magical reutterance that would enable her, like Anna Weamys, to have another chance to speak and be heard. But at most this edition can offer itself as a conjoined homage to both women: two women who, in their complicated relation to patriarchy, managed brilliantly the complexities of their womanhood. This edition of a long-silent woman of the seventeenth century is dedicated to her distant daughter of the twentieth. This book, Mom, is for you: gardener, traveler, teacher, community member, wife, and mother: an excellent woman among excellent women.

PATRICK COLBORN CULLEN
New York, 1994

INTRODUCTION

Life and Circumstances

A Continuation of Sir Philip Sidney's Arcadia (Wing 1189) is a text almost anonymous. According to the work's title page, its author is "Mris A. W."; according to tradition, A. W. is Anna (or Anne) Weamys. That is the attribution in the *Short-Title Catalogue*, and its source is Edward Arber's attribution in his edition of *The Term Catalogues*[1] in a notice for the 1690 Easter term of a second edition:

> Written by a young Gentlewoman, Mrs. A[nna] W[eamys]. The Second Edition.

Unhappily, Arber gives no source for his attribution.[2]

I have unearthed only one source for the attribution: one of the authors of the commendatory poems is the poet and essayist James Howell. In his *Epistolae Ho-elianae* (IV.xx) is a letter "To Dr. Weames":

---

1. In Volume II (for 1683–96) (London, 1905). *The Term Catalogues* were the quarterly lists of new books and reprints issued by the booksellers of London. John J. Morrison, of the Wing STC Revision Project, has informed me that no copy of a second edition has yet turned up. It may never have been published; entry in *The Term Catalogues* was sometimes no more than staking a claim.

2. Nicholas Barker, of the British Library, has written me that "the attribution is evidently of some antiquity, since it goes back to the first edition of the *General Catalogue* and the *Catalogue of the Thomason Tracts*. [Since Thomason has not indicated the attribution on the title page] I think that the only possible source of information for the attribution will be recorded on our 'fourth copies,' the authority file for the printed catalogue. Unfortunately these files are now inaccessible to us."

Arundell Esdaile, in his entry for "Weamys, Anne" in *A List of English Tales and Prose Romances Printed before 1740* (1912), cites as his source for the attribution: "*Term. Cat.*, ii.316." Interestingly, he includes a piece of information—"*For W. Miller*" (that is, printed for W. Miller)—not in Arber's edition of *The Term Catalogues*.

Arber's "Anna" and Esdaile's "Anne" is a difference reflected in all subsequent references to Weamys. What is more remarkable about the Arber and Esdaile entries is less this difference than their agreement on the spelling of the surname, since "Weamys" has many variant spellings (Wemys[s], Weam[e]s, Weem[e]s, and others). This may have been a coincidence, but it may also suggest the possibility of a common source for their attribution.

SIR,

I return you many thanks for the additionals you pleased to communicate to me, in continuance of Sir Philip Sidney's *Arcadia;* and I admired it the more, because it was the composition of so young a spirit: which makes me tell you, without any compliment, that you are father to a daughter that Europe hath not many of her equals; therefore all those gentle souls that pretend to virtue, should cherish her. I have herewith sent you a few lines that relate to the work, according to your desire.

[Howell quotes the commendatory poem.]

So with my very affectionate respects to your self, and to your choice family, I rest

Your ready and real
Servant,
J.H.
London, 9 Nov.[3]

Howell does not supply A.W.'s first name, but at least he confirms that she is A. Weamys. I have been unable to locate decisive evidence elsewhere for her first name, which tradition has as both "Anna" and "Anne." In this edition, I have chosen to follow the authority of *The Term Catalogues,* choosing "Anna" over "Anne" and "Weamys" over other spellings of the surname.

Dr. Weamys seems almost certainly to have been a Doctor of Divinity in the Church of England. The only figure I have been able to locate who fits this description is listed in *Fasti ecclesiae Anglicanae* as "Weems, or Wemys, Lodowick, prb [i.e. prebendary] Westminster,"[4] and is included as a "prebendary of the Fourth Stall of Westminster":

> Louis Way, sometimes written Lodowick Weems or Wemys, S.T.B., was nominated vice [in succession to] John Holt, and installed 5th Feb 1630–31.

He appears again in a calendar compiled by William Shaw of the royal-

---

3. Quoted from the ninth edition (London, 1726), which contains Book IV (unlike the 1650 edition, cited elsewhere, which contains only Books I–III). Howell does not give the year of the letter, but it would seem to be 1650 or slightly after since the collection of letters in Book IV was published as an addition to the 1650 edition of letters, and those letters that are dated by year are from the 1650s.

4. *Fasti ecclesiae Anglicanae, or A calendar of the principal ecclesiastical dignitaries in England and Wales…from the earliest time to year M.DCC.XV.,* compiled by John Le Neve, corrected and continued…by T. Duffus Hardy (Oxford: Oxford Univ. Press, 1854), III.353.

ist "plundered clergy," whose livings were sequestered and given to Puritan ministers:

> 22 April 1643: Lambourne (Essex) sequestered from Dr. Ludowick Weames to Gamaliel Carr.[5]

We cannot be sure that this is Anna Weamys's father, or even that the two references are to the same man, but his name, title, dates, and apparent royalist allegiance make him a reasonable candidate.

Whoever Howell's "Dr. Weames" actually was, Howell's letter makes clear that Anna Weamys was a member of an educated family and that her father was untitled. She would seem to have been of a "good" family, perhaps on the margins of the aristocracy, but not noble or aristocratic. Howell's letter gives us another insight that should not be passed over too quickly: Dr. Weamys runs against the conventional picture of male opposition to female writers. He seems to be an early version of a stage father, encouraging (or pushing) his young prodigy as he solicits commendatory letters for her book. Indeed, her father is one of the candidates for the person Weamys intends when she says in "The Epistle Dedicatory" that "my ambition was not raised to so high a pitch, as the title now manifests it to be, until I received commands from those that cannot be disobeyed." In any event, her father seems certainly to have been a major force behind the publication of her volume—along with Howell and possibly Henry Pierrepont.

The front matter of the volume is the source of what little else we can deduce about Anna Weamys.

1. She was a young woman born in the first half of the seventeenth century, perhaps around 1630. Her youth is emphasized throughout the front matter: on the title page: "Written by a young Gentle-woman, Mris A. W."; by H. P. M., "She's young" (line 20); and by James Howell, who suggests her youth when he praises her precocity: "So wits ask time to ripen, and recruit; / But yours gives Time the start, as all may see / By these smooth strains of early poesy" (lines 8–10). "Young," of course, is an elastic term, but the recurrent and extreme emphasis on

---

5. *A History of the English Church during the Civil Wars and under the Commonwealth, 1640–1660* (1900; reprint New York: Lenox Hill, 1974), II, 311.

her youth (she is, as Howell puts it, "so young") suggests that she was precocious. I am assuming the attribution of precocity does not go much beyond the age of twenty; hence my speculation that she was not much more than twenty when Howell wrote his letter, and was therefore probably born not much earlier than 1630.

2. She was unmarried. This (and her virginity) are likewise stressed in the front matter. H. P. M. describes her as "a maid" (line 32), F. L. as "virgin" (line 12).

3. She was a "gentlewoman." This is the description on the title page. Like "young," it is an elastic term. It can mean "a woman of good birth or breeding" or "a female attendant (originally a gentlewoman by birth) upon a lady of rank" (*OED*). Anna Weamys is always referred to as "Mistress," in contrast (for instance) to her dedicatees, Lady Anne and Lady Grace Pierrepoint ("Perpoint" is the spelling in Weamys), daughters of the Marquess of Dorchester. That fact, and Weamys's deferentiality to nobility in her dedicatory epistle and in her *Arcadia* itself, perhaps suggests the difference of rank between them.

More is known about some of the people connected with Weamys's volume—her printer, bookseller, and commenders—than about Weamys herself. Knowledge about their lives provides the most reliable information we have at this point for situating Weamys and her book. We will begin with her printer (William Bentley) and bookseller (Thomas Heath).

William Bentley (printer in London, at Finsbury, 1646–56?)[6] apparently enjoyed the favor of the interregnum government,[7] and was

---

6. Henry R. Plomer, *A Dictionary of Booksellers and Printers Who Were at Work in England, Scotland and Ireland from 1641 to 1667* (London: Blades, 1907), has 1656 as William Bentley's last date, but Paul G. Morrison, *Index of Printers, Publishers, and Booksellers in Donald Wing's Short-Title Catalogue …1641–1700* (Charlottesville: Univ. of Virginia Press, 1955) has found later references in Wing to him: 1668 (*Pharmacopoeia Londiniensis*) and, somewhat implausibly late for the same man, 1693 (Samuel Roycroft, *A Short History of Monastical Orders*).

7. Bentley is first heard of in 1646 when the Westminster Assembly of Divines proposed issuing a new and cheap edition of the Bible, and the project was awarded to him. This involved him in controversy with the Company of Stationers, who issued an order denying his workmen pension privileges. However, by the Act of 1649, and of 1652, Parliament supported Bentley's printing house by specially mentioning them as being exempt from the provisions of the Company of Stationers. See Plomer, *A Dictionary of Booksellers and Printers*, 22.

perhaps therefore a good printer for royalists interested in accommodating themselves to the parliamentary government (like Pierrepont, Howell, and Vaughan; see below). Specializing in political and religious works, he printed very few texts of imaginative literature. As far as Weamys is concerned, his most interesting venture is his publication in 1652 of Madame de Scudéry's *Ibrahim*, a work that resembles Weamys's *Arcadia* in that it is a romance written by a woman for primarily a female audience. *Ibrahim* was also, like Weamys's work, a joint venture with Thomas Heath.[8] Even more suggestive is the fact that Heath and Bentley were joined by a third man, Humphrey Moseley. Moseley is known now as the publisher of Milton's 1645 volume (among many other major works), but for our purposes his link with Bentley and Heath is important because he was James Howell's major publisher in the 1640s and early 1650s, publishing him fourteen times in that period. This is a small suggestion, but one of several, of Howell's possible role linking the major participants in the production of Weamys's volume.[9]

Thomas Heath (bookseller in London, 1648–55)[10] first appears as a bookseller in 1648, of Enrico Caterino Davila's *Continuation and Conclusion of the Civill Warres of France*. One of Heath's later volumes suggests a possible link to the Hispanist Howell, Augustin Rise's *The Rise and Fall of the Late...Count Olivares*.[11] In general, Heath's list is less religious and political than Bentley's. He has more continental writers (including Descartes) and more imaginative literature (including at least one other romance, William Sales's *Theophania*).

---

8. In 1653 Bentley and Heath linked up again to publish a play, *The Ghost, or The Woman Wears the Breeches*, and again in 1654 for a translation of Charles Sorel's *The Extravagant Shepherd*, which (as a pastoral "anti-romance") has a slight, if obverse, generic linkage to Weamys's *Arcadia*. In addition to romances, Bentley published another "ladies' text" of interest, *The Ladies Companion, or, A Table Furnished* (1654).

9. Another possible indication of a connection between Howell and Bentley is Bentley's publication in 1653 of Gonzalo de Céspedes y Meneses's novella, *Gerardo the Unfortunate Spaniard*. Howell had a life-long interest in Spanish culture, and in fact wrote a Spanish grammar and even a kind of travel guide to Spain for the foreign service.

10. Plomer, *Dictionary of Booksellers and Printers*, 95, has Heath first appearing as a bookseller (presumably of Weamys's *Arcadia*) in 1651, but Morrison, *Index of Printers, Publishers, and Booksellers*, has the first entry for Heath in 1648 and the last in 1655.

11. Count Olivares is mentioned at least twice in Howell's correspondence from Madrid (*Epistolae Ho-elianae*, III.xi and III.xviii).

According to Henry Plomer,[12] Heath issued an edition of Sir Philip Sidney's *Arcadia* in 1651. It is apparently this claim by Plomer that has led the author of the entry on Weamys in *The Feminist Companion to Literature in English* to assert that Weamys's *Arcadia* was "timed to coincide with a new edition" of Sidney's *Arcadia*.[13] This is an attractive hypothesis, but no such 1651 edition exists: it is not entered in the Stationers' Register; Thomas Heath makes no mention, as one would expect him to, of such an edition in his epistle to the reader; it is not listed in Wing, nor is it entered in Bent Juel-Jensen's inventory of editions of the *Arcadia*.[14] I suspect Plomer may have confused Weamys's 1651 title with Sidney's (as does the *National Union Catalogue* in one instance).

The next people referred to in the front matter of the volume are the members of the Pierrepont family of Dorchester. Weamys's dedication is: "To the two unparalleled sisters, and Patterns of Virtue, the Lady Anne and the Lady Grace Perpoint, daughters to the Right Honourable the Marquess of Dorchester." The dedication is not to Anne and Grace simply in themselves but to them as the children of the Marquess of Dorchester: which is to say that Weamys dedicates her work, in part, through the children to the father. Henry Pierrepont, first Marquess of Dorchester and second Earl of Kingston (1606–80), was a man of a certain fame, even notoriety. Politically, his sympathies were royalist; but, to the chagrin of some royalists, he compounded for his estate. Unable to make a living after the war, he went to London in 1649 and ended up studying law and medicine. Eventually he practiced medicine and became a member of the College of Physicians, which outraged some royalists, but earned him the praise of *Mercurius Politicus* (22–29 July 1658), the official journal of the Protectorate, for providing a model for the nobility. These activities suggest a compromising royalist politics comparable to the politics of at least two other men who were directly

---

12. *Dictionary of the Booksellers and Printers*, 95.

13. Ed. Virginia Blain et al. (New Haven: Yale, 1990).

14. "Some Uncollected Authors xxxiv, Sir Philip Sidney," *The Book Collector*, 11 (1961), 468–79. In his revision of his essay, "Sir Philip Sidney, 1554–1586: A Check-list of Early Editions of his Works," in *Sir Philip Sidney: An Anthology of Modern Criticism*, ed. Dennis Kay (Oxford: Clarendon, 1987), 289–314, Juel-Jensen again lists no 1651 edition.

or indirectly involved with Weamys's volume, James Howell and Richard Vaughan.

Weamys's dedicatory epistle supplies no specifics of her relationship to the Pierrepont children and their father; all she offers is discreetly generalized praise and generalized humility. However, it is not difficult to imagine Pierrepont as a supporter of Weamys's project, if not exactly her patron; he was a man known for his literary interests. William Munk quotes a description of him as "always much addicted to books,"[15] and Horace Walpole, in *A Catalogue of the Royal and Noble Authors of England*, says of him that he "appeared but little in the character of an author, though he seems to have had as great foundation for being so, as any on the list."[16] And so it seems possible that Pierrepont is indicated, or included, when Weamys claims that she "received commands from those that cannot be disobeyed."

As far as the Pierrepont children are concerned, Cokayne's *Complete Peerage* gives Anne's baptismal date as 9 March 1630, which would mean that she was twenty or twenty-one at the time of publication. Cokayne gives Grace's birth date as 1635, which would make her fifteen or sixteen in 1651.[17] Weamys's emphasis on aristocratic marriage may have been a reflection of Anne and Grace's eligibility. (Ironically, Anne's marriage to John Manners in 1658 led to one of the great marital scandals of the age,[18] and Grace never married.) Anne died in 1697, Grace in 1703: both lived long enough to have encouraged, had they been interested, a second edition in 1690 of the work that had been dedicated to them in their youth.

The remaining figures associated with Weamys's volume are the authors of the five commendatory poems: "H. P. M.," "F. L.," "F. W.," "Jam. Howel," and "F. Vaughan." What is most impressive about these

---

15. Munk is quoting from "a MS. of Dr. Goodall's in the College library," in his *The Roll of the Royal College of Physicians in London* (London, 1828), I.282.

16. Edinburgh, 1792, 41.

17. Antonia Fraser, however, in *The Weaker Vessel* (New York: Knopf, 1984), 299, claims Anne was seventeen when she married in 1658. Fraser's dates would require Anne to have been born in 1641 or 1640. However, Cokayne and the *DNB* agree that her mother died in childbed in 1639, so presumably Fraser is inaccurate.

18. Fraser, *The Weaker Vessel*, 298–305, has a lively account of this scandal.

poems is their extraordinarily intelligent invention. They are among the joys of the volume, and indeed I would say this is one of the better collections of such poems in the seventeenth century. They are also remarkably similar: all are in iambic pentameter couplets; all, with the possible exception of H. P. M.'s poem, are written in highly conceited, witty verse; and they tend to share some of the same conceits (based on metempsychosis, the virago/Amazon, the virgin) that play on the idea of the author's being a woman who is continuing a man's work. Moreover, while one can no doubt find some indication of resistance, largely they are remarkable for their openness to female authorship.[19] F. Vaughan, for instance, begins with the exhortation: "Lay by your needles, ladies, take the pen, / The only difference 'twixt you and men," and concludes the octave with "Since all souls equal are, let all be heard." And F. W., after a brilliant suggestion that Sidney's transmigration into Weamys is a form of literary cross-dressing (Sidney becomes, through Weamys, his own Zelmane), concludes with a provocative, almost Borgesian reinscription of authorship:

> ...for doubtless such is she,
> Perfection gives t' *Arcadia*'s geography.
> *Arcadia* thus henceforth disputed is,
> Whether Sir Philip's or the Countesses.

The exact referent for "Countesses" is unclear, but one of its referents is surely the Countess of Pembroke, which permits the author to play with the genitive ambiguity of *The Countess of Pembroke's Arcadia*. As a woman perfecting "*Arcadia*'s geography," Weamys becomes the means whereby male authorship of Arcadia (as a place to be "perfected" as well

---

19. Elaine Hobby, *Virtue of Necessity: English Women's Writing, 1649–88* (Ann Arbor: The Univ. of Michigan Press, 1989), 89, finds in the transmigration-conceit an effort at male reassurance that "the *Continuation* should not really be seen as a product of women's writing." This is possible, of course; but it is also possible that one of the authors using this conceit is a woman. Moreover, although two of the other terms used to describe Weamys, virago and Amazon, could be terms of abuse, they were also customary humanist terms of (usually) praise for a woman writer, and so they seem to be here. See "Women Humanists: Education for What?" in Anthony Grafton and Lisa Jardine, *From Humanism to the Humanities: Education and the Liberal Arts in Fifteenth- and Sixteenth-Century Europe* (Cambridge: Harvard Univ. Press, 1986), 29–57.

as a work to be "continued") is questioned, and even Weamys's own title for her work, *A Continuation of Sir Philip Sidney's Arcadia*, problematized.

The general excellence of the prefatory encomia suggests that Weamys, or someone she or her father was acquainted with, was connected with some highly accomplished writers who gave more than ordinary efforts in their praise of her. The volume as a whole seems to have been prepared with some care, but it is the care and attention given in the commendatory poems that is the most impressive part of its preparation.

Unhappily, we know nothing of the three persons (H. P. M., F. L., and F. W.) who are, like A. W. herself, identified only by their initials, though they all seem to have been male. One can speculate that H. P. M. may be Henry Pierrepont, Marquess, and that F. W. may have been a member of Weamys's own family, but there is no evidence for these speculations.

James Howell (1594?–1666) probably played a larger role in the publication of this volume than just writing a poem for it. His republication of his letter to Dr. Weamys in Book IV of his letters suggests continuing support of the book: the republished letter is, in effect, an advertisement for the book. Also, Howell seems generally supportive of women writers. In a letter to "Th. W.," for example, after praising the poem of Henry King, he adds that he finds "the same genius among the sisters" and praises Mrs. A. K. (Ann King) as a "tenth muse."

Howell is conceivably the main link between Henry Pierrepont, F. Vaughan, and Dr. Weamys. He was an important literary figure in his own right (he was, as Douglas Bush phrases it, "the supreme epistolizer of the age"[20]), and he had an impressive number of literary and political connections. While on a special mission to Spain (1622–24), he made the acquaintance of Sir Kenelm Digby and Endymion Porter; he knew Robert Sidney, for whose embassy to Denmark he was secretary; his *Epistolae Ho-elianae* find him corresponding with Lord Herbert of

---

20. *English Literature in the Earlier Seventeenth Century: 1600–1660*, 2nd ed. (Oxford: Clarendon, 1962), 206.

Cherbury, Edward Benlowes, and Sir Kenelm Digby, and even referring to Ben Jonson playfully and intimately as "my father."[21]

He was also himself a versatile and prolific writer. Among the writings that are potentially relevant to Weamys is *Dodona's Grove, or the Vocall Forest* (1640; Part II, 1650), a political allegory covering events between 1603 and 1640; by 1646, there had been three editions, a Latin version, and a French translation. It was, therefore, a work of some fame and one of Howell's signature pieces, and seems to be alluded to by F. Vaughan in her commendatory poem. Also of interest for our purposes are the political pamphlets of the 1640s, written from the Fleet after his arrest by order of the Long Parliament; they begin with a defense of the royalists but later become much more supportive of Cromwell, so that in respect to his political sympathies, Howell seems a royalist in the mould of Pierrepont and Vaughan.

Howell was in the Fleet from 1643 until 1650 or 1651.[22] During his imprisonment, he wrote prolifically; and presumably one of the things he wrote in the Fleet, or at least immediately after, was his commendatory verse for Weamys. Why Howell would have contributed a commendatory verse for Weamys is unclear: money and royalist connections leap to mind as possible motivations. It is possible that he became involved with the project through the Marquess of Dorchester. Pierrepont and Howell had had the occasion to meet before 1651: in 1642, the king made Pierrepont, who had represented Nottinghamshire in Parliament, lord lieutenant of Nottinghamshire, to help raise forces for the royal army; and in 1642, Howell was also in Nottingham,

---

21. *Epistolae Ho-elianae* (London, 1650): I.5.xvi (1629); I.4.xxvi (1629); I.6.xxii (1635). It should be noted, however, that Howell's letters are not known for a scrupulous adherence to fact when the famous are involved. The fullest and most sympathetic view of Howell as an historian is J. D. H. Thomas, "James Howell, Historiographer Royal," *Brycheiniog*, 9 (1963), 79–102. See also Patterson, *Censorship and Interpretation: The Conditions of Writing and Reading in Early Modern England* (Madison: The Univ. of Wisconsin Press, 1984), 210–18.

22. *Dictionary of National Biography from the Earliest Times to 1900* (*DNB*), ed. Leslie Stephen and Sidney Lee (London, 1885-1900). In its entry on Howell, *DNB* claims that he "was admitted to bail, and released from the Fleet in the same year [i.e. 1651]." However, William Harvey Vann, *Notes on the Writing of James Howell* (Waco, Texas: Baylor University Press, 1924), 9, claims that Howell was released from the Fleet in the general amnesty of 1650.

where he was sworn in as clerk of the council. If the two did not meet in Nottingham, they may have met in London, where Pierrepont moved in 1649. In any event, we do find Howell directing one of his epistolary essays to Pierrepont (*Epistolae Ho-elianae,* IV.xii). Unhappily the letter is not dated by the year, but it is in the same section (Book IV) as the letter to Dr. Weamys and presumably is dated around the same time. Its subject is appropriate for the royalist politics of Weamys's commenders: in a fascinating appraisal of Elizabeth I, Howell discusses the relation of popular opinion to the rise and fall of monarchs. Howell's concluding remark, however, is even more suggestive of a link between the two men:

> A speculation [about providence and "the genius of the times"] that may become the greatest, and knowingst spirits, among whom your Lordship doth shine as a star of the first magnitude; for your house may be called a true academy, and your head the capitol of knowledge, or rather an exchequer, wherein there is a treasure enough to give pensions to all the wits of the time.

Pierrepont's "academy" may be only an epideictic metaphor, but Howell seems to be alluding to the existence of an interregnum royalist academy, or salon, with Pierrepont as its focus. However this may be, it at least seems clear that Howell sees Pierrepont as a present or potential patron. Lacking the exact date of the letter, we cannot say more than that.

The connection between Howell and F. Vaughan is speculative, but my suspicion is that F. Vaughan is Frances Vaughan (née Altham), the wife of Howell's friend Richard Vaughan (1600?–86) of Golden Grove,[23] Carmarthenshire, the second earl of Carbery. Howell and Vaughan were both Welsh, both raised in Carmarthenshire. They may have known each other in Carmarthenshire, or later in Oxford: Howell entered Jesus College in 1610 and remained there until 1613; Vaughan

---

23. The Vaughans of Golden Grove should not be confused with Henry Vaughan's family, the Vaughans of Tretower, though both are of course Welsh families. I am indebted to Jane Collins, of the CUNY Graduate Center, for suggesting I explore the possibility that F. Vaughan is Frances.

entered Oriel College in 1612.[24] Howell had certainly met Vaughan by 1623. In a letter to Thomas Guin of Trecastle, Howell writes: "Mr. Vaughan of the Golden Grove and I were comrades and bedfellows here [Madrid] many months together" (*Epistolae Ho-elianae*, I.3.xix). Politics also united them: Vaughan was, like Howell and Pierrepont, a royalist who made peace with the interregnum government. Also like Howell (and, to a lesser degree, Pierrepont), Richard and Frances Vaughan had literary interests; they were patrons of writers, and are perhaps best remembered as providing hospital shelter to Jeremy Taylor, who dedicated works to Richard, his second wife (Frances), and his third wife (Lady Alice Egerton, Milton's "Lady" in *Comus*). Vaughan was also one of Howell's most generous patrons.[25]

Another link between Howell and Frances Vaughan is that she was the niece of his close friend, Richard Altham.[26] Moreover, the commendatory poems themselves suggest a link between them, for the poems seem to be designed as companion-pieces: they are placed side by side, they have identical form (six iambic pentameter couplets), and the last couplet of Frances Vaughan's poem alludes to Howell's perhaps most famous literary work, *Dodona's Grove* (while it alludes simultaneously to *her* own grove, Golden Grove):

> A single bough shall other works approve,
> Thou shall be crown'd with all DODONA's grove.

One suspects this witty, Marvellian compliment is not just to Weamys but to Howell, and that Frances Vaughan and Howell must have known each other, by correspondence if not more directly.

---

24. See A. Wood, *Athenae Oxonienses* (London, 1691), II, 265 (Howell) and II, 257 (Vaughan), and Vann, *Notes on the Writing of James Howell*, 5.

25. Thomas, "James Howell," 83. Howell apparently received patronage from Carmarthenshire families all his life.

26. In one of his most beautiful and moving letters, written upon his return from one of his continental trips, Howell greets Richard Altham: "Hail half my soul, my dear Dick" (I.2.ii). Even after Altham's death, we find him in 1642 writing Altham's sister, Elizabeth, now Lady Digby.

Frances Vaughan died in 1650, but that date need not rule her out as Weamys's F. Vaughan; nor need she be ruled out because of her addressing women, in the opening lines of the poem, as "you" and "your sex":

> Lay by your needles, ladies, take the pen,
> The only difference 'twixt you and men.
> 'Tis tyranny to keep your sex in awe,
> And make wit suffer by a Salic law.

This is a wonderful poem and a wonderfully feminist poem, regardless of the sex of the author; and unless evidence to the contrary emerges, I am inclined to assume Frances Vaughan its author.

The front matter of Weamys's volume remains our key source for her life and circumstances: her father (and perhaps Anna as well) was connected, possibly through Howell and/or Pierrepont, with writers of considerable accomplishment. Moreover, as the dedication, along with the dedicatory poem by (possibly) the wife of the Earl of Carbery, suggests, the Weamyses seem to have moved on the margins of aristocratic society, and their sympathies were almost certainly royalist. What we know of this text—its publication, its self-presentation, its dedication, its genre, its subject—supports the hypothesis that it was the production of some sort of royalist network. The politics of Pierrepont, Howell, and Vaughan were certainly royalist. In fact, it would not seem improbable that all of the commenders had royalist sympathies: they write in the heavily conceited style associated with writers of a royalist bent. Moreover, the work is dedicated—at a time when the Protectorate seemed firmly entrenched—to a noble family, and the form of the work is that of the romance. As Lois Potter has shown, "there were some literary forms which belonged specifically to the royalists," and the romance was one of those forms.[27] Indeed, Weamys's *Arcadia* celebrates the world of princes and princesses perhaps even more than most romances do; the work's dominant emotional register is awe of the glamor of the

---

27. *Secret Rites and Secret Writing: Royalist Literature, 1641–1660* (Cambridge: Cambridge Univ. Press, 1989), 80. See especially chapter 3, "Genre as Code: Romance and Tragicomedy." See also Annabel Patterson's chapter, "The Royal Romance," in *Censorship and Interpretation.*

royals, especially of the women, and its dominant political discourse is that of aristocratic hegemony.

Literary Background

For the literary (and social) contextualization of Weamys's *Arcadia*, the most general and most obvious point is also the most essential: it is a product of a traditional—that is to say, classical and mimetic—aesthetic.[28] Any cultural contextualization of an early-modern woman writer like Weamys is obligated to take into account the dominant aesthetic discourse, of inventing by means of derivation, she shares with the literary culture of her class and time. Otherwise we run the risk of misconstruing both her deference and her difference.[29] Weamys's *A Continuation* is especially vulnerable to being misconstrued: first, as "only" a "continuation"; second, as "only" the product of female aesthetic passivity and conservatism, or of the restricted aesthetic possibilities for women writers.

The powerfully intertextual aesthetic within which Weamys works discovers literary excellence in continuation almost as much as originality, in the relations of works almost as much as "the work itself." Its history is one of continuously reinscribed traditions and models, and its

---

28. The classic account of this tradition is Erich Auerbach, *Mimesis: The Representation of Reality in Western Literature* (1946; reprint Princeton: Princeton Univ. Press, 1953). Among the more important recent studies are Thomas M. Greene, *The Light in Troy* (New Haven: Yale Univ. Press, 1982), and G. W. Pigman, "Versions of Imitation in the Renaissance," *Renaissance Quarterly*, 33 (1980), 1–32.

29. Hobby, *Virtue of Necessity*, 89, argues that "Weamys's continuation of the unfinished stories…could hardly have been more self-effacing. She hides her name, merely identifying herself as 'a young gentlewoman, Mrs. A. W.,' and seeks only to give some shape to an extension of a man's work, using his characters solely." In fact, the four other (male) authors of continuations and supplements of Sidney's *Arcadia* also create "an extension of a man's work," three of them "using his characters solely." Even the exception, Markham, largely uses characters Sidney at least mentioned, and the few who are not in Sidney are mostly variants of characters in Sannazaro. Gender is no doubt involved in Weamys's choice of a "continuation," but it is not the only factor: class, youth—and genre—also play a role. Finally, while the use of initials may or may not be self-effacing, it is commonplace and crosses gender lines. In Weamys's volume, printer and seller are, of course, noted by name; but of the five authors (six, if T. H. is included), only Howell and Vaughan identify themselves by name, and one is male and one (I think) female.

production is characterized by what Barbara J. Bono has called (preserving the aesthetic's tension between repetition and contradiction) "transvaluations."[30] To take two obvious examples: Virgil's epic reinscribes Homer's, and Renaissance epics reinscribe both of them, and one another; Virgil's pastoral *Eclogues* reinscribes Theocritus, and Renaissance pastorals reinscribe both of them, and one another.

The structure of relations within this aesthetic discourse can easily suggest, to some, a binary passive/dominant relation of precursor and follower. The fact is—and this point is essential if we are to give Weamys, or any other woman writing within such an aesthetic, her due—that the characteristic production of this aesthetic discourse, independent of gender, is one of continuations: the continuation-as-sequel is simply the extreme production of the aesthetic. From the perspective of this aesthetic, the precursor-text of Weamys's *Continuation* is itself a continuation: *The Countess of Pembroke's Arcadia* (1593). Only the feminine genitive of the title stresses uniqueness; *Arcadia* is Sannazaro's title, and Sidney's work is replete with reworkings, and continuations, of his precursors' tales: Virgil, Heliodorus, Sannazaro, Montemayor, the *Amadis de Gaule*, and others.

Moreover, in the context of mimetic reinscription, the interest of works like Weamys and Sidney is to a considerable measure not only in what they are in themselves but in the theater of their intertextual relations. In an aesthetic of (re)sourcefulness, part of the inventive power of Weamys's work lies in the very area where we may locate its weakness: that is, in its derivations. Weamys's main source is the fragment of a male precursor, namely the unfinished *New Arcadia* section of the 1593 *Arcadia.* (The *New Arcadia,* first printed in 1590, is Sidney's revision, left incomplete at his death, of the *Old Arcadia,* an earlier version of his work not printed in its entirety until the twentieth century. The *New Arcadia* fragment was incorporated into the 1593 *Arcadia,* along with the last two and a half books of the *Old Arcadia.* For more details, see page xxxvi.) Weamys's having the fragment of a male precursor as the

---

30. *Literary Transvaluation: From Vergilian Epic to Shakespearean Tragicomedy* (Berkeley: Univ. of California Press, 1984), 1–6 *et passim.*

main source for her "continuation" does not inevitably suggest an espe-cially feminine subservience. In the Renaissance, the completion of another writer's text (Chaucer's, for example, by Spenser) is a fairly commonplace staging for (and of) the act of invention, as is the rein-scription of a writer's own earlier text as a fragment or a source to be completed or perfected by his own later version (for example, Sannaz-aro, Tasso, Spenser, and Sidney himself); and a good part of our interest is focussed on the way a later text stages and performs its relation to its precursor. And so it is with Weamys. Her decision to write a continua-tion of Sidney is by no means to be regarded, and disregarded, as a choice of female aesthetic docility. That demeans and, as I hope to show, misrepresents her. She is, in fact, placing herself on the same stage as the "learned Sidney" ("The Epistle Dedicatory"). The choice of that stage for any writer in the seventeenth century, especially a woman writer and even more especially a young woman writer, was an act of courage.

Weamys's *Arcadia* is a "mixed kind," that is, it is (like many if not most longer works of the period, and like Sidney's *Arcadia*) a composite of literary genres.[31] Of the two principal genres in Weamys, the pastoral and the romance, the romance is dominant. Of all the traditional genres, it is the romance that seems most to engender continuations. Its narratology is one of a continuing and seemingly inexhaustible produc-tion of event, with the characteristic romantic closure almost always potentially an opening for a new beginning, of yet more narrative "to be continued"; or as Bakhtin puts it, in romance there are "no necessary internal limits" on what is in effect an "infinite series" of events.[32]

---

31. The pioneer discussion is Rosalie L. Colie's in *The Resources of Kind: Genre-Theory in the Renaissance* (Berkeley: Univ. of California Press, 1973). Her work has been built on by, especially, Alastair Fowler, *Kinds of Literature: An Introduction to the Theory of Genres and Modes* (Cambridge: Harvard Univ. Press, 1982) and Barbara K. Lewalski, Paradise Lost *and the Rhetoric of Literary Forms* (Princeton: Princeton Univ. Press, 1985). See also Stuart Curran's excellent discussion of "composite orders" in *Poetic Form and British Romanticism* (New York: Oxford, 1986), 180–203. For Sidney, see Stephen J. Greenblatt, "Sidney's *Arcadia* and the Mixed Mode," *Studies in Philology* 70 (1973), 269–78.

32. M. M. Bakhtin, *The Dialogic Imagination*, ed. Michael Holquist (Austin: Univ. of Texas Press, 1981), 94.

Romance is a genre, as Patricia Parker has described it, of internal "detours, postponements, and suspensions"; it is characterized, as she says, by "'espace dilatoire'—both dilated and dilatory space—in which straightforward movement towards the end is opposed by delays, equivocations, and turnings."[33] The internal "espace dilatoire" of romance has an intertextual spill-over in works that continue precursor narratives and that are themselves made to be continued. The narrative momentum of romance to continuation generated some of the monuments of Renaissance literature; one might cite Boiardo's continuation of the matter of Roland, and Ariosto's continuation of Boiardo, and Spenser's of both of them, or Cervantes's continuation of the first part of his *Quixote*. The same momentum of the genre to continuation also generated some of the works that themselves generated Sidney and, at least indirectly, Weamys: Montemayor's *Diana* (which ends promising a conclusion and which generated the continuations of Gaspar Gil Polo and Alonso Pérez) and the twenty-one books (in its French version) of what may have been the most widely read book of fiction in the Renaissance, the *Amadis de Gaule*. Both these works deeply affected Sidney in the openness of their closure: they became paradigms of the literary work that ends by opening up into its own future possibilities and that defines itself as a participant in a process of engendering and re-engendering that need never end. The 1593 *Arcadia* ends with precisely such openness:

> But the solemnities of these marriages, with the Arcadian pastorals, full of many comical adventures happening to those rural lovers; the strange stories of Artaxia and Plexirtus, Erona and Plangus, Helen and Amphialus, with the wonderful chances that befell them; the shepherdish loves of Menalcas with Kalodulus's daughter; the poor hopes of the poor Philisides in the pursuit of his affections; the strange continuance of Claius' and Strephon's desire; lastly, the son of Pyrocles, named

33. *Inescapable Romance: Studies in the Poetics of a Mode* (Princeton: Princeton Univ. Press, 1979), 220. "Espace dilatoire" is a term employed by Roland Barthes, *S/Z*, trans. Richard Miller (New York: Hill and Wang, 1974), XXXII. Delay: "between question and answer [i.e., of the hermeneutic terms which structure the narrative 'enigma according to the expectation and the desire for its solution'] there is a whole dilatory area whose emblem might be named 'reticence,' the rhetorical figure which interrupts the sentence, suspends it, turns it aside" (75).

> Pyrophilus and Melidora, the fair daughter of Pamela by Musidorus
> (who even at their birth entered into admirable fortunes) may awake
> some other spirit to exercise his pen in that wherewith mine is already
> dulled.[34]

The ending of the 1593 *Arcadia* (a rewriting of the ending of the *Old
Arcadia*) in effect fragments the work in the act of finishing it. The end
becomes Sidney's invitation, to an imagined futurity, to begin again.
Another Sidneian invitation for more narrative, equally important to
seventeenth-century continuators, was expressed through the fragment
of the *New Arcadia*. Here was a work that was quite literally a fragment
needing to be finished: a revision (and in a sense a type of "continuation") of the *Old Arcadia* that was interrupted (so legend had it) in mid-
sentence by Sidney's death.

Weamys accepts Sidney's invitation, but the terms of her acceptance
are for an almost intimate intertextuality. If Sidney's work is an intertextual symposium, Weamys's is virtually a conversation with him. The literary background of Weamys's *Arcadia* is simple: it is almost entirely
Sidney himself. There is no indication that Weamys read, much less
wished to respond to, any of Sidney's sources: classical epic (Homer and
Virgil), Greek romance (*Aethiopica* and *Clitiphon and Leucippe*), continental romance (Sannazaro, *Arcadia;* Montemayor, *Diana*, and Gil
Polo's continuation; and the *Amadis de Gaule*). None of these does
Weamys seem to have a direct knowledge of, or even an indirect knowledge of except through Sidney. Nor (with the possible exception of
another seventeenth-century continuation of Sidney's *Arcadia*, Richard
Beling's *Sixth Book*) is there much strong evidence to suggest other literary influences on her, at least not specific ones. One suspects that she
may have been influenced by some of the "ladies' texts" of the time: for
example, conduct books (she is extremely attentive to protocol, especially the protocol of emotional expression) and the romances in

---

34. Quotations from the 1593 *Arcadia* are to the edition of Maurice Evans, *The Countess of
Pembroke's Arcadia* (London: Penguin, 1977). This is the only readily available modernized
edition of the complete 1593 *Arcadia,* which is the version of the *Arcadia* Weamys knew; hence
the Penguin edition is the one used throughout this volume.

English and French of the first half of the century, but that case remains to be demonstrated.

In her decision to continue Sidney's *Arcadia*, Weamys linked herself to the author who was probably the most widely read of the Elizabethans during her time, and indeed remained so until the eighteenth century, when his reputation declined. By the time of the publication of Weamys's *Arcadia*, Sidney's *Arcadia* (i.e., the 1593 *Arcadia*) had gone through eight editions (nine, counting the 1590 edition of the *New Arcadia*) and a total of eighteen issues.[35] Moreover, by mid-century there was a substantial body of literature reworking Sidneian materials in drama and verse as well as prose.[36] However, as far as I can tell, Weamys does not seem to have responded to this literature, even to the work—another neo-Sidneian romance by a woman—that one might most expect she would have responded to: Lady Mary Wroth's *The Countess of Montgomery's Urania* (1621).

---

35. See Juel-Jensen, "A Check-list of Early Editions" (1987), 291–301.

36. See Dennis Kay, "Introduction: Sidney—A Critical Heritage," in *Sir Philip Sidney: An Anthology of Modern Criticism*, 3–41. On, specifically, the *Arcadia*'s early reception and influence, see Victor Skretkowicz's survey in *Sir Philip Sidney, The Countess of Pembroke's Arcadia (The New Arcadia)* (Oxford: Clarendon Press, 1987), xliii–lii; and Paul Salzman, *English Prose Fiction, 1558–1700: A Critical History* (Oxford: Clarendon Press, 1985), 123–47. We do not know much about how Sidney was read in the seventeenth century. Mary Ellen Lamb, in her splendid study of *Gender and Authorship in the Sidney Circle* (Madison: The University of Wisconsin Press, 1990), 112–13, claims that "generally, men read the *New Arcadia* as a serious work, revealing either political insights...or moral guidance," and "as represented by seventeenth-century male writers, the primary response of women readers...was sexual arousal"; but she cites only Fulke Greville for the first claim, and three for the second (of which only one portrays "sexual arousal"). Lamb's lack of evidence does not mean that her speculation is implausible, only that evidence of such a clearly defined gender-difference in response is not readily available. It may well be that men responded more to the *arma* of romance, and women the *amor;* but it is also possible that men admitted less to responding to the "romance" of romance than did women, for reasons both social and aesthetic: to the extent that a work like the *Arcadia* could have any claim to aesthetic importance, it would have had to have been justified in terms of an aesthetic that privileged the heroic—as Sidney himself realized in his revision of his work. Moreover, women have been associated with the romance since the Greek romances, and the romance with them, often to the disparagement of both; and one will find male critics on both sides of the debate over romance in general and Sidney in particular. (See, especially, Kay and Skretkowicz, above.) Perhaps our most important evidence for how Sidney was read in the seventeenth century is to be found in how he was rewritten; the map of that territory is as yet unmade.

Presumably, the neo-Sidneian material that would have concerned Weamys most directly would have been her precursors in continuing and completing Sidney, but even here the evidence is slight for her using or even knowing them (Richard Beling again excepted). The material in question is usually divided into "supplements" and "continuations." To understand this distinction, it is important to know something about the text of the *Arcadia* in the seventeenth century. The original *Arcadia*, called the *Old Arcadia*, was a prose work in five acts, circulated in Sidney's lifetime and no doubt later, but as an entirety it was virtually unknown to subsequent generations until its rediscovery early in the twentieth century and its publication by A. Feuillerat in 1912.[37] Sidney's revision of the *Old Arcadia*, left incomplete upon his death, is called the *New Arcadia*, and was published in 1590. In the *New Arcadia* Sidney added new tales (most notably, of Amphialus and the Arcadian civil wars, Helen of Corinth, and the love of Parthenia and Argalus), and in general drew his work away from a pastoral-heroic-tragicomedy and closer to epic. In 1593, under the aegis of Sidney's sister, the Countess of Pembroke, a composite edition was published in five books: the two-and-a-half book fragment of the *New Arcadia* was completed by the last two-and-a-half acts of the *Old Arcadia*. The 1593 *Arcadia* was "the *Arcadia*" until the rediscovery of the *Old Arcadia*. As C. S. Lewis famously put it, "the composite text of 1593, and it alone, is the book which lived; Shakespeare's book, Charles I's book, Milton's book, Lamb's book, our own book long before we heard of textual criticism."[38] It was Weamys's *Arcadia*, too.

The composite text of 1593 was left with a narrative gap between the two sections: the *New Arcadia* section breaks off in mid-sentence with Pyrocles fighting Anaxius, and the *Old Arcadia* section begins with the safe return of Philoclea and Pamela to their father's house. There were two attempts in the seventeenth century to bridge this gap; these are the so-called "supplements." The first was by William Alexander (published

37. *The Prose Works of Sir Philip Sidney*, IV (Cambridge: Cambridge Univ. Press).
38. *English Literature in the Sixteenth Century* (New York: Oxford, 1954), 333.

with the later issues of the edition of 1613),[39] the second by James Johnstoun (published, with Alexander, in the edition in 1638); both are short, about twenty folio pages. These so-called "supplements" are usually distinguished from the three "continuations" (discussed below) of Markham, Beling, and Weamys; but the supplements are also continuations in that they continue the narratives of the *New Arcadia*, and actually conclude one of the narratives (of Philisides) that Sidney mentions at the end of the 1593 *Arcadia* as a subject for later pens.

Weamys does not seem to have been influenced by either of the supplements, except possibly by choosing not to follow them. Indeed, she notably departs from two of their narrative choices. The first concerns Anaxius, whom Pyrocles seems on the verge of vanquishing as Sidney's Third Book breaks off: both Alexander and Johnstoun have him die; Weamys has Pyrocles extend him mercy, only to have him killed later in the battle over Erona. The other important choice, made by all three writers, concerns the fate of Philisides/Sidney; all three writers have him die, though Weamys's version is quite different from the men's. The main narrative material of the supplements—that is, the events permitting Philoclea and Pamela to return home from Amphialus's castle—Weamys simply ignores. When we encounter the two couples in Weamys, they are at Basilius's Arcadian retreat waiting to get married and delaying their marriage until they've heard from their wounded former captor and cousin, Amphialus. It is not clear whether Weamys is assuming the events of one of the supplements and of the *Old Arcadia* or merely circumventing this narrative problem. In any event, she incorporates none of the plot developments in either of the supplements or in the *Old Arcadia* section of the 1593 *Arcadia*.

Three works are generally classified as "continuations" of the *Arcadia*: Gervase Markham, *The English Arcadia*;[40] Richard Beling, *A Sixth Book*

---

39. The date once given for the first publication of Alexander's supplement, 1621, has been corrected by Juel-Jensen, "A Checklist of Early Editions" (1987), 295–96.

40. *The English Arcadia* is in two parts: the first (published in 1607, but probably finished before the end of the 1690s) is 142 pages quarto; the second (published in 1613) is 119 pages quarto.

to the Countesse of Pembrokes Arcadia;[41] and A.W.'s *Continuation*. The
shared rubric conceals the fact that what links them is more their difference from the "supplements" (they do not try to bridge the two parts of
the 1593 *Arcadia*) than their similarity. Markham's work has little
resemblance to either Beling or Weamys. Unlike them, he sets his events
a generation after Sidney's; and while, like them, he continues (frag-
mentarily) Sidney's narrative of Helen and Amphialus, largely he is concerned with creating new narratives: he deals with two characters
(Pyrophilus and Meliodora) Sidney alludes to at the end of the *Arcadia*
as narrative possibilities for future authors, and he introduces entirely
new characters and events, though often obviously derived from Sidney's.

Of the continuations and supplements of the 1593 *Arcadia*, Beling's
Sixth Book is the only one for which a reasonable case could be made
that it influenced Weamys. What follows is as systematic a case as I can
make for that influence.

1. Both works take as their main occasion the marriage of the princes in
   Arcadia. However, Beling has only Pamela's and Philoclea's marriage,
   whereas Weamys uses the Arcadian marriages as a way of framing a climactic marital tour de force: four aristocratic couples (Pamela and
   Musidorus, Philoclea and Pyrocles, Helen and Amphialus, Plangus
   and Erona) are married at the same time, only to be followed by a
   fifth, pastoral marriage of Urania and Strephon.

2. The marriage festivities become the occasion to continue and com-
   plete Sidney's narratives: in Beling, the narratives are told by (and of)
   Amphialus and Helen; in Weamys, the narratives are told by (and of)
   Strephon and Urania.

3. In both works Helen and Amphialus are reconciled (though in different ways) and married, and the last major event of Beling's *Sixth Book*
   is the pastoral festivities celebrating that marriage.

4. Both works conclude with a pastoral framework occasioned by a

---

41. According to Juel-Jensen, "A Check-list of Early Editions" (1987), 299, Beling's *Sixth Book*
was first published separately in 1624 in Dublin, and it was first published with the *Arcadia* in
the edition of 1627.

noble marriage (Helen and Amphialus's in Beling; the four aristocratic couples in Weamys).

5. Although Beling does not resolve the narrative of Strephon's and Claius's love for Urania (though they do appear in a lament for Urania), he does resolve Sidney's pastoral narrative of "the shepherdish loves of Menalcas with Kalodulus' daughter" (in which the elder Corydon vies with the younger Menalcas for Kalodulus's daughter) in much the same way Weamys resolves the conflict of the elder Claius and the younger Strephon over Urania: Musidorus is asked to choose the victor, and he chooses (as does Weamys's Musidorus, in consultation with Pyrocles) the younger shepherd over the elder.

6. Beling concludes by leaving Basilius and Gynecia "to the happy quiet of their after-life"; Weamys concludes by having her two main couples end "their days in peace and quietness."

There are also important differences. First, Beling's Erona-Plangus narrative, as told by Amphialus, ends tragically with the death of both. Second, Beling's *Sixth Book* concludes with eclogues, just as the 1593 *Arcadia* (with the exception of Book Five) concludes each book with eclogues. Weamys has no eclogues, in fact no poetry; however, the pastoral events at the end of her book may be intended as an analogue to Sidney's and Beling's pastoral endings. Finally, and most importantly, Weamys's *Arcadia* is not a "sixth book" of the 1593 *Arcadia;* as we will see, it is closer to being a continuation of the *New Arcadia*, but is in fact (by virtue of its synopses) more independent and self-contained a work than Beling's.

One may go so far as to claim that Weamys found in Beling a model for a Sidneian "continuation," but it is Sidney, of course, who constitutes her chief relationship. Of the narratives that Sidney at the end of the 1593 *Arcadia* proposes for later writers, Weamys chooses only those that are fragments of Sidney's. Unlike Markham, and to some extent Beling, she is not interested in his suggestions for new narratives. At the same time, her opening sentence, which is modelled on the *New Arcadia*'s famous opening sentence (see page lxxi), suggests that she wishes her work to be seen as not solely a "continuation" but also an independent work: her own new *Arcadia*. Weamys's opening sentence does not just copy and overgo Sidney; it re-initiates the act of writing the *Arcadia*. This sentence is an overview of the main action of the *Arcadia*—more precisely the main action of the *New Arcadia:* that is, Weamys alludes to Basilius's retirement to the Arcadian countryside and Pyrocles's and Musidorus's courtship of his daughters. She does not, however, mention the resolution of these narratives in the *Old Arcadia* section of the 1593 *Arcadia:* there, after the trial, the two main couples are married (though Sidney does not actually describe the "solemnities of these marriages"). Weamys does not really continue Sidney's main narrative so much as conclude it, and that conclusion is effected through an announcement by a minor character, Clytifon: Weamys has Basilius send Clytifon as an ambassador to Amphialus

> …to certify him of his cousins' deliverance out of his castle, by the prowess of Prince Pyrocles and Musidorus; and how they disguised themselves for the love of Pamela and Philoclea, with all the several attempts that they practiced to obtain their desired enterprise (as their bringing Anaxius to submit to their mercy, Pyrocles having granted him his life on condition he would acknowledge it) and finally to give him notice that the nuptials of Pyrocles and Philoclea, with Musidorus and Pamela were only deferred for the time they could hear from Amphialus. (30–31)

This material is the substance of Alexander's and Johnstoun's "supplements," or bridges, between the two parts of the composite 1593 *Arcadia*. What is striking about this brief, almost parenthetical, "bridge" of Weamys is that it is not in the least designed, as was theirs, to link the *New Arcadia* with the *Old*, but to link the *New Arcadia* with her *Arcadia*.

Indication that Weamys is using any material from the 1593 *Arcadia* other than the *New Arcadia* section is in fact very slight. She perhaps vaguely alludes to the *Old Arcadia* section in her account of the trip to Arcadia made by Evarchus (Sidney's Euarchus): "And after many strange accidents had apparently been discovered, as the famous Sir Philip Sidney fully declares, Pyrocles and Musidorus were found to be alive; and now he [Evarchus] tarried in Arcadia to see his blessedness completed in their marriages" (39–40). But even here Weamys rewrites Sidney's account, for she has Evarchus visit Arcadia because he desires to assuage his grief over the apparent deaths of his son and nephew, not (as Sidney has it) because he is shipwrecked on the Laconian coast on his way to Byzantium (1593 *Arcadia,* V.2). Moreover, Weamys makes no mention of the other principal events of the *Old Arcadia* section of the 1593 *Arcadia,* namely Pamela and Musidorus's aborted elopement, the discovery of Philoclea and Pyrocles sleeping side by side, or the trial over the apparent murder of Basilius. Nor does Weamys acknowledge Pyrocles's public disclosure in Sidney's trial scene of Basilius's attraction to him in his Amazonian disguise; for in her own judgment scene, when Pyrocles and Musidorus are adjudicating the question of whether Claius or Strephon should have Urania's hand, Pyrocles observes that Basilius fears "my discovering his courtship" (78).

Some evidence for Weamys's use of the *Old Arcadia* appendage is perhaps found in her account of Plangus's journey to Evarchus for military assistance, but even here the evidence is equivocal; for while in Sidney that visit takes place in the *Old Arcadia* section, the visit has already been mentioned at the end of Basilius's account of Plangus in the *New Arcadia* section. Moreover, almost all of Weamys's account of Plangus in Macedon is her own invention, and even the points of contact between the two versions show important differences. Both Sidney and Weamys have Euarchus judging Artaxia and Plexirtus, but in Sidney Euarchus makes the judgment in his capacity as King, and his judgment is death to the murderers; in Weamys, he is appointed Judge of the Sessions, and his judgment is public execution for Plaxirtus, but he leaves ambiguous what will be done to Artaxia ("remember she is a woman"). Moreover, while Sidney has Euarchus make Plangus the head of a naval operation, proceeding to Armenia by way of ship, Weamys makes him "the general of my army" and goes on foot. Nothing in Weamys's account of Plangus in Macedon, then, requires Sidney's account as a point of origin.

One other possible basis for a claim for Weamys's use of the *Old Arcadia* section of the 1593 *Arcadia* is that Pyrocles's and Musidorus's adjudication of Strephon's and Claius's claims for Urania may be seen as a counterpart of Sidney's trial scene, but there is nothing in Weamys's "trial" that necessarily assumes Sidney's as a background: though exegetically illuminating, the linkage of the two is probably more fortuitous than designed.

In sum, even the strongest case for Weamys's borrowing from the *Old Arcadia* section of the 1593 *Arcadia* would not disturb the claim that for the most part she ignores it and focuses instead on completing the narratives of the *New Arcadia* section. This, I should hasten to add, is not the same thing as to suggest that she was using the 1590 *New Arcadia*. Clearly she knew and used the 1593 *Arcadia;* otherwise she would not have known Sidney's account of the origin of Strephon's and Claius's love for Urania, which is found only in the First Eclogues of the 1593 version of the *New Arcadia*. It is possible, nonetheless, that Weamys makes the somewhat daring manoeuvre of not accepting the claim of Hugh Sanford (the Countess of Pembroke's secretary) that the *Old Arcadia* conclusion of the 1593 *Arcadia* was "no further than the author's own writings or known determinations could direct" ("To the Reader"). Whether entire or partial, her erasing the second part of the 1593 *Arcadia* is a forceful indication of her determination to write her own work.

The possibility of an aggressive erasure should not be ruled out too quickly, for Weamys does not hesitate to write and write out Sidney. As I hope to demonstrate, one reason Weamys's *Arcadia* has so much synopsis of Sidney is not just to comply with Sidney or even to situate the reader, but to situate herself by rewriting Sidney; and one reason she intercepts Sidney's narratives earlier than her own narrative requires, and why at the same time she silences so much of her characters' Sidneian past, is that it allows her to reshape his narratives to her own end(ing). That end is the resolution of all the dangling narratives of the *New Arcadia* in a triumphant marriage-day scene. Nothing more strongly attests to Weamys's desire to create her own *Arcadia* than her ending. The marriages of Pamela and Philoclea to Musidorus and Pyrocles are alluded to, almost off-handedly, by Sidney at the end. They are the very be-all and end-all of Weamys's work, and Weamys has chosen to give center stage only to the narratives from the *New Arcadia* that can be reshaped to her end—not Sidney's trial of the young by the elderly but the triumph of youth in multiple marriage. This does not mean Weamys does not problematize marriage (she does so, I believe, through the figure of the chaste heroine), but largely her work reinscribes the "heroic" Sidney for women through the elaborate foregrounding of the "marriage plot." If Weamys were a Victorian woman novelist, we might find her emphasis on marriage and sentiment subservient and conventional, but in her own historical context, marriage and romance have at least the potential to be empowering: they are the agency for her appropriation of a masculine text.[42]

In sum, the author of *A Continuation of Sir Philip Sidney's Arcadia* is no mere docilely derivative woman writer appending herself to a man's work. With the exception of Markham (who is writing a different kind of work), Weamys is more willing to rewrite Sidney, sometimes directly, sometimes obliquely by omission, than are her male counterparts. Moreover, what the first sentence of her work suggests, the rest of the work tends to confirm: Weamys has decided, largely if not entirely, to continue the *New Arcadia* section of the 1593 *Arcadia* and largely to erase the *Old Arcadia* section. That decision reflects a more complicated agenda than her work's actual title may suggest: she is writing a work that is not just what it calls itself, "a continuation of Sir Philip Sidney's *Arcadia*," but one that deserves to be called, like Sannazaro's *Arcadia* and Sidney's, Anna Weamys's *Arcadia*. Hence that, not *A Continuation*, is the short title I have used throughout this volume.

The narratives from the *New Arcadia* Weamys continues are these: Plangus's love of Erona; Helen's love of Amphialus; Claius's and Strephon's love of Urania; the tale of Mopsa; and the love of Philisides. These narratives comprise Weamys's selection of her Sidneian past. As a "continuator," one of the major choices she faces is what to do with her characters' Sidneian past, for their past (a considerable one in most instances) is the main limit of her invention. In retelling their past, she can reinscribe her own Sidneian past. That, at any rate, is the angle of approach I will use in the following account of Weamys's deployment of

---

42. A thorough survey of the range of feminist readings of romantic love can be found in the introduction to the admirably nuanced study by Elaine Hoffman Baruch, *Women, Love, and Power: Literary and Psychoanalytic Perspectives* (New York: New York Univ. Press, 1991).

Sidneian narrative. (Readers unfamiliar with Sidney are alerted to the fact that a summary of the Sidneian narratives Weamys develops is included in Appendix 3, Narrative Sources, along with a Synopsis of the 1593 *Arcadia* and a List of Characters.)

Plangus and Erona, the hero and heroine of Weamys's first narrative, have a substantial Sidneian past, structured around *amor insanus*. The world of Sidney's Plangus is defined by the mad love of his father for a married woman who ultimately becomes his queen and who turns the king against Plangus, sending him into exile with his cousins, Tiridates and Artaxia in Armenia; the mad love of his cousin, whom Plangus initially supports in his efforts to force love from a woman (Erona) who does not love him; and perhaps even his own mad love, which spurs him on to raise forces in civil insurrection against his aunt, who has provided him sanctuary. Erona's mad love is for an unworthy suitor, Antiphilus, and her love indirectly causes her father's death and imperils the integrity of her own kingdom and royal succession (she is willing to let Antiphilus marry Artaxia, while she remains his second wife). What is so striking about Weamys's Plangus-and-Erona narrative is that she largely eliminates Sidney's linking Plangus and Erona in terms of *amor insanus*. Weamys supplies very little of Erona's obsession for (as she spells his name) Antifalus,[43] and we never learn how destructive Erona's erotic past has been. The result is a portrayal of Erona almost entirely as a victim of Artaxia's ruthlessly exercised power.

A similar simplifying of the Sidneian scene occurs in the opening scene of the work. Weamys solicits our sympathies for the lover, Plangus, as he struggles to protect Erona against Artaxia's vindictiveness; but in order to create this almost operatic scene, Weamys must downplay the complicating dissonance of Plangus's past: he is, after all, speaking to his cousin, who has given him protection in his exile and against whom (for largely personal and romantic reasons) he has created civil

---

43. Sidney's spelling, "Antiphilus," reflects the somewhat allegorical aspect of his character. The spelling in Weamys may, or may not, reflect her indifference to, or ignorance of, the allegorical dimension of Sidney. However this difference is to be accounted for, it has seemed to me best to preserve it. Hence in this essay as in the edition, when Weamys's dominant spelling of a character's name differs from Sidney's, I retain "her" difference, though that difference may well not literally be hers but instead her amanuensis's or her printer's.

unrest in her kingdom. Weamys's reshaping of Plangus's Sidneian past permits her to make him *her* character in *her* work: unlike Sidney, her aim is not to create a scene of moral ambiguity for adjudication, but to create a more compellingly dramatic scene in a world that is largely, as she constructs it, a series of scenes in a theatre of sensibility and cruelty.

Weamys's opening scene signalizes her difference from Sidney both substantively and formally. She initiates her "continuation" of Sidney by intercepting his Plangus-Erona narrative in its middle; she begins, in a sense, *in medias res*. She also begins with a rather lengthy synopsis. Nothing might seem more compliant than a synopsis, but what is most striking about Weamys's synopsis is that she begins it with a scene that is not in Sidney. Sidney has the "principal noblemen" of Armenia produce an agreement that will end civil strife and culminate in a combat-to-the-death between Pyrocles and Musidorus and two knights of Artaxia's choosing; in contrast, Weamys portrays an encounter between Plangus and his aunt in which he begs for Erona's life. The resulting agreement is the same in Sidney and Weamys, but the encounter of aunt and nephew is not in Sidney. If the action of Weamys's narrative is more theatrical than Sidney's, so is its format: in a move characteristic of her, Weamys transforms Sidney's narrative into dialogue. Weamys's opening episode, therefore, like many other openings in works that are self-consciously intertextual, is a mixed signal defining what her work is and what it is *not*—a complicated gesture of deference and difference.[44]

In her other major aristocratic narrative, that of Helen and Amphialus, Weamys works in much the same fashion as she did with the

---

44. One other narrative difference between Weamys and Sidney should be noted. Weamys keeps the occasion of Plangus's relation of his story to Basilius: Basilius learns of Plangus's story as Plangus is passing through Arcadia on his way to Macedon to persuade Euarchus to help him avenge the death of Pyrocles and Musidorus and to rescue Erona from Artaxia. However, Weamys alters the scheduling of the relation: in Sidney, Plangus relates the apparent death of the princes to Basilius while they are, unbeknownst to him, alive but disguised in his own kingdom; in Weamys, however, Plangus relates "all circumstances" (which presumably would have included some mention of the princes' deaths) to Basilius, but Basilius knows the princes are alive (and undisguised) in his kingdom and his daughters are in fact engaged to them. This creates a potential narrative glitch in Weamys, unusual for her, and she seems to have been aware of the problem. Her generalized phrase, "all circumstances," seems designed to evade the narrative difficulty (its vagueness keeps open the possibility that Plangus may not have mentioned their deaths), and she places Pyrocles (and presumably Musidorus) off stage, so Plangus does not commit the absurdity of lamenting their deaths in their own presence.

Erona-Plangus narrative: a reinscription of Sidney by means of a romantic reconstruction of his characters' past. In Sidney, both Helen and Amphialus are deeply problematic characters, ethically, with considerable strength matched by considerable weakness. Weamys largely elides the ethical and legal issues, so central to Sidney, of Amphialus's involvement in treason and civil war; for her, his treason is important insofar as Helena fears Basilius may use his offence as a "fair pretense to take away his life" (32): a romantic issue. (I hasten to add, however, that it was no doubt prudent for a writer of royalist sympathies writing around 1650 not to pursue too forcefully the subject of the prosecution of perpetrators of treason against a lawful king in a civil war.) So, too, Amphialus's "ill usage in his castle" (34) of Philoclea and Pamela, in Sidney an issue replete with political and legal problems, becomes an issue for Weamys insofar as it affects the course of desire: Weamys will not have Amphialus and Helena marry until Amphialus has begged and received forgiveness from Philoclea. Weamys also rewrites Amphialus's feelings for Helen: in Sidney, Amphialus is actively hostile to Helen (her imprudent revelation of her love for him, to a friend of his who was courting her, led to a mortal duel between Amphialus and his friend, with the subsequent death of his friend's father); in Weamys, he is merely unresponsive to Helena because of his overwhelming love of Philoclea. In this narrative as in the earlier one, then, Weamys is largely uninterested in the ethical ambiguity of her characters' past: her work is to end with a marriage, not a trial.

The last third of Weamys's *Arcadia* is pastoral; it contains the Uranian narrative (the pursuit of Urania by Strephon, Claius, Lalus, Antaxius, and Lacemon), the completion of Mopsa's tale, and the death of Philisides. I will discuss them in that order, but first a few general observations should be made on Weamys's and Sidney's relation to the pastoral. To begin with, they are formally different. Sidney (and Weamys's possible additional source, Richard Beling) follows Sannazaro in having a prose section succeeded by an eclogue or group of eclogues, sung by shepherds; and in all three writers, the poetry provides the Virgilian signature of their works. Weamys does not make her shepherds into classical ecloguists, and she claims no Virgilian pedigree for herself.

Sidney and Beling are also like Sannazaro in articulating the so-called "pastoral idea": a complex of attitudes—an opposition to courtly show, aspiration, and honor; a preference for the mean estate, simplicity, and humility; a longing for a golden age—that is a characteristic strategy (if not necessarily the point of view) of much Renaissance pastoral. Weamys is not especially interested in this aspect of the pastoral.

The pastoral is a deeply, though usually obliquely, political mode; and in terms of class and gender its history is divided between nostalgia and subversion, even within the same work. One of the most persistent stagings of the pastoral's politics, the aristocratic birth of an apparent shepherd, is notably absent in Weamys. What interests her more (in Urania above all, but also in Strephon and, to a lesser degree, Claius) is what can be called "aristocratic approximation," that is, the approximation of aristocratic refinement of sentiment and gesture as a mechanism of social mobility.

Weamys, and largely Sidney, too, divides her rustics into two types: "real" rustics (Mopsa and her family) and "literary" rustics. This division is epitomized above all by the gulf between the two shepherdesses, the "real" rustic Mopsa and the "literary" pastoral Urania. Mopsa epitomizes the intractable limitations of her class as much as Urania epitomizes transcendence of her class. Mopsa is Sidney's and Weamys's Gryll: pushy and ugly, afflicted with bad taste and social pretension, she is a kind of grotesque soubrette. The amusement at her expense at once forgives and contains her. Unlike Urania and Strephon, she cannot approximate aristocratic sensibility; she can only parody it.

Weamys's portrayal of her "literary" rustics stems ultimately from the ancient pastoral device of portraying aristocrats in the guise of shepherds, a device that in the Renaissance manifests itself in the Platonic or Petrarchan shepherd who approximates the refined sentiments of the ruling classes. This is what Sidney is working with in Strephon and Claius, as is Weamys; but with Weamys it is significant that the literary shepherd who most transcends her class is a woman, Urania. Strephon, it is true, becomes Sir Strephon at the end of the work; and while he has done much to merit his knighthood, not the least of those merits is that he is Urania's husband and, as her husband, he must be worthy of her. It is Urania, more than her husband and certainly more than his rival Claius, who is least contaminated by the foolishness and bad form of "real" rusticity; and it is Urania, more than any of the shepherds, and arguably even more than the aristocratic figures, who most embodies the refinement of sentiment and gesture associated with the heroes of aristocratic pastoral. Urania is the supreme embodiment in the work of the code of gentility or sensibility; and for Weamys, as for numerous other writers at least since the sixteenth century and the emergence of a strong middle class, it is this code, with its emphasis on delicacy of feeling, that permits the approximation of the presumed sensibility of "the gentles" by the less well-born.

Weamys never really allows this code to pose a radical challenge to patriarchal class distinctions, but it does permit some mobility. It is in fact the most democratic of the social codes in Weamys: it links all her "good" characters, independent of class and gender, from Strephon to Musidorus, Urania to Philoclea. In this respect it is markedly different from the heroic code in Weamys, which is much more rigidly gender- and class-defined. The heroic code is notably limited to men (Weamys includes no female warriors like Sidney's Parthenia), and the male shepherds, while capable of stalwart deeds, never become heroes in the sense that the aristocratic males do. Through the code of gentility, Urania can approximate her female aristocratic counterparts much more closely than Strephon and Claius can approximate their male counterparts through the heroic code. Indeed, the most interesting aspect of masculine social mobility in Weamys is that its agency is primarily through a code that (unlike the heroic) not only crosses genders but is predominantly associated with women, especially Urania. To a degree, the male pastoral heroes are allowed to rise socially insofar as they become heroines. However, the very nature of the agency allowed them for mobility also forces them to share, albeit partially, in the inaccessibility of the heroic to Weamys's heroines. Weamys's text, moreover, seems ambivalent about the male shepherds' gender-definition, for while Strephon's and Claius's delicacy of feeling makes them worthy of Urania's sensibility, it also leads them to an extravagant loss of emotional control, which in Weamys is a characteristically feminine debility. It is the two shep-

herds' feminine debility, coupled with their falling short in heroic conduct, that defines the limits of their approximation of aristocratic
masculinity. The feminine is deployed at once to enable and contain
masculine social climbing.

Even more rigid than the heroic code in Weamys is the relation of
romance and marriage to class and gender. At least a flirtation with marital class-crossing, usually manifested in the inappropriate love of an
aristocrat for a shepherdess, is deeply embedded in the history of the
pastoral romance from *Daphnis and Chloe* on; but Weamys's pastoralism does not even play with this possibility.

Nor is there any of Sidney's Arcadian play with gender-crossing in
the staged homoeroticism of Pyrocles and Basilius. It says a great deal
about Weamys's pastoralism that it finds no place for the potentially
destabilizing paradoxes of the Amazon or the cross-dresser. (This
absence is all the more striking in the context of the use, by the authors
of the commendatory poems, of gender-crossing and cross-dressing to
define Weamys herself in her relation to Sidney.) The dominant wish of
her pastoralism is for domestic and social harmony or, to use the last
words of her work, "peace and quietness," and in this context it is
appropriate that for her the dominant code that relaxes class and gender
distinctions is sensibility.

Traditionally, the green world of the pastoral provides the occasion
for characters to come into their own identity. That is certainly true of
Weamys as a writer. Perhaps one reason she seems so much more
sophisticated a writer in the pastoral section is simply that she is more
experienced, but it is also possible that she is liberated by the fact that
her pastoral narratives have a less fully developed Sidneian past. In her
main pastoral narrative, the love of Strephon and Claius for Urania,
Weamys uses the greater part of what Sidney had presented, but that
was no great restriction on her, for the Urania narrative is not developed
very much in Sidney. The origins of the Urania narrative are contained
in Lamon's eclogue in the First Eclogues at the end of the first book of
the 1593 *Arcadia* (they are not included, however, in the 1590 *New
Arcadia*), but the reader first encounters the Urania narrative at the very
beginning of the work. The 1593 *Arcadia* begins with the ending of the

Urania narrative, with Urania's departure, followed by Strephon's and Claius's pursuit of her.[45] Sidney's Urania narrative is thus ideal for a continuator: Sidney gave it pride of place—and yet left it fragmented, so the narrative provides an ideal point of attachment (to a privileged origin, Sidney) and of detachment (an open space for the continuator's own invention).

Interestingly, of the Arcadian prose romancers that followed Sidney, the only two who saw the full narrative potential of the Uranian fragment were women—Weamys and, earlier in the century, Lady Mary Wroth. And while both women writers found in the absence of Urania a site of invention, their Uranias could not possibly be more unlike. Wroth's Urania, unlike Sidney's, is no mere absence for male Petrarchan projection and transformation, but at the same time Wroth's Urania is far from Weamys's figure, an object of desire who longs to escape her own desire and agency. From the beginning, Wroth's Urania is an agent, and it is she who (despite the otherworldly suggestion of her name and Sidney's portrayal of her) pragmatically provokes action in the emotionally enfeebled Perissus and proceeds to pursue her own desire. Moreover, unlike both Weamys and Sidney, Wroth constructs her Urania into one of the staples of Greek and pastoral romance, the shepherd whose birth is in fact aristocratic. Sidney employed this device in the *Old Arcadia* in his portrayal of Strephon and Claius, but not Urania, and he dropped it in the *New Arcadia*, where the two shepherds, instead of recovering aristocratic origins, transcend their class origins by means of their Platonic and romantic transfiguration. Weamys follows Sidney's romantic transfiguration of Strephon and, to a markedly less degree, the older Claius; but it is the object of their desire, Urania, who is most transfigured and who most transcends her class. It is perhaps fair to say, in summary, that both Weamys and Wroth find in the Uranian absence the space for the creation of a heroine, for female presence; both locate in Sidney's Urania the site for women writers to idealize women. Beyond that, they seem as different from each other as from Sidney.

---

45. In a witty play on his work's generic mixture, Sidney begins his heroic narrative, the adventures of Pyrocles and Musidorus, *in medias res* through a pastoral narrative that is also begun *in medias res*.

Weamys's first and defining point of intervention into Sidney's narrative is her rewriting the reason Sidney gives for Urania's absence in the *New Arcadia* section of the 1593 *Arcadia.* Sidney begins the *New Arcadia* with Strephon and Claius on the Grecian shore staring into sea at the absence left by the departed Urania and remembering her in reflections on how their love for her has transformed them. Though Sidney informs us how Urania left (she dismounted her horse, and Strephon and Claius escorted her to a boat), he does not tell us why she left. Sidney's enigmatic representation of desire, remembrance, and absence encourages at least the possibility of a Platonic, even allegorical reading. Certainly Sidney seems to encourage a "literary" explanation. Weamys does not, and she is quite remarkably, even forcefully, different from Sidney on the point of Urania's absence. She does more than merely fill in the Sidneian gap of Urania's motivation; she in effect rewrites Sidney's account of Urania's departure. Her Urania has not been politely escorted to a boat by Strephon and Claius; she has been abducted: "rudely carried away" by Antaxius (who is, as in Sidney, a wealthy suitor pressed on her by her parents). This rewriting of Sidney reflects Weamys's very different purposes: the first, as in all her narratives, is to arrange for her character to be married; the second is to make Urania a feminine—and equally important, youthful—victim of parental power and values, and of masculine desire. To underscore this, Weamys follows this first abduction with yet another, by Lacemon, a *miles gloriosus* who actually tries to rape her and who kills her pet sparrow.

Whereas in Sidney the absence of Urania largely provides the occasion for male desire, it is that and more in Weamys. For her, Urania's continuing flight and absence become a sign of a flight from desire, as its subject as well as its object. The image of Urania bursting in on Claius and Strephon, screaming "murder" as Lacemon pursues her, is one side of her, her flight from brute male desire; this is the side that links Urania to romance heroines such as Sidney's beleaguered Pamela and Philoclea. The other side is her inner flight from desire itself, an apparent absence of erotic will. After Strephon kills Lacemon, Urania returns to her parents, but even after their deaths, when she is free to choose her own mate, she chooses not to: "it hath been always contrary to her chaste disposition to accept of the least motion concerning a married life" (75). She ultimately surrenders her preference for chastity only because she perceives the lives of her friends, Claius and Strephon, "in jeopardy"; and in order to avoid injuring either of them, she proceeds to recreate her parental relationship by surrendering her choice to Pyrocles and Musidorus.

Weamys largely portrays her heroine as the object of other people's will, and to the extent that she has agency it is expressed in a desire for freedom from all agency: freedom not just from the willful agency of male desire but from her own will as well, in effect, an almost absolute independence of the construction of self around agency. Hence, when Urania feels she cannot avoid marrying, she transfers the agency of her choice to the princes. Weamys does not permit Urania even the agency of erotic preference. Weamys's readers are allowed to hope that Urania gets the younger shepherd for her mate (and Weamys actually encourages our hopes, for she exaggerates Sidney's emphasis on the difference in age between the two shepherds, and she makes the elder Claius the moral as well as physical inferior of Strephon, which he is not in Sidney), but Urania herself is not allowed that hope. We may see in her behavior a reaction formation to masculine will, but that may be our own way of disabling the heroine. For Weamys, it seems, the value of the Uranian presence, in the kind of world Urania inhabits, lies in the very absoluteness of her character's absence of erotic selffulness, an absence whose distinct value is the challenge it makes to the insistence of desire and to the erotically and romantically defined self. She is the opposite of Weamys's two other heroines, who are (like her heroes) defined by romantic desire, even romantic obsession. This is not to say that Weamys ranks Urania's relation to desire over Philoclea's and Pamela's, rather that Weamys uses the chaste heroine to problematize the romance form's own ideology of desire. Urania is the result, admittedly incomplete, of a woman writer's effort to create within a romance a heroine who transcends romance.

Interlaced with the Urania narrative is Weamys's other main pastoral narrative, Mopsa's tale. Weamys's decision to interlace two of Sidney's incomplete pastoral narratives is truly inspired: it allows her to counterpoint the crude rusticity of Mopsa with the Platonic pastoralism of the Urania narrative, but above all it allows her to develop an aspect of her own talent, the comic, that links her to Sidney. We may doubt how Weamys read the romantic Sidney, but not how she read the comic Sidney. Indeed, of all the prose continuators, it is Weamys who best understood Sidney's comic genius and the only one who saw the potential of the Mopsa fragment. (It is not one of the narratives in Sidney's list at the end of his work.) Mopsa's tale may be one of the less subtle occasions of Sidney's comic genius, but it is brilliant nonetheless. It is equally brilliant in Weamys. In Sidney, Mopsa's tale is a kind of prose balladmonger's mingling of folklore with learned, aristocratic material (in particular, Apuleius's tale of Cupid and Psyche). By democratic standards, Sidney is ruthlessly condescending to Mopsa's pretension and ineptitude, especially as he contrasts her ineptitude with the aristocratic grace of Philoclea. Weamys is merciless, too, but perhaps not quite so much as Sidney. She cleverly reuses Sidney's device of interrupting the loquacious Mopsa. Sidney had had Philoclea interrupt Mopsa, thus making her tale a fragment. Weamys also has Mopsa interrupted, but by fellow rustics Strephon and Claius, whose pastoral (as opposed to Philoclea's aristocratic) gentility contrasts with her rustic boorishness. It is at least arguable, then, that Weamys may have intended, in her interruption's substitution of a polished rustic for an aristocratic interrupter, a partial dissociation of her own ridicule of Mopsa from class and background; but frankly I doubt that. Largely, Weamys does not seem to have the "profound ambivalence" about upholding the established system that Patricia Meyer Spacks[46] discovers in the eighteenth-century novelists of sensibility to whom Weamys, like Sidney, in many ways points. She no more questions the centrality of aristocratic values than does Sidney, and those values underlie the ridicule of her comedy as much as the idealization of her romance.

---

46. *Imagining a Self: Autobiography and Novel in Eighteenth-Century England* (Cambridge: Harvard Univ. Press, 1976), 63.

The final Sidneian pastoral narrative Weamys completes is Sidney's self-portrayal as Philisides. Weamys's narrative takes up less than two pages, but it is crucially placed at the end of a narrative tour de force. In a witty play on Sidney's failure to complete the *New Arcadia* (and, from one perspective, the 1593 *Arcadia* too), Weamys ends her *Arcadia* in a brilliant coda of endings. We expect the solemnities of the aristocratic marriages to be the triumphal finale (that is clearly what the work has been leading up to), but Mopsa's interruption delays that finale. Then the Urania narrative interrupts Mopsa's finale, and Mopsa's tale is followed by the completion of Strephon's tale. At last, with the Uranian narrative seemingly finished and all the couples married and ready for bed, the work seems ready itself to be put to rest, but then the Uranian narrative erupts for a surprise coda of its own: Lalus (the shepherd who kept Urania from being raped by Lacemon) rushes in, claiming Urania for his own, and the princes must dismiss his case. But the work is still not over: the night creates a new ending, the death of Claius; and his death is followed by the death of another "despairing shepherd," Philisides, who is found dead of a broken heart on Claius's tomb.

For a work that continues and completes an incomplete work, Weamys's coda of continually deferred completion is a formal masterstroke. The placement of Sidney/Philisides in the midst of this coda of completions can certainly be read in terms of an agonistic literary relation: the strong poet is murdered by the belated one, her triumph over his incompleteness asserted by the emphatic completeness of her own multiple endings. Some of that may be there, but the major point of Weamys's giving her precursor the last narrative seems to me memorial and celebratory—in Sidney's own terms. It is helpful in this respect to compare Weamys to the two other continuators, Alexander and Johnstoun, who also portray the death of Sidney (as Knight of the Sheep and Knight of the Star, respectively). They, unlike Weamys, have Sidney dying as he did in life, of a thigh wound from an arrow: a heroic death. Weamys's Sidney, however, is not the Sidney dying at Zutphen, but the literary Sidney, the Arcadian Sidney, and so his death is fictionalized in terms of his fiction, not his life; he dies as he portrayed himself in the *New Arcadia*, as a lover and a poet, and a poet with a secret love:

a romantic death. In her precursor's secret Weamys might well have found a tempting place for overgoing him: she might have told his secret, thereby bringing to a tight, definitive close not only his work but also his self-presentation. William Alexander, her one predecessor who deals with Philisides's secret love, does reveal Sidney's secret: while dying, Philisides reveals the name to Musidorus, who later reveals the secret to Pyrocles. Weamys lets us know there is a secret love, and says nothing more. In her coda of closures, she leaves only one tale incomplete, and that is Sidney's own; she encloses the fragmented precursor in closures, but leaves some space open for him in her ending as he had for her. A more elegant statement of Weamys's literary relation to Sidney would be difficult to imagine.

Weamys's romantic rather than heroic portrayal of Philisides is in effect an image of her relation to Sidney: largely, the romantic Sidney, the Sidney who points to eighteenth-century novels of sensibility. The narratives Weamys chooses to complete are all, with the possible exception of Mopsa's tale, romance narratives. As we have seen, Weamys tends to simplify the moral past of Sidney's (now her own) characters, downplaying them as the objects of moral judgment (whose denouement is a trial) and foregrounding them as romantic subjects (whose denouement is a marriage). Moreover, in Weamys Sidney's romance narratives tend to become, even more than in Sidney, narratives of sensibility, in which tears flow copiously and delicacy of feeling is the virtue that links the sexes and makes romantic marriage possible. Her narratives are also, again more than Sidney's, narratives of romantic languishing: male and female may languish in different ways, but languish they all do. The only character who is free of languishing, though she is not free of the requirement of marriage, is Urania. In addition, the romances of all of her characters are explorations of "triangular" desire: not always specifically in René Girard's[47] sense of the term, but often in that sense, and certainly always in the simpler sense of desire mediated with or through a third person. Moreover, the desire of all of the central

---

47. See the classic statement in chapter 1 ("'Triangular' Desire"), *Deceit, Desire, and the Novel: Self and Other in Literary Structure* (1961; Baltimore: The Johns Hopkins Univ. Press, 1965), 1–52.

characters ends in marriage. Only minor characters end up unmarried, and most of those end up dead: Anaxius, Plexirtus, Claius, and Philisides—though the only two characters in her fiction who actually die for love are male.

In her revision of Sidney, Weamys would seem to fit the stereotype of the female "romantic" reader of Sidney as opposed to the male "heroic" reader of Sidney. This image runs the risk of reducing an early-modern woman to a Victorian cliché, and so what I have tried to emphasize in this account of Weamys as a continuator of Sidney is her agency, not her subservience. From this perspective, the process governing Weamys's relation to Sidney is one of romantic reinscription, a female appropriation of a male text through romance. Reinscription for Weamys is not just a revision by reseeing; she quite literally rewrites his text. Weamys reinscribes the male precursor-text by means of the representation of women in terms of the principal agency, real and fantasized, open to most women of her class, namely romantic agency. (As Virginia Woolf famously described it, marriage is "the one great profession open to our class since the dawn of time," and we have not, in the seventeenth century, reached the point where romantic agency has lost its ancient power as a youth's principal challenge to patriarchal family structures.) Contrary to the way s/he is usually characterized, the "romantic" or "sentimental" reader or writer is, from this standpoint, potentially a "resisting reader"[48] of male texts, and what may represent to post-Victorian eyes clichéd docility may in fact be more accurately a form of romantic resistance and reinscription. In the rewriting of, especially, heroic texts, sentimentality need not be confused with compliance. Romanticizing is

---

48. The term, of course, is Judith Fetterley's, in *The Resisting Reader: A Feminist Approach to American Fiction* (Bloomington: Indiana Univ. Press, 1988), esp. xi–xxvi. Fetterley's argument seems in part a feminist appropriation for the female reader of the creative misprision of the writer, as Harold Bloom described it: "the poet's deliberate misinterpretation, *as a poet,* of a precursor poem or of poetry in general" (*The Anxiety of Influence* [New York: Oxford, 1973], 43). Caroline Lucas, *Writing for Women: The Example of Woman as Reader in Elizabethan Romance* (Philadelphia: Open University Press, 1989), has fruitfully employed Fetterley's term for her own strategy of reading Elizabethan romances in the context of "feminist reader-response criticism" and "reading 'against the grain'" (26). Weamys, it seems to me, provides a historical model for both Bloom's "creative misprision of the writer" and for Lucas's "resistant" feminist re-readings of male-authored texts.

the principal agency of Weamys's resistance in the mimetic act, her chief way of establishing her own difference in the act of continuation. Weamys is a cautious resister, and the moments of her resistance may only be intermittent fissures in the mimetic compliance of the work, but those moments seem to me significant and interesting.

All of this notwithstanding, it would be a distortion of Weamys to overemphasize this resistance. It is probably we, more than she, who feel uncomfortable in her role as a continuator, we, more than she, who have difficulty with her compliance, so that ironically we may become her resisting reader trying to control her compliance. In any event, I should not wish this introduction's emphasis on Weamys's difference from Sidney—a difference attributable at least in part to gender—to obscure her quite substantial links with him. Some would emphasize the link of class—not that the two are of the same class but that they both identify with aristocratic values. I would like to emphasize another link, one that by emphasizing the discourses of gender and class we may forget, and that is youth. The connection of romance and youth (specifically, the privileging of youthful desire) is as old as the Greek romances' roots in New Comedy; as much as gender or class it has a claim to being the dominant discourse of romance. The discourse of youth is possibly even stronger in Sidney than in earlier romance writers. Though he was probably revising the *Old Arcadia* in his late twenties and early thirties, Sidney began the *Arcadia* in his early twenties, and the revision preserves the earlier version's emphasis on youth. The *New Arcadia*, especially, is pervasive with a strong mistrust of the older generation: Basilius and Gynecia are sexually rapacious, while keeping their daughters under rein; even Philanax and Euarchus seem cruelly just in the trial scene, certainly ethically ambiguous; and, of course, there is Cecropia.

As for Weamys, one can probably account for her work as much by characterizing her as a *young* writer as by characterizing her as a woman writer. The Sidneian portrayal of an older authority gone awry is not, however, a focus of hers: her resistance of age is less through representation than through nonrepresentation. The old kings are very much in the background: Evarchus is barely mentioned except briefly in his role of assisting Plangus's rescue of Erona, and Basilius's main role is to plead in behalf of "dotage" (Claius's) to Pyrocles and Musidorus. Genecea (Sidney's Gynecia) is mentioned, but the only woman of an older generation who has a real presence is Artaxia, and her villainy defeated, she vanishes into widowhood after surrendering the throne to the younger Plangus and his bride. Weamys awards power and love to the young. This is seen throughout: the multiple marriage that is the *telos* of her work represents the discourse of youth as much as of gender; the entire work satisfies the fantasy of the agency of youthful desire and the marriage of young people according to their own desires. Equally revealing of Weamys's partiality to youth is her counterpart (whether or not intended) to Sidney's climactic trial scene, namely the princes' judgment of Strephon and Claius: the same princes who in Sidney were judged by their elders, now control the verdict; and their verdict goes against old Basilius's recommendation of the older Claius and for the youthful Strephon.

Weamys does not represent the success of youth in terms of romantic agency alone. Though less represented than alluded to, their political agency is also important. In the next-to-last sentence of her work, Weamys alludes to her youthful couples' assumption of the thrones of their kingdoms. Remarkably, that is no sooner mentioned than, in the very next sentence (the last of the work), they abdicate for their children. At the end of the *New Arcadia*, Sidney also has his youthful characters assume roles of political power, but he stops there. Weamys carries the discourse of youth farther: it is not enough for the young to gain power; they must be prepared in time to surrender it to the next generation. Nothing so strongly testifies to the power of the discourse of youth in Weamys than that the final act of her work is the abdication of those she has brought to power.

Weamys's final link with Sidney—the heroic Sidney—is tenuous, and it should not be exaggerated in the interest of protecting her from the "emasculation" of women through romance. Nonetheless, while romance may comprise the greater part of Weamys's world, it is not all of her world. The battles of heroic romance are largely absent, but there is a convincing account of Plangus's military strategy in the initial encounter between Plangus's forces and Plaxirtus's (53), and vivid death scenes for both Anaxius, who gnashes his teeth in anger as he falls to Pyrocles's feet, and for Plaxirtus, "dying with bitter groans and frantick speeches" (61) as his horse tramples on him. There is also a recurrent awareness of the political importance of protocol and ceremony. For instance, Weamys acknowledges the importance of aristocrats' courting the favor of the populace in the wedding arrangements Clytifon suggests for Helen and Amphialus: the wedding in Arcadia is to be followed by one in Corinth so Helen's people will not feel slighted. One might note, too, Weamys's awareness (through Kalodolus) of the need to establish a clear policy for disbanding the troops after the civil conflict in Armenia. There are other instances, but all of them would not suggest more than an intermittent concern with politics and power. For the most part, Weamys is less interested in the actual exercise of power than in what she no doubt was more acquainted with: powerlessness and the ceremony of power. To the extent power concerns her it is as a means to an end. What that end is, is expressed beautifully in the last words of the book:

> Then after all ceremonies [were] accomplished, they retired severally to their flourishing kingdoms of Thessalia and Macedon, and Armenia, with Corinth, where they increased in riches and were fruitful in their renowned families. And when they had sufficiently participated of the pleasures of this world, they resigned their crowns to their lawful successors, and ended their days in peace and quietness. (105)

This is, from one perspective, a typical romance ending: the characters marry and live happily. What provides just enough swerve to animate the convention is the last sentence: her characters know enough about psychology not to keep the young out of power for too long, and they know enough about politics to assure lawful succession by resigning their crowns in their lifetime, and so they "ended their days in peace and quietness." There is an elegant economy in the wisdom of this happy ending, made all the more moving in the historical context of its author: the young woman who wrote these lines was writing in all probability during or slightly after the civil wars; for her, the longing for orderly succession and for days of peace and quiet was far from being only a sentimental rite of romantic closure.

It is passages like this that remind one that it is easy to underestimate Weamys's work: this short "continuation" is more, at times much more, than a footnote in the seventeenth-century history of Sidney's influence. The almost madcap comedy of the Mopsa episode, the shrewd charm of the pastoral scenes, and the formal invention of, especially, the last part of the work: all suggest a writer who is learning, and learning very quickly, how to play with and against tradition. However, as far as we know, her *Arcadia* is as far as she got. For some reason, she seems not to have written, or at least she did not publish, another word. Perhaps she married, or died, or simply went on to other things. At any rate, this is all she left us: a work worthy of both gratitude and regret.

Bibliographical Note

The bibliography for Weamys is negligible. The longest and most valuable account for her work is Americus G. D. Wiles's chapter on her in his unpublished dissertation, "The Continuations of Sir Philip Sidney's *Arcadia*" (Princeton University, 1933). As an overview of Weamys's relation to Sidney and the continuators, Wiles's study is generally reliable, but the critical commentary suffers from his rigid insistence on aligning Weamys's work with Sidney's and valuing her only for complying with what he assumes Sidney would have done. Bridget G. MacCarthy, *Women Writers: Their Contribution to the English Novel, 1621–1744* (Cork: Cork University Press, 1944), 64–68, emphasizes the differences between Weamys and Sidney; she finds that Weamys avoids "the swaying garrulity of Sidney's style, and expresses herself in a style which, though certainly romantic, is clear, straightforward and economical," and she emphasizes Weamys's ability to "keep one eye on real life," and her characters' "energy and commonsense in achieving their purposes." Paul Salzman provides an invaluable generic contextualization of Weamys in two chapters on "The Nature of Seventeenth-Century Fiction" and "Sidney and the First Generation of Seventeenth-Century

Fiction" in *English Prose Fiction, 1558–1700: A Critical History* (Oxford: Clarendon, 1985). His treatment of Weamys is unhappily brief, and largely a response to Bridget MacCarthy. In a paragraph on Weamys in her chapter, "Fact and Fiction: Lady Mary Wroath and Anne Weamys," Dale Spender, *Mothers of the Novel* (London: Pandora, 1986), claims that Weamys "made a contribution towards the evolution of realism in fiction, and towards the women's novel." Elaine Hobby's *Virtue of Necessity: English Women's Writing, 1649–88* (Ann Arbor: The University of Michigan Press, 1989) is a landmark study in the field of its subtitle, but Weamys receives little more than a page (89–90) in a chapter on "Romantic Love—Prose Fiction." A note in *The Feminist Companion to Literature in English*, ed. Virginia Blain et al. (New Haven: Yale, 1990) claims that Weamys "reckons to capture his [Sidney's] spirit in a plainer style." A brief entry for Weamys appears in *A Biographical Dictionary of English Women Writers: 1580–1720*, ed. Maureen Bell et al. (Boston: G. K. Hall, 1990), 209–10.

TEXTUAL INTRODUCTION

Textual History

The first, and possibly only, edition of *A Continuation of Sir Philip Sidney's Arcadia* (Wing 1189) is the 1651 octavo edition, printed by William Bentley and sold by Thomas Heath. Copies of the 1651 edition are located at Yale, Harvard, the Folger Shakespeare Library, the Newberry Library, Texas (Austin), Michigan (Ann Arbor), the Huntington Library, the William Andrews Clark Memorial Library (UCLA), Princeton, Durham University, the Bodleian Library, and the British Library. The text of the corrected reprint, upon which the modernized edition is based, has been transcribed from the Folger copy of the 1651 edition. I have collated the Folger, Yale, and British Library copies, finding no variants. I have also checked the Harvard and Newberry copies to see if they share the most notable misprints shared by the Folger and Yale copies, and they do. It therefore seems likely that the author did not check proof. This does not mean, however, that the volume was carelessly produced. The small size of the volume suggests a fairly modest production, but the printing is fairly high quality: there is care in the format (especially the borders of the front matter), and the press work is even and good, with no unusual number of errors. There is, however, a notable increase of errors in the second half. Also characteristic of only the second half is the use of the apostrophe, placed before the *s* in proper names ending in *s,* to signify possession: e.g., *Claius* and *Venus.* This may suggest either a rush job or a change of type-setter, though the volume seems to have been the work of a single print shop.

A second edition is listed in *The Term Catalogue* for May, 1690,[1] but it may not have appeared (entry in *The Term Catalogues* was at times no more than staking a claim), and according to John Morrison of the Wing STC Revision Project, no copies are known to have survived.

---

1. *The Term Catalogues, 1668-1709 A. D.*, ed. Edward Arber (London: Privately printed, 1903-06), II.316.

Editorial Principles

In an effort to address the needs of as wide an audience as possible, this volume includes both a modernized, annotated edition (based largely on the editorial principles of the Oxford Sidney) and a corrected reprint of the 1651 text (based largely on the editorial principles of the Cambridge Sidney) of Weamys's *Arcadia*. As discussed below, a modernized text has seemed essential if the needs of undergraduates and other nonspecialists are to be addressed. At the same time, a corrected reprint is of obvious value to specialists, and for this audience the modernized text can serve as an interpretive gloss. However, I hope that the inclusion of the original text will be useful not only to those already experienced in seventeenth-century women's writing, but also to those in whom the modernized edition has kindled a desire to be so, and will encourage them to refer to the text upon which their modernized edition is based.

The Modernized Edition

The aim of the modernized edition is that of the Oxford Sidney of Jean Robertson (*Old Arcadia*)[2] and Victor Skretkowicz (*New Arcadia*)[3]: which is to say, in Robertson's words, "to produce a clean, readable text" (lxvi) in a modernized format. The decision to modernize Weamys's text did not come easily. The trend of the times is largely against editorial intervention, especially by a male editor of a female author's text. Thus, I have decided to follow the principles of conservative modernizing of the Oxford Sidney. To the extent this edition departs from the Oxford editors' principles, it is in the direction of less rather than more editorial intervention.

My decision to modernize is based on the following arguments. First, if a modernized edition (Oxford/Clarendon) is appropriate for Sidney, it is appropriate for his continuator. For years the standard scholarly edition of Sidney was Feuillerat's extremely conservative text (Cam-

---

2. *The Countess of Pembroke's Arcadia (The Old Arcadia)* (Oxford: Clarendon, 1973).

3. *The Countess of Pembroke's Arcadia (The New Arcadia)* (Oxford: Clarendon, 1987).

bridge, 1912). Unhappily, it was an edition more often quoted from than read. Furthermore, as Robertson puts it, "As there is no holograph, there is little point in preserving the idiosyncrasies of one particular scribe" (lxix) or printer. We have no way, in the absence of a holograph, of knowing whether or not the punctuation and spelling are Weamys's, and as I said above, it seems fairly certain that Weamys did not proof-read the text. The punctuation, then, may very well be in part her scribe's or her printer's, so that a modern editor's insistence on non-interference may ironically perpetuate the original interference.

For me, however, the decisive reason for a conservative modernizing of Weamys is this: she has been ignored for over three centuries; it would be a dreadful irony to edit her in such a way as to assure her continuing to be ignored. Weamys's text is not unreadable for most modern readers, but accidental differences of punctuation and spelling make it more inaccessible than it need be. The modern reader is a visual reader, and yet many, if not most, early-modern printed texts seem in varying degrees to continue to be part of an oral or at least aural tradition. Romances, especially, seem designed to be read aloud. If we are not deal-ing with, strictly speaking, an oral tradition of composition, we are almost certainly dealing with a text written with an awareness of its potential status as a text to be read aloud, a writerly orality for a poten-tial aural audience. The heavy punctuation, the loose construction of long prose units (they are not always modern sentence units), the abun-dance of what we would call "sentence fragments" in Weamys's text sug-gest the text's orality/aurality, and in truth the text is more readily enjoyed read aloud than on the page. It is difficult to read the 1651 edi-tion and not feel that the printed text is a mere ghost of a speaking voice.

This edition, though modernized, has tried (to use the words of Sara Jayne Steen) to express "a responsibility to a woman" by "interfer[ing] as little as possible with the *sound* of [her voice]."[4] I am not sure that, with

---

4. "Behind the Arras: Editing Renaissance Women's Letters," in *New Ways of Looking at Old Texts: Papers of the Renaissance English Text Society, 1985-1991*, ed. W. Speed Hill (Binghamton, NY: Medieval & Renaissance Texts and Studies, 1993), 231. Steen's essay is one of such subtlety, moral and intellectual, that I regret not being able to follow all of her recommendations.

this particular text, establishing an unbending rule preserving old spelling and punctuation necessarily results in preserving the sound of the voice, at least not for the visual reader of printed texts. Weamys's text has an unusually large number of difficult patches. Individually, they may not always be daunting, but cumulatively they can be, and this cumulative difficulty is made all the more acute for readers who are also trying to make sense of the intricacies of Sidneian plots unfamiliar to them. Such readers, had they had available to them only an old-spelling edition of Weamys, would have heard little of the "sound of her voice" through the static. This, at any rate, has been my experience. As an experiment, I have had graduate students and colleagues (the presumed audience of this edition) read a typescript of parts of the original text, and consistently they have found the punctuation, especially, of the original perplexing and often confusing. As a result, Weamys emerges for them—quite wrongly, I think—as a rather graceless stylist. I am far from denying that she can be graceless, and I have done my best not to create an arabesque out of a fall, but most of what seems graceless to a modern reader is in fact a defacement through a historical shift in punctuation practices. Modern repunctuation can often bring out, or at least imply, the verbal and intellectual structures that the text actually has (and almost certainly had in its original status as an aural text), and for which the original punctuation of the printed text is now, and possibly was then, not always adequate for the solitary visual reader. Indeed, when I have found passages unclear, the surest way I have found to break through the incoherence is to read them aloud; and often the latent, if loose, structures of the speaking voice have emerged. Most readers will not read the text aloud, and I have tried to use modern punctuation as a way of enabling the modern (that is, the solitary, visual) reader to approximate the text's aurality and to help her hear, especially in the intricacies of the text's longer units, the punctuating clarity of the lost voice of the tale's teller.

Finally, the decision to modernize Weamys's text has been made easier by the inclusion in this volume of the corrected reprint of the 1651 text, on which the modernization is based. Furthermore, for those who wish a facsimile of the 1651 edition, an extremely convenient and inexpensively bound copy-flo of the text is available from the Yale University Library.

The governing principle behind all my decisions in modernizing the 1651 text is the assumption that I should intervene no more than is necessary for the sake of reasonable clarity. The resulting methods are as follows.

Spelling. Spelling is for the most part normalized. My exceptions are these:

1. retention of the old usage of *other* for *others* in its single appearance

2. retention of archaic prefix *a-* to participles; e.g., *astealing* and *asounding*

3. retention of older grammatical forms like *swom, strook, brake, shew, trode, tare* (for tore), but modernization of preterite formations like *whisht, stopt,* and *staid*

4. retention of the division of reflexive pronouns as two words: *my self, her self,* etc. Meanings significantly change when *self* collapses into one word. I won't speculate on what the change is, but important issues of subjectivity are potentially involved, especially for contemporary readers; and since clarity is not at stake, I have seen no reason to intervene with original usage.

Proper names are standardized. The text's spellings of the names of Sidney's characters and places are not always consistent and do not always agree with modern standardization of Sidney's names. (For that matter, of course, there are variants within Renaissance editions of Sidney's *Arcadia,* and one or more of these may have influenced Weamys or her printer.) Names in this edition are standardized according to the dominant forms in the text, independent of whether or not they agree with the standard forms in Sidney. (The exception is the name of Sidney himself, which is "Sydney" in Weamys.) Consequently, some of the names in this edition are slightly different from those in the Oxford Sidney and in the Penguin edition of the 1593 *Arcadia:* it is *Plaxirtus,* not *Plexirtus; Clytifon,* not *Clitophon; Antifalus,* not *Antiphilus; Evarchus,* not *Euarchus; Genecea,* not *Gynecia; Citherea,* not *Cithera; Kaleander,* not *Kalander; Kalodolus,* not *Kalodoulus* or *Kalodulus.* Where there is no dominant form, I have chosen the spelling that agrees with the standard Sidneian spelling.

Capitalization. It is simpler, but potentially simplifying, to eliminate all old-style capitalization of common and abstract nouns; and I have not done so, for it is probably as dangerous to assume that such capitals mean nothing as to assume that they all signify emphasis, reverence, or abstraction. In any event, modern punctuation allows, if it does not always require, the use of significant capitals of this sort. I have kept capitals for sacred places (Heaven, the Temple [of Hymen]), sacred names/powers (the Gods, Providence, Fortune), titles (King, Queen, Prince(s), Princess(es), Her/His Majesty; My Lord and My Lady as prefixes to a proper noun and as addresses), some terms of address (Cousin, Sir, Madam), and some abstractions (Patience, Mercy). Eliminating these capitals would have meant eliding some of the more important and persistent political discourses of the work (of rank, of decorum) and their aesthetic matrix (romance).

Punctuation. This is by far the most important area of modernization. Because it is the one in which most help can be given and most damage done, I have intervened as little as possible. I have not broken up the long colon-punctuated units into shorter sentences, except as a last resort. Indeed, in the repunctuation of these long units, I have preferred to use their own cement, colons and semicolons, to keep them together and avoid breaking them into shorter modern sentence units.

Like much early-modern vernacular prose, the comma-punctuation is heavy to the point of confusion for the modern reader, and I have occasionally lightened the punctuation when clarity seemed at stake. However, in some instances of comma pile-up, phrases and clauses seem to belong to the material both before and after them; in these instances of syntactical ambiguity, I have let the original punctuation stand unless total confusion would result.

Possessives are given their apostrophes. When this involves an important editorial choice of singular or plural, I have noted that choice, and in one instance I have let the ambiguity stand. Possessives formed by the possessive pronoun (e.g., Plaxirtus his) are made to conform to modern usage.

Parentheses are reasonably common in Weamys (as in Sidney), and I have not hesitated to use them. Speeches are enclosed in inverted commas. "Sentence fragments" or "incomplete sentences" are incorporated into neighboring sentences when the sense permits; otherwise, they are left to stand on their own. Italicization of proper nouns is dropped.

Use of brackets. Brackets have been used sparingly when there is a lacuna in the text and when editorial intervention has been necessary to avoid incoherence. Bracketed editorial intervention that is not self-explanatory is explained in footnotes.

The clearest way of demonstrating the editorial principles of this edition is to compare a passage from the 1651 text with its modernized counterpart. I choose as my example the most extreme instance of the modernization principles of this edition; the reader can be assured that nowhere else has there been quite so much intervention with the 1651 text. The passage is the opening of the work:

> In the time that *Basilius* King of *Arcadia*, with *Genecea* his Queen, and his two renowned daughters, the Paragons of the World, *Pamela* and *Philoclea*, were retired from the Court to a private lodge amongst the shepherds, there to refresh themselves with their pleasant & harmless sports. In the time that *Pyrocles*, son and heir to the good *Evarchus* King of *Macedon*, disguised himself to an Amazonian Ladie, for the love of his Venus, the sweet *Philoclea*. And *Musidorus* Prince of *Thassalia* disrobed himself of his glorious rayment, and put on Shepherds weeds, for the sight of the stately *Pamela*. And when *Cupid* displayed his quivers throughout his circle, and brought the famousest Princes in the world to adore his mothers beautie: Then Prince *Plangus*, son to the King of *Iberia*, at the first view of *Erona*, a Queen in *Lydia*, was made a Prisoner to her who was a Prisoner. And he whose resolutions were altogether fixed on the rare beautie of *Erona*, resolved with himself, either to release his incomparable Jewel out of a dolefull Prison, or else to loose his life in the enterprise.

A reader familiar with Sidney's *Arcadia* will probably find that this passage poses no difficulty: she takes it for the synopsis it is and does not inspect it too carefully. A reader less familiar with Sidney is likely to be confused by the punctuation, and a reader lost at the beginning is likely to be a lost reader indeed. Such readers *need* this synopsis, and for such readers the synopsis makes Weamys's "continuation" a work capable of standing on its own.

The above passage is filled with parenthetical commas used almost exclusively to identify the characters by their noble titles. For the sake of clarity, in the modernized text (beginning on page 13) I have replaced parenthetical commas with parentheses. I hope the result makes the passage usefully synoptic, for that is what Weamys wishes it to be. But I hope, too, that the modernizing, by clarifying Weamys's careful linking of names with parenthetical titles, allows a gesture of real wit and charm to emerge in the midst of the synoptic density. Weamys gives her characters the same titles Sidney gave his characters (King of Arcadia, Queen of Lydia, and Prince of Iberia, and so on), with this one exception: she diverges from her male precursor for the titles of Pamela and Philoclea. For them she creates a new and grander title than the one Sidney gave them, the princesses of Arcadia. For Weamys, they are more than princesses, they are paragons, and they are more than princesses of Arcadia, they are "paragons of the *world*." What Weamys offers in the midst of what may seem to be mere synoptic compliance is a disarming but powerful gesture of difference, and it is surely not unimportant that her difference concerns young women.

A similar effect, of difference in mimetic compliance, is achieved in the syntax of the passage. The original punctuation creates the impression of a syntax loose to the point of ineptitude. The syntax *is* loose (it does not aim for the elaborate rhetorical architecture of Sidney), but it is not incoherent. For (at least) the modern reader, the original punctuation, by creating a series of "fragments," obscures the larger architectural design of the opening passage. The loss of this design entails not only a loss of clarity but also a loss of invention, for it is through the design of the opening "sentence" of her work that Weamys suggests both her attachment to and detachment from Sidney. I have repunctuated the entire passage, eliminating what for the modern reader may seem a series of unconnected fragments and replacing them with a series of colonic units in a large and (I find) rather elegantly sustained structure. My repunctuation is designed not to impose modern sentence structure where there is none but to bring into relief a colonic structure, characteristic of much early-modern writing, that the original punctuation tends to obscure. The recreation of this large, sentence-like unit has the result of foregrounding a stylistic statement of Weamys's difference from Sidney in the very act of imitating him. Weamys begins her "continuation" of Sidney with a summary of his plot that takes the form of an imitation of the first sentence of his *New Arcadia:*

> It was in the time that the earth begins to put on her new apparel against the approach of her lover, and that the sun, running a most even course, becomes an indifferent arbiter between the night and the day, when the hopeless shepherd Strephon was come to the sands which lie against the island of Cithera....

Weamys signals her difference from Sidney by doubling his "in the time that" clause. Moreover, by her eliminating Sidney's initial "it was," she more forcibly and daringly delays periodicity by suspending the creation of a main clause for over a page of her text. (One might also note that Weamys also shows her difference from Sidney in her avoidance of his periphrasis; it is not generally true that Weamys's style is simple, but it is comparatively direct.) Instead of an inept series of fragments, Weamys's beginning is a strategically paradoxical tour de force of deference and difference: in a beginning of delayed periodicity, she combines synoptic directness in an act of stylistic playfulness with her precursor, and in an act of what seems to be extraordinary compliance (in synopsis and imitation), she establishes the space of her difference. Weamys's opening sentence is thus a stylistic paradigm of her relationship to her precursor: in the act of staging her work's past she problematizes her own past as a writer. It is therefore fitting, in terms of Weamys's complicated relation to Sidney, that her long opening synopsis should lead into another synopsis of Sidney (the Erona-Plangus narrative), but one that begins with an episode (the meeting between Artaxia and Plangus) entirely of her own invention.

I hope this comparison has helped to illustrate, and perhaps justify, the principles of the modernized edition. I am well aware, however, that no one method of modernizing will satisfy all readers: even with the comparative stability of modern punctuation, the prose you have just read most of you would at points punctuate differently, and there is no doubt that none of us would modernize Weamys in quite the same way. I myself would not: I have experimented with at least a half-dozen versions, and I am sure that, given the time, I would continue producing other versions. There is no one way. One does not modernize without accepting compromise, nor without hoping that this compromise brings to a writer previously lost to almost all of us a new audience.

The Reprint Edition

The conventions of transcription for the corrected reprint of Weamys's *Arcadia* are essentially those of the Cambridge Sidney (*The Prose Works of Sir Philip Sidney,* edited by Albert Feuillerat [1912]): "the text adopted is printed without any deviations from the original in the matter of spelling and punctuation, save those recorded [at the end of the volume]. These exceptions consist of evident misprints which it has been thought useless to preserve" (I, ix). This means that the only changes I have made in Weamys's text as it appeared in 1651 are of obvious and incontestable misprints.

I have silently corrected dropped letters (fond[*n*]ess, page 131; withi[*n*], page 155; [*c*]orps, page 159; S[*t*]rephon, page 179); an added letter (acc*c*ident, page 176); turned letters (glorio*n*s, page 117; Fo*n*ntain, page 165; allusio*u*s, page 175); foul-case letters (A*m*axius, page 132; c*h*allenge, page 146; Antax*t*us, page 183); faulty spacing (pit ie, page 179; the e, page 179); dittography (*a a* reasonable company, page 151; Ph*iy*siognomies, page 185); and transposed letters (Ura*i*na, page 189; Cli*fti*on [for Clytifon], page 141). Certain possible misprints are preserved on the grounds that they conceivably fall within the normal variation of an old-spelling text: P*æ*mela, Basili*æ*us, Str*æ*phons, B*i*silius, Sort*æ*sia. "Waw" (page 154) is almost certainly a misprint for "way," but even so, as a Scottish word for "wave," it may reveal something about the amanuensis, the printer, or even Weamys herself.

I have corrected the punctuation only in instances that are incontestably printer's errors: on page 155, a second comma has replaced an unmatched parenthesis; on page 158, a comma, originally inserted between a preposition and its object [into, rags], has been placed after the object; and on page 184, a colon placed between subject and verb [they : had] is placed after the verb. I have decided not to replace the few instances of commas, semicolons, and (presumably) dropped punctuation at the end of sentences and paragraphs on the grounds that insertion of a period might conceal a possible lacuna. I have also decided not to replace question marks used as semicolons or exclamation marks. Semicolons are used frequently enough as commas that replacing them would move this reprint unduly in the direction of a critical edition. The same principle has determined my decision to let stand one of the most notable features of the second half of the original text (beginning on page 155), namely the ten instances of the apostrophe placed before the terminal *s* in proper names, used primarily to signify possession (e.g., Claiu's). Finally, where an italicized word begins with a roman capital letter, or is followed by a roman punctuation mark, those have been normalized to accord with modern usage.

The original text has a few instances of words apparently omitted by the printer in the process of typesetting, or perhaps omitted in the manuscript itself. I have decided not to note those gaps in the reprint since, first, their existence and exact location are not beyond question and, second, the gaps have been noted, through the insertion of brackets, in the modernized edition. Other probable, but not certain, misprints include two instances in which a sentence seems to be broken between the end of one paragraph and the beginning of the next; I have let these stand since they are not self-evidently printer's errors (they may, for example, reflect the imperfect state of the text the printer was working from), and in any event the emendation has been made in the modernized edition.

Like the Cambridge Sidney, this reprint does not note the page numbers or the hyphenated words in the original text. Unlike the Cambridge Sidney, however, this edition makes no effort to preserve the original typography: old-style long-*s*'s, ligatures, and a tilde (in its single use) are not retained; *v* used for *u* (in three instances) has been converted to *u*.

A CONTINUATION
OF
SIR PHILIP SIDNEY'S
Arcadia

To the Two Unparalleled Sisters, and Patterns of Virtue, The Lady Anne and the Lady Grace Perpoint,

Daughters to the Right Honorable the Marquess of Dorchester.

If I had not observed that the greatest humility reigns in the bosoms of the noblest personages, I should not presume to dedicate this most unworthy fabric to Your Honors, especially when I consider the poorness of my endeavors and admire the learned Sidney's pastimes; whereof I beseech you charitably to believe that my ambition was not raised to so high a pitch, as the title now manifests it to be, until I received commands from those that cannot be disobeyed. But however, if Your Ladyships will graciously vouchsafe to peruse such a confused theme, I shall harbor the better opinion of it and shall acknowledge my self, as in all gratefulness,   10

Your Honors' devoted Servant,

A. W.

Lines 4–5. **the learned Sidney's pastimes**: i.e., his *Arcadia*. Weamys seems to accept the common Renaissance view of the romance as a mere amusement or diversion.

Line 9. **theme**: matter or subject, possibly with the sense of a school exercise.

The Stationer to the Ingenious Reader

Marvel not to find heroic Sidney's renowned fancy pursued to a close by a feminine pen: rather admire his prophetical spirit now as much as his heroical before. Lo, here Pygmalion's breathing statue, Sir Philip's fantasy incarnate: both Pamela's Majesty and Philoclea's Humility expressed to the life in the person and style of this virago. In brief, no other than the lively ghost of Sidney, by a happy transmigration, speaks through the organs of this inspired Minerva. If any critical ear disrelish the shrillness of the note, let it be tuned to Apollo's lyre, and the harmony will soon be perceived to be much better, and the lady appear much more delightful to her Musidorus. So wisheth

Thine and Her Servant,

T. H.

Title. **Stationer**: publisher, bookseller.   **ingenious**: discerning.

Line 3. **Pygmalion**: a sculptor who fell in love with his own statue of a woman; in answer to his prayer, Aphrodite (goddess of love) brought the statue to life.

Lines 4–5. **Pamela's Majesty and Philoclea's Humility**: The distinction drawn here is suggested in Sidney; Sidney's Kalander, for example, says "methought there was…more sweetness in Philoclea but more majesty in Pamela" (I.3).

Line 5. **virago**: heroic or man-like woman; Amazon. The term was commonly applied to a learned woman (see Anthony Grafton and Lisa Jardine, *From Humanism to the Humanities* [Cambridge: Harvard Univ. Press, 1986], 210–18).

Lines 6–7. **transmigration**: the rebirth of the soul after death in another body.

Line 7. **Minerva**: the goddess of wisdom and warfare, usually represented in the arms of war.

Lines 8–9. **the shrillness of the note…Apollo's lyre**: i.e., the shrillness of the (Sidneian?) music as played on the rustic flute (as opposed to its sweetness on the lyre). The rustic flute, or the pipes, was a musical instrument invented by Minerva (to whom Thomas Heath compares Weamys); the lyre is the instrument traditionally associated with Apollo, god of poetry. Probably the most famous appearance of these two rival instruments is in the musical contest between Marsyas and Apollo, when Apollo's lyre defeats Marsyas's Minervan flute and Apollo subsequently has Marsyas flayed alive (see Ovid, *Metamorphoses,* 6:382–400); this myth would seem to be in the background of Heath's conceit, as may be the related myth of Midas and the singing contest between Apollo and Pan (*Metamorphoses,* 11:146–193).

Line 10. **Musidorus**: the beloved of Sidney's heroine Pamela.

On the Ingenious Continuation of Sir Philip Sidney's *Arcadia*, by Mistress A. W.

No thing doth greater disadvantage bring
Than by too great commending of a thing;
Thus beauty's injured, when the searching eye,
Deceiv'd by others' over-flattery,
Finding that less was magnifi'd before,   5
Thinks there is none, because there is no more.
Art suffers too by this, for too great praise
Withers the greenness of the poets' bays:
For when men's expectations rise too high,
There's nothing seen or read will satisfy.   10
This fault is epidemical; do but o're-look
The stationer's stall, 'tis spoke in ev'ry book:
Where some are so voluminous become
With prefaces of this kind, as scarce a room
Is left for th' author's self. But I can quit   15
My self of this: till now I never writ.
Nor had I done it now, but that a She
Did tempt my pressing for her company;
From whence when she's returned, pray use her well:
She's young, but yet ingeniously will tell   20
You pretty stories, and handsomely will set
An end to what great Sidney did beget,
But never perfected; these embryons she
Doth midwife forth in full maturity.
Nor is't, where things are left undone, a sin,   25

Title. **Ingenious**: characterized by unusual invention, originality, or genius.
Line 8. **bays**: the crown of laurel leaves awarded to the best poets.
Line 23. **embryons**: embryos.

5

To seek to end what greater ones begin.
Therefore whoe're reads their ingenious style,
Not with a frown compare them, but a smile.
She does not write for critics, for whoe're
Loves for to be censorious, forbear.   30
Then this of both, let nothing else be said:
This Sidney's self did write, but this a maid.

                                        —H. P. M.

To the Ingenious Lady, the Author of the Continuation of Sir Philip Sidney's *Arcadia*

Fair author! though your sex secure you so,
That all your dictates will for classic go,
Yet to be lik'd thus only will sound less
Our approbation than our tenderness,
Because the civil world will judgment spend   5
That we are bound in manhood to commend,
Taking our praises' level from that sight
Of what you are, more than from what you write.
Whence critic-wits this nice pretense will find,
That we our courtship speak, but not our mind.   10

    But when they single each respect apart,
Viewing the virgin there, and here the art,
Their prejudice will then to wonder reach,
Not spent on both united, but on each.
For though the stars shine in a beauteous sphere,   15
Yet are they not more stars for shining there,
But would boast luster of as great a force,
Though their containing orbs were dim and course.

                          —F. L.

Line 2. **dictates**: dictated utterances (?).

Line 11. **single each respect apart**: separate out each aspect.

Line 15. **sphere**: one of the concentric spherical shells in which stars and planets were set, according to ancient astronomy.

Line 18. **orbs**: spheres, orbits.   **course**: "course" as orbit, but also "coarse."

On the Continuation of Sir
Philip Sidney's *Arcadia*,
by Mistress A. W.

Much of the terrene globe conceal'd doth lie,
Cheating the searcher's curious industry:
Arcadia too, till now, but partly was descried;
Sidney her beauty view'd, fell lovesick and died
Ere he could show the world her perfect state   5
And glory, interrupted by his fate.
Amazement at her frame did him betray,
In each rare feature too too long a stay,
Till being benighted, left imperfect this
Earth's paradise, to possess one perfect is.   10
In pity o' th' loss, and to repair't, believe
His gallant generous spirit a reprieve
From's sleeping dust hath purchas't, death's malice
Defying with a timely metempsychosis,
He breathes through female organs, yet retains   15
His masculine vigor in heroic strains.
Who hears 't may some brave Amazon seem to be,
Not Mars but Mercury's champion, Zelmane.
And well he may: for doubtless such is she,

Line 1. **terrene**: terrestrial.

Line 2. **curious**: careful, clever, as well as the modern sense of inquisitive.

Line 7. **frame**: proportion, proper organization of features.

Line 14. **metempsychosis**: reincarnation.

Line 18. **Not Mars but Mercury's champion, Zelmane**: i.e., Sidney's reincarnation into the Amazon Weamys is as the champion of not the god of war (Mars) but the god of eloquence, inventor of the lyre (Mercury). Mercury's proverbial skill at deception may be alluded to by way of Zelmane, the Amazonian disguise Pyrocles assumes in order to woo Philoclea in Sidney's *Arcadia*.

Perfection gives t' Arcadia's geography.
Arcadia thus henceforth disputed is,
Whether Sir Philip's or the Countesses.

—F. W.

Line 20. **Perfection**: completion.
Line 22. **Countesses**: probably singular possessive and presumably the Countess of Pembroke.

To Mistress A. W.
Upon Her Additionals to Sir
Philip Sidney's *Arcadia*

If a male soul, by transmigration, can
Pass to a female, and her spirits man,
Then sure some sparks of Sidney's soul have flown
Into your breast, which may in time be blown
To flames, for 'tis the course of enthean fire   5
To warm by degrees, and brains to inspire;
As buds to blossoms, blossoms turn to fruit,
So wits ask time to ripen, and recruit;

    But yours gives Time the start, as all may see
By these smooth strains of early poesy,   10
Which like rays of one kind may well aspire,
If Phoebus please to a Sidneian fire.

                    —JAM. HOWEL.

Line 5. **enthean**: divine inspiration, *entheus ardor.*   Line 8. **recruit**: strengthen, flourish.
Line 12. **Phoebus**: Phoebus Apollo, god of the sun and of poetry.

On the Continuation of Sir Philip Sidney's *Arcadia,* by Mistress A. W.

Lay by your needles, Ladies, take the pen,
The only difference 'twixt you and men.
'Tis tyranny to keep your sex in awe,
And make wit suffer by a Salic law.
Good wine does need no bush, pure wit no beard;   5
Since all souls equal are, let all be heard.
    That the great world might nere decay, the main,
What in this coast is lost, in that doth gain:
So when in Sidney's death wit ebb'd in men,
It hath its spring-tide in a female pen.   10
A single bough shall other works approve,
Thine shall be crown'd with all DODONA's Grove.

                     —F. VAUGHAN.

Line 4. **Salic law**: a law excluding females from dynastic succession.

Line 5. **Good wine...bush**: good wine needs no advertisement. An old proverb based on the custom of hanging out branches of ivy (perhaps as the plant sacred to Bacchus, god of wine) as a vintner's sign; hence, a "bush" became the sign-board of a tavern (*OED*). As Elizabeth Hageman has suggested to me, F. Vaughan's use of this proverb, in conjunction with her use of "beard" to signify "male," may echo Shakespeare's Rosalind in her epilogue to *As You Like It.*

Line 7. **the main**: the high sea. The sense is that the world never really decays because whatever land the coast loses, the sea gains.

Line 12. **Dodona's Grove**: the ancient oracle, where the will of Zeus was declared by the wind rustling through the trees. Cf. F. Vaughan's witty comparison of a crown of "a single bough" to a crown of "all Dodona's Grove" to Marvell's similar conceit in "The Garden" (stanza one).

A Continuation of Sir Philip Sidney's *Arcadia*

Wherein is handled the Loves of Amphialus
and Helen Queen of Corinth, Prince Plangus
and Erona: With the History of the
Loves of old Claius and young
Strephon to Urania

In the time that Basilius (King of Arcadia), with Genecea (his Queen), and his two renowned daughters (the Paragons of the World), Pamela and Philoclea, were retired from the court to a private lodge amongst the shepherds, there to refresh themselves with their pleasant and harmless sports: in the time that Pyrocles, son and heir to the good Evarchus (King of Macedon), disguised himself to an Amazonian lady for the love of his Venus (the sweet Philoclea), and Musidorus (Prince of Thessalia) disrobed himself of his glorious raiment and put on shepherds weeds for the sight of the stately Pamela: and when Cupid displayed his quivers throughout his circle and brought the famousest Princes in the world to adore his mother's beauty: then Prince Plangus (son to the King of Iberia) at the first view of Erona (a Queen in Lydia) was made a prisoner to her who was a prisoner, and he, whose resolutions were altogether fixed on the rare beauty of Erona, resolved with himself either to release his incomparable jewel out of a doleful prison or else to lose his life in the enterprise.

10

Line 1. **Arcadia**: a country in southern Greece associated with pastoral poetry. See map of Greece and Asia Minor on page 213.

Line 5. **harmless**: innocent.

Line 13. **Lydia**: the name of Erona's kingdom in the *Old Arcadia* (the *New Arcadia* has "Lycia"). This is one possible, but slight, indication that Weamys knew the *Old Arcadia*.

13

Then he became an humble suitor to Artaxia, Queen of Armenia,
under whose custody the fair lady was, telling her his life was bound
20 up in Erona's. And then would he vow it was pity so sweet a creature
should pass by the pleasures of her life in so solitary a place. And
sometimes he would pray for her, and then again he would praise
her. But Artaxia would no ways be persuaded to any compassion: the
more he desired, the more she denied, which he perceiving, with a
soft voice and deep sigh he brake out into these words:

"Great Queen, if my grief and groans cannot mollify your heart,
nor the remembrance that once I was your beloved kinsman, nor yet
the beauty of Erona can be a sufficient remedy to cure your anger;
yet call to mind she was your royal brother's mistress; and can you
30 imagine that he would have endured the thought that Erona's blood
should so innocently be shed! no, but assure your self that whensoever a drop of it is spilt, out of his ashes there will rise a revenger to
root you out of your kingdom."

But Artaxia arose out of her throne with a graceful majesty, and
did protest she would be revenged on her brother's murderers: "For,"
said she, "although my brother did love and honor Erona too well,
yet her hate of him was the cause of his being slain, and of his subjects' overthrow. And, Prince Plangus, if your affections be never so
extremely set upon Erona, yet I am resolved to keep her lie in my
40 power. But because you shall have no occasion given you to brand
me with the title of Tyrant Queen, in the word of a Princess I do
promise you that if within two years after the day of my brother's

Lines 18–184. The first pages of Weamys's narrative paraphrase and rewrite the Sidney's tale of
Plangus in the 1593 *Arcadia*, II.29. Weamys's paraphrase of Sidney here can be unusually
difficult to follow, and readers are referred to the account of the Sidneian background in the
Appendices; see especially the summary of the Erona-Plangus narrative in Appendix 3A
(Narrative Sources).

Line 29. **your royal brother's mistress**: Artaxia's brother, Tiradates, was desperately in love
with Erona, to the point of trying to win her by waging war on her kingdom.

Line 35. **her brothers murderers**: Pyrocles and Musidorus.

Line 39. **keep her lie**: force her to remain(?). It is possible that "lie" is a misprint for "life."

death, you can procure Prince Pyrocles and Musidorus to accept of a combat against two others of my choosing, to obtain the liberty of Erona; if they overcome those knights of my electing, that day shall Erona be at her own disposal: but if my champions manifest their valor to that height as to receive the victory, the same day Erona's body shall be consumed to ashes, and I shall endeavor to gratify their courage."

Plangus joyfully accepted of this proposition since he could 50 obtain no better. And well he knew the Princes cared not for their proud looks, nor feared the glittering of their swords; yet little did he know the craftiness of Artaxia. But such subtle policy seldom ends with an happy conclusion.

And now in hopes of a prosperous journey, he bends his course towards Greece, there to deliver his message, upon which his life depended. But he had not travelled many days before he had surprised a letter; the superscription was to Plaxirtus, brother to Leonatus, King of Paphlagonia; he, without fear or dread, brake it open and read it. He had no sooner perused it over but that he wished it 60 closed again. Then cried he out aloud, "Can it be possible? is Artaxia such a deceitful politician? can her lips utter that which is so far at distance from her heart? and can flattering make her seem the less cruel? No sure, her very name will be hateful to all posterity."

"See here," saith he to some of his servants that were with him, "see here a letter from Artaxia to Plaxirtus, how she praises him for a treacherous act, how she condoles with him for the death of Pyrocles and Musidorus, the two gloriousest Princes that ever lived in the

---

Line 48. **gratify**: reward.   Lines 57–58. **surprised**: intercepted.

Line 66. **a letter from Artaxia to Plaxirtus**: In the 1593 *Arcadia* (II.23), this letter is a forgery by an "old knight, still thirsting for revenge" on Plexirtus (Sidney's spelling). See the entry for Plexirtus in Appendix 2 (List of Characters).

Line 67. **condoles with**: The standard meaning, "expresses one's sympathy with," seems not to fit the context; if that is the meaning here, then the usage is presumably ironic or suggests Artaxia's duplicity.

world, how she promises him to end the tragedy with a comedy; she
70 tells him the Gods set to their help to revenge her brother's death;
and then she acknowledges her self and her kingdom his, according
to her proclamation."

Thus Plangus was breathing out his griefs, but had not altogether
eased himself before he was interrupted by a messenger who (not
being accustomed to compliments), came to him and certified him
that he came from Armenia, and that he was servant to that nobleman to whom Artaxia and he reposed so much confidence in, to
intrust Erona to be under his charge; and that now, contrary to the
articles agreed upon between them, Plaxirtus had brought the news
80 to Artaxia of the death of Pyrocles and Musidorus, which had been
procured by his contrivance; and, said he, "She hath married him in
requital. And by this time he hath besieged my Lord's castle where
Erona is confined. Then my Lord, having intelligence of it, immediately sent me after you, to let you understand that he was not furnished with conveniences well enough to hold out long: therefore as
you love Erona, so come with speed to relieve her. Now I have finished my message, and I must be gone." So with less reverence than
he used when he came, he hastily went his way, Plangus being cast
into such an astonishment that he let him go at his pleasure, without
90 so much as inquiring after Erona's welfare. But at length he roused
himself out of his amazement, and then would have poured out his
soul in complaints, had he not espied his newsmonger galloping
almost out of his sight; then sending his eyes after him, he made a
virtue of necessity, and [his eyes] contented themselves that they
were spectators of the nimble nag, which shewed his unwillingness
to rest his foot upon the ground before he entered his native soil.

Line 70. **set to**: have added (?).   Line 75. **compliments**: polite ceremonies, courtesies.

Line 81. **by his contrivance**: i.e., by Plaxirtus's plot to have Pyrocles and Musidorus killed on
board the ship he had furnished them, in the 1593 *Arcadia* (II.24).

Lines 81–82. **in requital**: as a reward.   Line 87. **with less reverence**: i.e., with fewer formal
gestures of respect, such as bows and farewells.

This tempted Plangus to discover his fancy, which he did in these terms: "Certainly," said he, "there is a charm in beauty that beasts do homage to and must obey that now makes the nag to trip so fast away to do Erona service. Shall I then be worse than a beast? No. Although I cannot pass along with thee, yet my heart shall always keep before thee. And, dear Erona, though now I turn my face from thee, yet my deeds shall always declare to be for thee and shall endeavor to clear the clouds that now obscure thy brightness."

Thus, between hope and despair, he mounted his horse, and commanding his servants to follow him, he resolved to go into Macedon to report the news to Evarchus of his son's and nephew's death. For he was persuaded that Evarchus would not be backward from bringing to due punishment the causers of his unspeakable loss. And by that means he thought he might handsomely shew his valor and prove it upon his lady's enemies. Yet sometimes fears would make conspiracies within him and almost overwhelm him until he recalled his senses and considered that it was not a daunted spirit that could serve Erona. Then setting spurs to his horse, he travelled in a night and a day without once opening his lips, silence in his opinion being the best companion to a troubled mind.

But at last he entered into the pleasant country of Arcadia, which was adorned with stately woods. No cries were heard there but of the lambs, and they in sport too sounded their voices to make their playfellow lambs answer them again in imitation of the like. And the abundance of shady trees that were there were so beautiful with the sweet melody of birds that anyone, save love-sick Plangus, might think it a sufficient harmony to draw away their delight from any other vanity of the world. Besides, there were the shepherds piping to their pretty shepherdesses, whilst they cheerfully sang to pleasure them again. In this sweet place, he sat himself down with an

100

110

120

Line 97. **discover his fancy**: reveal, by speaking aloud, his inner musings (or, perhaps, amorous inclination).

intention to rest his wearied limbs under a branched tree whilst his
servants refreshed themselves and baited their horses, but no ease
could be harbored in his disquieted heart, his eyes being no sooner
closed but that he imagined he saw Erona burning in their unmerci-
ful fire: at which sight he staringly opened them and determined
with himself that since sleep would procure no comfort to him other
than tragical scenes, he would never enjoy any contentment before
he had settled Erona in her throne in safety.

He had not been long in this perplexity before he was kindly
examined the cause of his sadness. Plangus, hearing the question and
musing extremely who it should be that to his thinking should ask
so strange an one, heaved up his head, which before he had carelessly
held down; and seeing only an ancient man attended by his two
daughters, and hoping he would be a companion suitable to his disposition, he courteously answered him that it would be but a trouble
to him to understand the occasion of his grief, "for," said he, "it will
be too melancholy a story to rehearse to you, unless you were in a
capacity to help me."

"It is possible I might do you service," replied the old man; "for
now you are in Arcadia, where I am King, and having retired from
my court to a private lodge, which is seated in a grove hard by, I with
my two daughters, happening now to walk for recreation into this
pleasant place, and I perceiving you being a stranger, lying in such a
forlorn posture, I must confess it was incivility in me to disturb you,
but my compassion would submit to no causalities that could hinder
my desired knowledge. And now I hope it will be no inconvenience
to you to relate your own history to me."

But Plangus with humble reverence excused his denial and
beseeched Basilius first to grant him his pardon, since it was a fault

---

Line 128. **baited**: fed.

Lines 146–47. **having retired from my court**: Basilius, with his wife and daughters, has retired
to the Arcadian countryside in an effort to escape the destiny prophesied by an oracle (see the
1593 *Arcadia*, II.28).

Line 151. **causalities**: causes, but possibly a misprint for "casualities" (chance events).

of ignorance and not of perverseness. And that he promised himself that he would choose rather to be his chirurgeon to heal his wounds than in the least to mar or make them.

Basilius would suffer him no longer to go on with his frivolous civilities and, telling him they should serve his turn, made him sit down. Then Plangus related all circumstances in the same manner that afterward the divine Philoclea sweetly declared to her lover, the admirable Pyrocles. And believe me, she told it with more liveliness and quickness of wit than Plangus did himself; for oftentimes his thought was strayed from his story to sigh with gazing upon the splendor of Pamela and Philoclea, for he conceited that in their beauties he might see Erona's. But alas poor Prince! Cupid in that had blinded him, for although Erona might deserve a large share of praises, yet the two sisters could not be paralleled. But when he had concluded his passionate relation, he earnestly craved release of Basilius, who answered him that he governed a quiet and a peaceable country and that he should very unwillingly teach his people the way of dissension, but yet he would command a guard of Arcadians to conduct him safe into Macedon.

Plangus, in lowly submission, congratulated with Basilius for that favor, believing that time and entreaty would amplify his goodness according to his ability. Then as he was appointing a place where the Arcadians should meet him, his servants presented themselves to him and certified him that the day was far spent and that it would be necessary for him to go to the next town and there to lodge that night. Plangus very well liked of their advice that he might have the more freedom to contrive his best way to act his part he had already

---

Line 157. **chirurgeon**: surgeon.

Lines 161–63. **Then Plangus related...Pyrocles:** There is a possible narrative glitch in Weamys's revision of Sidney's scheduling of Plangus's relation of his history to Basilius. See Introduction, page xlv, note 43.

Line 166. **conceited**: imagined.

Lines 167–68. **Cupid...him:** Cupid himself is traditionally portrayed as blindfolded.

Line 170. **release**: permission to leave.   Line 175. **congratulated with**: thanked.

begun to play. Then after they had ended their sundry discourses, he parted from Basilius and the two surpassing sisters.

Now Erona's beauty had grounded such an impression in his heart that no other thought but of her perfections could enter into his. She was his image, her he worshipped, and her he would forever magnify. And until he came near the city, he busied his fancy in extolling his lady. But there he was received by the governor of the town with as great gallantry as could be expected, considering the short warning Basilius gave them, there wanting no cost that might be pleasing either to his eye or taste. A stately supper being provided which was garnished with a royal banquet sent from Basilius, and all was finished in so gorgeous a manner that Plangus did assure himself he was no ordinary, nor yet unwelcome, guest. But all the sweet music with the plenty of delicates was no more to Plangus than the remembrance of his own misfortune. Yet having a princely care not to show himself unthankful to the meanest supporter of his undeserved festivals, he would oftentimes praise them for their bounty to him, a stranger and one that was no way able to make them the least requital, but they replied that his acceptance was as much and more than they deserved or expected. Then after they had a good while parleyed together upon several occasions, the citizens returned to their houses, and Plangus went to his lodging, then prostrating himself before Cupid for his happy success in fulfilling of his own desires, beseeched him to unite Erona's affection as firmly to him as his was unmovable to her, and that both might be so well preserved that at length they might enjoy the happy fruition of real friendship between him and Erona, at whose name he ended; and as if he received his life from thence, he fell into a little slumber, which continued for so short a time that when he awaked, the clouds were not separated to give way to the approaching day that was then extremely wished for by him, who determined to spend the hourglass of his life in defense of his esteemed mistress.

Line 191. **cost**: costly thing.   Line 196. **delicates**: delicacies.

By that time he had run over his thoughts to the end of his intended enterprises, Phoebus spread his beams over his curtains, which cast so great a reflection upon him that though his eyes were still dissembling sleep, yet the sun's brightness made him gaze about him, and seeing it so sweet a morning, he believed it to be an emblem of his prosperous success. In this persuasion he arose, and 220 charging his servants to be in a readiness, he walked into a gallery, where multitudes stood waiting for his presence, he kindly saluting them and repeating his former speeches of courtesy and gratitude, he commanded his man to bring out his steed; and then taking his leave of the Arcadians, saving the residue which Basilius appointed to wait on him, he raised himself upon the beast, which gently received him, as willing to bear so loved a burden, and sprightly ambled along: but Plangus was forced to hold his bridle, and teach his nag his bounds were no further than his commission, by reason of a calling from a young shepherd, who speedily running to Plan- 230 gus, and in a breathless manner he certified him that he was sent by his Lord Basilius to excuse his absence, the occasion being his retiredness to so private a place, that with no conveniency he could entertain him there agreeable to his greatness, nor yet to remove so far so suddenly.

Plangus requested the shepherd to return his thanks and obedience to his sovereign, and seeing it was a matter of no greater importance, he would endure no longer hindrances, but set spurs to his horse and galloped away with all expedition: but not without some turbulent passages that he was fain to endure, before he could attain 240 to his desired haven: yet at last he arrived under the dominions of

---

Lines 232–33. **his retiredness**: See note to lines 146–47.

Line 240. **passages**: events.　　**fain**: obliged.

Lines 241–406. Plangus's journey to Macedon is mentioned at the end of Basilius's tale of Plangus in the *New Arcadia* section of the 1593 *Arcadia* (II.29). The sojourn itself is briefly sketched in the *Old Arcadia* section of the 1593 *Arcadia* (V.2), but Weamys's account—the encounter with Kalodolus, the dialogue with Evarchus, Evarchus's appointment as Judge of the Sessions to legitimize his judgment of Artaxia and his authorization of troops, the oracle—is almost entirely her own invention. See Appendix 3A (Narrative Sources).

Evarchus in Macedon, where he was welcomed by a company of
dolorous persons, who without entreaty would participate with him
in his sorrows: but alas! there were few comforters, all the people
seeming like shadows, in regard of the miss they had of their young
Prince, who after he had brought so many Kings in subjection under
his prowess and valor, should now himself be lost, none knowing
where or how, but perpetually harkening to several relations, which
put them into more fears and doubts every day than they were in
before.

Musidorus wanted not bewailing neither; for well they knew
Pyrocles's life was bound up in his and that he loved and respected
the Macedonians as much for Pyrocles's sake as he did the Thessalians for his own sake, and that they learned one another virtuous
qualities, which were equally distributed between them; therefore
the whole kingdom groaned under burdensome calamities for their
witnessed loss: but by the entrance of Plangus, who was a stranger to
them, their complaints were turned into whisperings, and their sighs
into listenings, all being earnest to know who he was and the cause
of his posting from city to city towards the court. Some would
believe the worst, and then would swear they did see sadness in his
face; others would persuade themselves, it was his hasty travelling
that made him seem careful. But Plangus, not staying to harken to
their mistrustful uncertainties, kept on his former pace till he was
come within a mile of the palace, where he was stopped by one
Kalodolus, an ancient servant belonging to Musidorus, who hearing
of the coming of a foreigner, and infinitely longing to hear from his
dear master, and meeting Plangus, he fell down at his feet, and
besought him to have commiseration upon him, and tell him of the
safety of Musidorus.

This request silenced Plangus for a while, who could not imagine
what reply to make to him but having considered a little better of it,

---

Line 254. **learned one another**: "taught one another" or, possibly, "learned one another's."

he brake his silence on this fashion: "Sir, it grieves me extremely that I cannot give you such satisfactory answer as I wish I could: however do not afflict your self, for I dare assure you that he is happy, being a more glorious Prince and far greater than all the kingdoms of the world could make him."

"Why? Is he dead?" said Kalodolus; "then all virtue is fled away: but I will follow thee, Musidorus, where're thou beest, I will not stay behind." Then snatching out a rapier from him that was nearest him, he would have sent his soul to Pluto, had it not been prevented by the quick eye of Plangus who apprehending his danger, leaped upon him and with violence wrung the rapier out of his hand, but yet he would not be pacified for a time, nor persuaded from practicing his intended mischief, till reason overswaying his patience made him become a moderator of his own rashness; for said he, "What good can my death do to Musidorus? shall I my self destroy, and do my Prince the wrong? no, I will live as long as fortune pleases and guide my steps about the world till I have found his tomb, where I will solemnize such obsequies as may be thought worthy to be titled the funeral of so worthy a Prince. Then I will weep my self to tears upon his grave to water that illustrious plant that certainly must needs spring up and flourish; for it is impossible so rare a thing can be obscured in the earth."

Here Kalodolus's speech was stopped by a flood that would endure no longer to be hid within his aged carcass. And the noble Plangus answered him with sighs as if his heart would break: then they both looked so steadfastly in pity upon one another that if a painter had been present, he could not take nor have a livelier masterpiece of sorrow than this lover and servant represented, they being both void of comfort and equally afflicted, until Plangus plucked up his dead spirits and advised Kalodolus to cease his complaints and

280

290

300

Line 281. **Pluto**: Roman god of the underworld and the dead.
Line 296. **carcass**: body.

not to suffer grief to overrun his patience, for since Musidorus was dead, the only service he could do for him was to help forward the revenging of the actors in his death. And then he required him to direct him the way to Evarchus: which command Kalodolus instantly obeyed and guid[ed] him through stately courts, paved all with marble, and compassed in with marble pillars that were adorned with such goodly proportioned statues that had not Plan-

310 gus been employed with matters of consequence, he would not so regardlessly have passed by them without prying into their story, which might perhaps have been beneficial unto him to know the several tricks of warlike Hercules, as was there curiously engraven by famous antiquaries. But Plangus's thoughts were higher flown than these portraitures could reach to; those he valued like shadows in comparison of his valiant enterprises that artificially his invention would lay before him, as if it were accomplished already. And in that unsatisfied persuasion he was brought to Evarchus, whose sight awakened him from his fabulous fantasy. And then with a sad rever-

320 ence he kneeled down.

But the good King would not suffer that, but lifting him up, he entreated him to use no such ceremonies, but to discourse that which he earnestly wished to know without any delays. So Plangus being extreme willing to fulfill Evarchus's charge, though first to bring him by degrees to the hearing of those mournful tidings, he began with this prologue:

"Most gracious Sir, did I not consider your wisdom in governing your passions far surmounting other men's, I should not so abruptly presume to be the messenger of such unfortunate news as now I am.

330 But since my life is hazarded in several respects, I know your good-

---

Line 307. **guid[ed]**: The word is "guiding" in the original text.

Line 313. **curiously**: skillfully, exquisitely.

Line 316. **artificially**: i.e., in artfully constructed fantasies.

Line 330. **hazarded**: imperiled.

ness will no way persevere against me, for necessity hath no rule, and that is the reason which now enforces me to manifest that unto you which I am loath to utter: but I assure my self that Your Majesty will no way despise the sovereign salve called Patience, that is a present remedy for all afflictions.

"Know then, great King, that the mirrors of virtue, the famous Pyrocles your son and Musidorus your nephew, are treacherously slain by the bloody plot of Plaxirtus (false brother to Leonatus, King of Paphlagonia) and revealed to me by the surprisal of a letter of congratulation from Artaxia (Queen of Armenia), under whose power Erona (Queen of Lydia) is a prisoner; and without speedy succor, she will be put to death in the cruellest way that can be imagined, by the same instruments that exposed her champions to theirs: but yet, Sir, they have left behind them so precious a name that their adversaries cannot blemish: and so long as their better part flourishes on earth, all the reality that can be shewed for the lesser is to go on courageously and revenge your loss, and to give Apollo thanks for their leaving so glorious a memory behind them."

Thus Plangus ended, without further mentioning Erona, until Evarchus's grief was somewhat digested: which he did perceive extremely to oversway him by the changing of blood in his face that perpetually going and coming would sometime wax pale and wan, and then would flush, as if he threatened to make Plaxirtus smart for all his villainy. And in this conflict of sorrow and anger he continued a great space: but at last they both yielded to reason, and Evarchus wisely became the Judge of the Sessions; for said he:

"It is justice to bring murderers to their deserved punishments. And because you, Prince Plangus, testify your self to be such an affectionate friend to my dear children, shew your self one in their revenge; you I will entrust to be the general of my army; prove as

340

350

360

Line 331. **persevere**: "be steadfast," or possibly "be severe" (Latin *perseverus*).
Line 339. **surprisal**: interception.

valiant now as you have ever done; let all your aim be at Plaxirtus; and if possible, convey him hither alive, that he may die a public spectacle of shame and terror before all the people. And I give you free liberty to use your power in the release of that distressed lady you spake of, for certainly their hearts are infinitely hardened for any mischief: but for Artaxia, remember she is a woman, and subject to degrees of passion as well as man. But alas! she desired the destruction of Pyrocles and Musidorus, and now she hath rendered her recompense to Plaxirtus for that abominable deed. O, the thought of that action reaches further than my compassion: but I will resign my power to you. Therefore though you grow victorious, yet strengthen your self with discretion, and let not rashness nor faintheartedness prevail over you. Now go on with your intentions, and prosper, whilst I end my days in solitariness."

370

Evarchus had no sooner done, but he bowed to the earth, as if he wished to be there quickly; and then after he had signed a commission for raising of an army, he withdrew into his chamber, and Plangus waited upon him to the entrance, and so they parted, one to temperate melancholy, the other to hope intermixed with cares: for though Plangus was loaded with troublesome employments, yet those he took for refreshments because the foundation of them was laid for Erona's sake. But Evarchus grieved, as he had too just cause, to think that he should never more behold the joy of his heart again; and so he continued without the least show of a contented mind, yet not with a desperate rage. A large and rare theme might be chronicled of his wisely governed passions; but that is too pregnant a virtue for my dull capacity to go on with.

380

Therefore surrendering that to sharp wits, I will only mention Plangus's happy success that he obtained in Macedon; for in short

---

Lines 368–69. **her recompense**: i.e., her marrying Plaxirtus as a reward for his arranging the death of Pyrocles and Musidorus. See lines 65–72.

Line 385. **theme**: discourse.

time he levied an army sufficient to conquer all Armenia, every one 390
being desirous to revenge their Prince's quarrel and thought it a preferment to be the meanest soldier; then being all in a readiness, they
march away. But Plangus, before he went, sent his ambassadors to
Delphos to know the oracle his destiny, and just as he was managing
his army in their march, they returned with this answer:

> That he should be victorious over his enemies, if so be he would
> be vigilant in guiding his forces in a way of deliberation; and
> not to venture to shew his valor, in overrash attempts in a
> bravado before his mistress, which oftentimes hath been the
> cause of the routing a magnificent army: but he must 400
> remember the eyes of all the world were upon him as their
> defence and shield, whose wisdom must preserve them from
> their furious enemies.

This oracle infinitely comforted Plangus; and when he had given
thanks to Apollo for his proclaimed prosperous fortune, he kept on
his march to Armenia, whom we will leave for a time.

Now I will discover some passages that passed between Amphialus
(nephew to Basilius, the King of Arcadia) and Helena (Queen of
Corinth), how that after she had carried him away in a lighter from
Arcadia, what bitter complaints she made for him, until she had 410
brought him to Corinth; that would be too pitiful a subject to stay
on; therefore leaving that to several conjectures, I will only rehearse
those particulars that united those rare persons together to both
their abundant felicity.

Line 407. **passages**: events.   Line 409. **lighter**: litter, carrying chair.

Lines 409–11. **how ... Corinth**: In the 1593 *Arcadia* (III.24–25), Amphialus attempts suicide
out of guilt for his complicity in his mother's treason and abduction of Pamela and Philoclea,
as well as his inadvertent contribution to her death, and the narrative breaks off with Helen of
Corinth (who has desperately and unrequitedly loved him) conveying him on a litter from
Arcadia to Corinth for medical help. Apart from this, the entire Helen-Amphialus narrative is
Weamys's invention. For the Sidneian background, see the entry for Helen in Appendix 2 (List
of Characters) and Appendix 3в (Narrative Sources).

When Helena had conveyed her beloved Amphialus to her renowned city Corinth, and lodged him in the richest furnished chamber that could be devised (yet all she thought too mean for such an incomparable guest), then she advised with her skilful chirurgeons how she might have his wounds healed, and had always an

420 especial care to see the salves applied to them her self; and when all was finished, she passed away the day with sighs by senseless Amphialus, who lay so quietly that for a great time none could perceive the least motion of life in him: but at last the chirurgeons avouched they could find warm blood strive for life in his (now in all likelihood) curable wounds. Which speech of theirs did make Helena wash her fair face with her tears for joy, when before it had not touched a drop of water from the time that she found Amphialus in so woeful a condition. Then began she to discourse with him, as if he could mind her what she said:

430 "Tell me, dear Amphialus," said she, "what occasion have I given you to make you hate me? have I not ever honored and loved you far above my self? O yes! and if I had a thousand lives to lose, I would venture them all for your sake. But since that is an impossible thing, propound to me the most probable way for me to purchase you, and I dare undertake it, be it never so dangerous: but if it be the Princess Philoclea that lies as a block in my way, so that I must either continue where I am, or else stumble over it and be made quite hopeless, yet let me counsel you as a faithful friend not to engage your affections to one that is so negligent of it, but rather bestow it upon me

440 that will accept of it. Oh hear me, and have pity on me, O Amphialus, Amphialus!"

Then she flung her self down upon his bed with a resolution not to stir before she had discerned some sign of life in outward appearance. And as she was earnestly looking upon him, she espied his eyes astealing open; but immediately, with a long-fetched sigh, he closed

---

Lines 428–29. **mind her**: perceive.

them up again, as grieving for their tenderness they could not gaze upon beauty. But Helena, replying with twenty to his one, went on with her love-sick speeches:

"Alas poor Prince!" said she, "is it thy hard fortune to receive thy life again in sighs? hath such ill-favored spleens no place to settle in   450
but in thy noble breast, which shines in goodness? Cheer up, dear Prince, and let not thy greatest foe find cause to tax thee with the least blemish."

Longer she would have proceeded in her bemoaning of Amphialus, had she not been interrupted by the chirurgeons that were in the chamber, and hearing her voice, came instantly to her, and kneeling down, entreated her to abandon the chamber, for as much as her presence and complaints caused disturbance in Amphialus and procured nothing but that which was hurtful to her own person: and then they assured her that if she would forbear his company,   460
they could perfect the cure in half the time that otherwise they should be constrained to be tedious in, by reason that her sad speeches would ground such an impression in him in his weakness, that it would be as much as their skill could reach unto to keep his wounds from growing worse than better. These persuasions of the chirurgeons had a very great influence over Helena, and she forsaking her former passions, guarded her self with a long robe of wise considerations and departed his chamber without any shew of fondness, to the admiration of all beholders. Yet she never neglected the care of Amphialus, but diligently inquired after his amendment that   470
she might know all passages as punctually as if she had been with him. In this golden mean of Patience she continued so long till

---

Line 450. **spleens**: passions, especially melancholy.
Line 462. **tedious**: slow, long.   Line 468. **considerations**: reflections.
Lines 468–69. **fondness**: doting.   Line 470. **amendment**: recovery.
Line 471. **passages**: incidents, events.   **punctually**: exactly.
Line 472. **golden mean**: moderation.

Amphialus had revived somewhat his decayed spirits, and the chirurgeons had so well overcome his wounds that by degrees he was brought to walk about his chamber; but always he would be crossing his arms, knocking his breast, and breathing speeches to himself in so woeful a manner as would make the hardest heart burst into a deluge of tears. Yet all this time he never examined by what means he was conveyed thither, nor any other question that concerned Helena's or his own condition. And so for a great while he imprisoned himself in such ignorance, till by the coming of a young gentleman, named Clytifon (son to Kaleander, a noble man of Arcadia), his concealed estate and all other circumstances that had happened in Arcadia from his departure from thence were declared to Amphialus's wonder and astonishment.

For this, Clytifon was sent as an ambassador to Amphialus from his uncle, the King of Arcadia, to congratulate with him for his recovery and to certify him of his cousins' deliverance out of his castle by the prowess of Prince Pyrocles and Musidorus; and how they disguised themselves for the love of Pamela and Philoclea, with all the several attempts that they practiced to obtain their desired enterprise (as their bringing Anaxius to submit to their mercy, Pyrocles having granted him his life on condition he would acknowledge it); and finally to give him notice that the nuptials of Pyrocles and Philoclea, with Musidorus and Pamela, were only deferred for the

480

490

Line 487. **congratulate with him for**: rejoice at.   Line 488. **certify**: assure, inform.

Line 488. **his cousins' deliverance**: Amphialus's mother, Cecropia, married the brother of Basilius, the father of Pamela and Philoclea. Towards the end of the *New Arcadia* section of the 1593 *Arcadia* (III.2), Cecropia, in an effort to thwart Basilius's dynasty, abducts Philoclea and Pamela, imprisoning them in Amphialus's castle. The rescue is Weamys's invention. See Appendix 1 (Synopsis).

Lines 489–90. **they disguised themselves**: In the 1593 *Arcadia,* Pyrocles disguised himself as an Amazon (Zelmane) and Musidorus as a shepherd (Dorus) in order to woo Philoclea and Pamela, respectively. See Appendix 1 (Synopsis).

Line 492. **Anaxius…mercy**: This is Weamys's invention: the *New Arcadia* section of the 1593 *Arcadia* (III.29) breaks off with Anaxius combatting Zelmane/Pyrocles.

time they could hear from Amphialus. This was the chief of Clytifon's ambassage, which he carefully obeyed.

But before he entered into Corinth, the city swelled with rumor,
every one being greedy to know that which nothing concerned
them. But Clytifon, knowing it was not a time of dalliance, hastened   500
to the palace, where he was waited for by Helena, whose watchful
eyes and attentive ears could not pass by any suspicious whisperings,
but would always make strict inquiry of the cause of them. So now
she, believing the credible report, would needs come down her self,
attended with a train of ladies, to welcome the ambassador to her
court, when as soon as she perceived a glimpse of him, she perfectly
knew him to be that noble Clytifon, whom before she had been
beholding to for his excellent company. Then whilst she was showing her courtesy to him for his former civilities, he with an humble
reverence, yet supported with a garb of majesty, came to her after the   510
manner of an ambassador and present[ed] mighty high commendations to her from all the Princes that resided in Arcadia. She
besought him to accept of such poor entertainment as her ability
could make him. Then leading him into the presence (it being in the
afternoon) she commanded a delicate collation to be set before him,
which was fulfilled so quickly and so decently that Clytifon could
not choose but sit and extol their comely order, and within awhile
fell to eating those rarities that Helena had provided for him; but she
would not be persuaded to taste of any, her troubled mind was too
full of jealousies and fears to think of pleasing her appetite. Some-   520
time she mistrusted that Basilius had sent for Amphialus to be tried

---

Lines 496–97. **the chief of Clytifon's embassage**: the main part of his ambassadorship.

Line 500. **dalliance**: idle delay.   Line 502. **pass by**: let pass, ignore.

Line 511. **present[ed]**: The word is "presenting" in the original text.

Line 514. **the presence**: the presence-chamber, the reception room in a palace.

Line 515. **collation**: meal.   Line 516. **decently**: properly.   Line 521. **mistrusted**: dreaded.

by the law for his mother Cecropia's stealing away his daughters that he might have a fair pretense to take away his life. But quickly she vanquished that doubt by another that she imagined to be most probable, which was that Philoclea's heart might be mollified and that she underhand had made choice of Clytifon to be her proxy, in wishing Amphialus to pursue his former petition to Philoclea that she with the more modesty might grant him his request. This fancy of Helena made such a wound within her breast that a thousand of sighs had free passage there, and in silence she did think out her complaints, until Clytifon had disordered the artificial curiosities with tasting of their goodness and had sufficed his natural hunger. Then Helena, taking him aside from the company that came to gaze upon him, with many shows of grief she conjured him that if ever he had been real to any friend, to shew himself one to her, who vowed faithfulness and secrecy: but yet if it were a matter of such weighty importance as he could not repose so much confidence in her, being a Princess of another country, yet she entreated him to certify her whether it concerned Amphialus, or in his her own ruin.

Clytifon had hardly patience to hear her out, but removed her fears on this manner: "Cheer up, great Queen," said he; "those cloudy shadows of discontent and fears never do good, but hurt and wrong your beauty that otherwise would be the sweetest, and the singular flower that could be found in the large garden of the world. Cheer up then and rejoice at joyful tidings: for to the amazement of all, the two ever-blessed Princes, Pyrocles and Musidorus, are by many strange accidents found to be alive, though disguised within my sovereign's lodges, from being gallant soldiers, the one to a woman, the other to a comely shepherd, which was brought to pass by the industry of blind Cupid, who takes pleasure in wounding the best of undaunted spirits. But yet he hath dealt so favorable with

---

Line 531. **artificial curiosities**: artistically arranged, or designed, delicacies.
Line 548. **sovereign's**: i.e., Evarchus's.

these incomparable persons that he hath equally wounded Pamela and Philoclea to them again: so that now Arcadia waits only for the nuptials' finishing to be made happy in having so glorious a Prince to reign over them, and that is delayed only for the time that they might hear from my Lord Amphialus."

Helena's joy at the hearing of this news was too great for my dull expression, yet after she had moderated her excessive mirth and brought it within the bounds of reason, she feared that Amphialus would be so overcome with despairing grief that nothing but death could end his misery. Then fell she at Clytifon's feet and begged of him not to be overhasty in declaring his ambassage to Amphialus, but to compass him in by degrees to the hearing of it. This request of hers Clytifon courteously promised to perform. And she, guiding him to Amphialus's chamber door, desired him to walk in, and departed.

But Amphialus espying Clytifon, and leaping upon him, and then lovingly embracing him, said, "How doest thou Clytifon? thou lookest as if thou meanedst to chide me; but spare your labor, I will do that my self, nay, and more if Philoclea would command it; let her desire my heart and she shall have it, and with mine own hand I'll pluck it out to give her, yet think it all too little to excuse my crime." "But she is gracious and noble," answered Clytifon, "and will be readier to forgive than you can be to beg your pardon of her." "But I will never presume to ask forgiveness," replied Amphialus, "since I deserve all punishments." "Though you do," said Clytifon, "yet if you will present your self into her in an humble and submissive way, and cast off your former suit, I durst assure you she would not only grant your life but would also receive you to her favor as her near kinsman." "If I could think so," replied Amphialus, "I should be highly contented far above my deserts or wishes." "And," said Clytifon, "would you be pleased to hear that she were married to another

560

570

580

Line 558. **excessive mirth**: extreme delight.   Line 562. **ambassage**: message.

or else likely to be so suddenly?" "Yes, with all my soul," answered Amphialus, "but yet upon condition that it may be to her all flourishing happiness. As for my own particular, that is the least thing I regard or hope for, only (as I said before) that the Princess Philoclea may be endowed with all felicity: that will procure to me an uncontrolled blessedness."

590   Then Clytifon asked him if he would accept of him to be the bearer of a letter from him to Philoclea, which he promised carefully to deliver, if it were such an one as might be received without scruple. Amphialus answered he would gladly write to Philoclea, but it should no way be prejudicial to him, he intending only to manifest his grief for her ill usage in his castle, and to let her know how ready he was to welcome any punishment she would inflict upon him. Then after more such speeches passed between them, Clytifon rehearsed the truth of his message which at first Amphialus heard with trembling, until Clytifon remembered him of his former discourse that nothing that could make Philoclea happy should ever

600   make him unhappy. Then rousing up himself, he wished Clytifon to leave him to his privacy, that he might have the more liberty to indite a letter worthy of her acceptance, Clytifon being to carry it away the next morning. So he, without the least contradiction, left Amphialus, who being alone fell into a passion (as afterward he confessed) that had almost made him senseless, until time that wears out all things recalled his memory back to him again, which first discovered it self thus:

"Alas, miserable Amphialus! thou employest thy self to extol thy rival, and meanest to make it thy recreation to do so always. Now I

610   can remember the Amazon lady that fought so gallantly with me in

---

Line 594. **her ill usage in his castle**: See note to line 488.   Line 597. **rehearsed**: recounted.
Lines 609–16. **Now I…timorousness**: Amphialus alludes to his first encounter with Zelmane/Pyrocles (1593 *Arcadia*, II.11).

the Arcadian woods for the Princess Philoclea's glove; what blows she strook at me, and with what nimbleness she avoided mine when I aimed at her in mine own defence. I must confess it daunted me to see a woman rant so over me, but yet it made me the more admire her valor and brought down my former loftiness to wonder at my timorousness. But since she is discovered to be the noble Pyrocles, I shall be so far from hiding that disguised exploit of his that I shall blazon it about the world in triumph as an honor for me to be overcome by him; and it shall never be said that envy of my rival shall make me obscure his worth, for I shall applaud his wisdom in making so rare a choice. Nor did I ever hear of any that could deserve him better than the divine Philoclea. Then grieve no more, Amphialus, at thy lady's happiness, since in hers all thine consists; but prepare thy self to obey her commands, be they never so contrary to thy nature."

With these resolutions, although with a shaking hand, he began to write his letters. But Clytifon, as soon as he came out of the chamber, was received by Helena, to whom he related Amphialus's and his whole discourse. And she, being in hope to make him a fortunate messenger for her proceeding, used him with all the courtesy that could be. And then by her favors she enticed him to her bait and made him as much her humble servant as he was Amphialus's: for then he had promised to be a nimble post to them both, and he must be conducted to his lodging, and Helena to her closet: where she began too hard a task for her distracted mind: a letter she did write unto Philoclea, but that did no way please her, it was not sufficiently adorned with rhetoric for so rare a Princess. Another she did like reasonable well, but that was so blurred with her tears that the

620

630

Line 612. **strook**: struck

Line 614. **rant**: storm violently.

Line 633. **post**: messenger.

best of eyes could not read it. More she wrote, and found blemishes
640 in them all. But at last being tired with scribing so long upon one
subject, she resolved that the next should go whate're it were, which
in earnest proved the worst of all. But yet because you shall
understand the inditement of it, it is set down as ensueth. The
superscription was, *For the virtuous Princess Philoclea.*

> Sweet Princess,
> Did I not hear in what raptures of happiness your divine self is
> involved, or could I in the least comprehend the splendor of
> your goodness to spread upon your distressed cousin Amphi-
> alus, I should willingly resign up all my claim to felicity, so that
650 > you, of far worthier endowments, might enjoy it. But since it
> hath pleased the Destinies to place you in the highest
> firmament of contentment, that you may with the more ease
> behold the calamity of your admirer, let me therefore entreat
> you to shew your compassion to him by mildness, and suffer
> his punishment may be sincere affection to me; and you will
> infinitely above measure oblige your devoted servant,
>
> HELENA of Corinth.

Often did she peruse this letter to find out cavils in it, until sleep
would endure no longer to be resisted nor hindered from seizing on
660 so pure a soul, which she evidenced by letting her letter fall out of
her delicate proportioned hand that held it: then fell she into slum-
bers, and starts would now and then affright her, but those she
ended with sighs, and fell asleep again, and then she passed away the
remainder of the night with variety of dreams, until the approaching
day roused up her senses and remembered her it was high time for
lovers to be stirring. Then she, being always mindful of such obser-

---

Line 640. **scribing**: writing.   Line 642. **in earnest**: in reality.
Line 651. **the Destinies**: the Fates, the three goddesses who control human destiny.
Line 658. **cavils**: faults, especially unfair or quibbling faults.

vations, took her letter, and making it fortunate with her prayers, she carried it into the presence, where she stayed for Clytifon, who was receiving his farewell of Amphialus.

For after Amphialus had finished his humble suit, as he termed it, and had endured a tedious night, Clytifon must needs be sent for to prescribe the likeliest medicine for a lovesick remedy. Clytifon could not be asked an harder question, for he himself would gladly have taken physic, had he been sure of the cure. "Tell me, Clytifon," said he, "is there no help for a troubled mind? no cordial to bring sleep into these eyes of mine?" "If you will submit your actions," replied Clytifon, "to my approbation, I will set you in a perfect way of quietness, though it should procure mine own endless misery." "He deserves no physician," answered Amphialus, "that will not accept of his advice, when it is so freely proffered him." "Know then," said Clytifon, "your only way to obtain contentment is to honor, nay, and love her who so entirely loves and respects you." "O stay there," cried out Amphialus, "and do not weigh me down with clogs of grief. I am balanced sufficiently already. Why do you with more burdens strive to sink me? Nothing but Philoclea's commands I find can enter into my heart, and they may strike me dead. Fly then, Clytifon, fly as swiftly as Phoebus can, and make a quick return to let me know Philoclea's censure equal to my deserts." With these words he gave Clytifon his letter, and with a sad gesture turned away. But Clytifon without deferring went his way, though first he received Helena's, and with many protestations vowed to further her undertakings.

And now I will leave these two lovers in longing expectation of his return, and will trace along with Clytifon to accompany him, he being destitute almost of any comfort by reason his affections were

670

680

690

Line 671. **tedious**: troublesome.   Line 684. **balanced**: ballasted, weighed down.
Line 687. **Phoebus**: in classical mythology, Apollo as the sun god; hence, the sun.
Line 690. **deferring**: delay.   Line 691. **Helena's**: i.e., Helena's letter.

so extremely engaged to Helena's beauty, that nothing but envious death could assuage it. This caused such a conflict to arise between Cupid's discharged bow and Clytifon's making his own wounds to gape with contrarying the God of love's commands and hastening
700 from the mistress of his desires to gain her to another, that oftentimes he was turning back to discover his intentions to her. But this design he vanquished by confuting himself.

"It is true," said he, "I ride apace towards mine own overthrow; but since it was her charge, how dare I harbor a thought of refusing? No, it is her gracious pleasure to vouchsafe me to be her messenger. And shall I lose her esteemed favors, which I infinitely hazard if I do not manifest my faithful endeavors in gaining Amphialus to be her husband? But I will choose to be her loyal servant rather than to her sweet self an importunate suitor. And I should account myself ever
710 happy, could it lie in my power to further hers; but I am unworthy to receive such a title as a poor instrument to redeem Her Majesty to her former felicity: however I will shew my willingness by my nimbleness. And then teaching his steed to give a gallant caper, he speedily rode away, and without the least hindrance he quickly set footing in the country of Arcadia, where he was welcomed by peals of bells and shoutings of people, with variety of sports contrived by young children: besides the pleasant shepherds blowed their pipes, whilst the pretty shepherdesses chanted out their praises of their great God Pan. All these harmless pastimes were ordered so conveniently that
720 he might have a perfect view of them as he went by: and all was to declare the joy they conceived for Clytifon's safe return, whose stay they heard was the only delayance of the Princess's nuptials. And as he rode along, the silly lambs did welcome him with leaps, whilst the fox that lurked in his private corner to catch them discovered himself to do homage unto Clytifon, and by that means lost his game; yet he, cheering himself up with hopes of a more plentiful prey here-

---

Line 701. **discover**: reveal.   Line 702. **confuting**: vanquishing, proving himself wrong.
Line 719. **harmless**: innocent.   **ordered**: arranged.   Line 724. **discovered**: revealed.

after, returned to his former craft and received that misfortune as a just recompense of his carelessness.

Thus Clytifon's thoughts were taken up by sundry objects till he had traced along ground so far as to the city of Matenia: there he might see noble personages glory with their employment, and to esteem themselves to be regarded were they not set to work. There he might behold the palace richly furnishing, and all the houses gaudily decking up. There he might hear of abundance of several inventions for masques and other curious sights that might be delightful to the eye. But Clytifon passed by all these rare scenes, they being (in comparison of his fantasy) by him reputed superfluous.

And now his eye was fixed upon the lodge that shadowed the wonders of the world and was seated about two miles distance from Matenia. Thither with eagerness he goes, where he was only saluted by the diligent servants that directed him to the grove adjoining to the lodge, where the Princes just before were walked for recreation. Then as he went gazing about him, he discerned Evarchus, King of Macedon, who signified his joy for his son's and nephew's (to him) revived lives by his lifted up hands and eyes, which with great devotion he rendered to the Gods in thankfulness.

For it happened after Plangus's departure from Macedon with an army, Evarchus, fearing his love-lines would give opportunity for sadness to overcome his languishing spirit, made a journey into Arcadia to visit his ancient friend Basilius. And after many strange

730

740

750

Line 730. **Matenia**: Mantinea.

Lines 733–34. **furnishing…gaudily decking up**: furnished…grandly decked up.

Line 734. **several inventions**: diverse ideas (i.e., for the subjects of masques).

Line 738–39. **shadowed the wonders of the world**: i.e., sheltered Pamela and Philoclea.

Line 740. **only**: specially, pre-eminently.   Line 742. **were walked**: had walked.

Line 748. **love-lines**: i.e., Evarchus's love for his apparently dead son and nephew. Presumably, "love-lines" is "loveliness" (as it is on page 46), with "lovely" having its older sense of "loving."

Lines 747–49. In the 1593 *Arcadia* (V.2), Euarchus arrives in Arcadia because of a storm, not (as Weamys has it) because of a desire to assuage his grief; encountering Arcadia in the midst of civil dissension because of Basilius's exile, he determines to persuade his friend to resume his authority.

accidents had apparently been discovered, as the famous Sir Philip Sidney fully declares, Pyrocles and Musidorus were found to be alive; and now he tarried in Arcadia to see his blessedness completed in their marriages. And in the meantime he dispatched a messenger to Plangus to encourage him with those welcome tidings. And then the good King confined himself wholly to the continual praises of the divine providence for his unlooked for comfort. And now straying from the rest of the princely company, he fell to his wonted contemplations and never moved from his devout posture, till Clytifon's sudden approach into his sight made him start and withal raised him.

Then Evarchus examined him how the noble gentleman Amphialus did, but Clytifon was so mightily dashed with his disturbing of Evarchus that he let silence be both his answer and pleader for his presumption, which Evarchus perceiving, brought him into that solitary arbor where Pyrocles in his disguisement had the privilege to resort. There sat Basilius with Genecea, his Queen, and he lovingly condoling with her for her former sufferings that she was then asounding in his attentive ears, but at Evarchus's and Clytifon's entrance they rose up, and graciously saluting Clytifon, they commanded him to repeat those adventures that had befallen him at Corinth, if they were remarkable; but Evarchus prevailed with them to have patience, that Philoclea, whom it most concerned, might hear as soon as any; then they all went to the young Princes, and found them so well employed that had they not espied them, they would in pity have passed by and not disturbed them.

Pyrocles and Musidorus being seated upon a fountain's brim (where in the middle Cupid's image was placed, ready the second

---

Line 751. **accidents…discovered**: incidents…made known. Weamys is perhaps referring to the series of events (in Book Five of the 1593 *Arcadia*) leading up to the trial of Pyrocles and Musidorus and the disclosure that the two heroes are in fact alive.

Line 753. **he**: Evarchus.   Line 763. **dashed**: abashed.

Line 766. **in his disguisement**: i.e., when Pyrocles was disguised as the Amazon Zelmane.

time to have wounded them), but they, not minding him, strived
who should with the comeliest grace and highest rhetoric extol their   780
mistresses, whilst the fair Pamela with lovely Philoclea tied the truest
lovers-knot in grass that ever yet was tied, and now and then would
pick a flower to shew their art to tell the virtue of it: in these harmless pleasures their parents found them busied.

Then Basilius, coming to Philoclea, told her that Clytifon had
brought her news of her servant Amphialus, and she, modestly
blushing, replied that she should be glad to hear of her cousin's
health; then Basilius desired them all to sit down that they might
lend the better attention to Clytifon; but he, in reverence to his sovereign, would stand till Basilius laid his commands upon him to the   790
contrary: then Clytifon recounted all circumstances saving that
about himself, as I have set down; and when he had ended, he presented Philoclea with Helena's and Amphialus's letters, which she
courteously received, and when she had broken them open, she read
them, but with such crystal streams all the time dropping from her
rosy cheeks that had Venus been by, she would have preserved them
in a glass to wash her face withal, to make her the more beautiful;
and then her servant Pyrocles gently wiped them away; but seeing
them yet distil, he was angry, and shewed it on this manner: "It is a
hard riddle to me," said he, "that a lover should write such a regard-   800
less letter to grieve and mar that face that he so much adored." He
would longer have chid Amphialus, but that Evarchus advised him
to take the letter from his sorrowful lady, which she willing resigned
unto him; and he read as followeth:

For the Incomparable PRINCESS, the Princess Philoclea.

Madam,
I am confident you have heard what affection I have harbored
in my heart, your (though unknown to me) most barbarous

Line 799. **distil**: drop.   **on**: in.   Lines 800–801. **regardless**: unworthy of regard, careless.

810 usage, and that I might clear mine innocence of such an heinous crime, with what a tragical act I heaped up misery upon misery, which hath infinitely overwhelmed my distracted soul; and now I only rest in expectation of your commands. I beseech you let it be so pitiful, that it may procure eternal ease to my extreme perplexity; and nothing can diminish that but death by your appointment; and that to me shall be most welcome; and I shall account my self happy in obeying your desires at the last moment, which I vow to accomplish whate're it be with cheerfulness; and with this undaunted resolution, I will ever continue to be,

820   Your faithful, though unworthy Servant,
                                                    AMPHIALUS.

Whilst Pyrocles was reading this, the sweet Philoclea stopped the remainder of her tears, till she had taken a view of Helena's. Then she entreated her Pyrocles to read over her cousin Amphialus's lines to her again. And she attentively listening to his passionate phrases, the second time she renewed her weeping deluge: but the stately Pamela said her cousin did wisely to cast himself into the power of her sister; he knew her clemency, and considered it was his safest way to do so before he set footing in Arcadia.

830 Then they all persuaded Philoclea not to grieve for that which she might remedy, and advised her to go and write a letter to Amphialus, and in it to command him to put in execution Helena's demands. She immediately arose, and at her rising made the flowers to hang down their heads for want of her presence: but her breath, being a

---

Lines 807–10. **I…crime**: Amphialus's (or Weamys's) sentence is garbled. The sense seems to be: "I am confident you have heard: [1] what affection [for you] I have harbored in my heart; [2] [my remorse for] your (though unknown to me) most barbarous usage; and [3] [in order] that I might clear mine innocence, with what a tragical act I heaped up misery upon misery," etc.   **crime**: That is, Amphialus's complicity in his mother's, Cecropia's, abduction and "most barbarous usage" of Philoclea and her sister, and his own treasonous refusal to yield to Basilius's authority.

Line 813. **pitiful**: compassionate.   Line 823. **Helena's**: i.e., Helena's letter.

sweeter perfume than the scent of the choicest flowers, made her careless of their sorrow; for she, not minding them, went her way; and Pyrocles, who could be as well out of his life as from her company, followed after her and would needs wait upon her to the lodge; and there he stayed till she had written her letter. Which she had no sooner ended, and Pyrocles perused, but that ingenious Clytifon was ready upon his horse to receive it that he might with speed convey it to Corinth. So after abundance of commendations from Philoclea to Helena and Amphialus, he parted, and without any remarkable passage, he quickly attained to his journey's end: where he was received between hope and fear by Helena, who hearing of his return, withdrew into a private room, and then sent for him; but as soon as he was entered into her sight, she cried out:

"Good Sir, do not break my heart with delayance; is there any possibility for me to live? if there be none, O speak, that I may die! and end my fears: for if Amphialus's doom be death, I am resolved not to live one minute after him." But Clytifon, as desirous to give her ease as she could be to ask it of him, answered that now the joyful time was near at hand that Amphialus and she should be united together and should flourish with all happiness that could be imagined. "I beseech you do not flatter me," said Helena; "such vain persuasions will do no good, but make my fall the higher and so more dangerous." "Madam," replied Clytifon, "let me beg the favor of you to believe me, and if I have told you any falsehood, say I was never trusty to my friend, and you cannot punish me more to my vexation: but here is a letter from my lord to Amphialus that will verify me of the truth." Upon this Helena was brought to believe that felicity to her that she so long hath wished for, and caused vermilion red

840

850

860

Line 848. **delayance**: delay.

Line 860. **a letter from my lord**: i.e., Philoclea's letter. This transferred usage of "lord" for "lady" is not without precedent; e.g., in *The Merchant of Venice* (V.iii.2), Portia speaks of herself as "the Lord / Of this fair mansion, master of my servants."

to dye her cheeks in preparation to receive their welcome guest: and then her earnestness grew impatient of deferrings, she longing to pry into Philoclea's letters; therefore sealing up her lips from further questions, she directed Clytifon to Amphialus, and then she left him.

Amphialus in the meantime, whose bowels earned for Clytifon's return, listened to all whisperings. So then he seeing the attendants 870 so busy in their private discourses, he inquired whether Clytifon was come, just as he entered his presence. Then after due civilities passed between them, Clytifon delivered up his charge to Amphialus, who used many ceremonies before he would presume to touch it; but when he was better advised, he joyfully embraced it and by degrees he intruded upon it, for first he brake the seal and then he made his protestation:

"Now I do vow and promise before Cupid, whose dart hath so cruelly wounded me, and before Venus, to whose beauty I am so much a slave, never in the least to resist Philoclea's lines; but I will 880 shew my duty to her by my willingness to obey her pleasure. And you, my lord Clytifon, with this noble company are witnesses of this my protestation."

Thus concluded he his solemn vow, and then he carefully unfolded the treasure of his life, with a belief that every fold drew him nearer than other to Paradise: and when he read it, the curious-est eye could not espy the least motion of discontent to reside in him; but he rather seemed as a conqueror that had suddenly surprised unlooked-for comfort, which much conduced to the joy of the beholders. And when he had fully delighted his eyes with Philo-890 clea's gracious lines, he changed his note from admiring her perfections, to blazon his now amorous phrases of Helena's worth; and

---

Line 868. **bowels earned**: heart yearned.   Line 885. **other**: the other.

Lines 885–86. **curiousest**: most scrutinizing.

Line 891. **blazon**: publicly celebrate, often by means of a formal catalogue of attributes.

then the sweet behavior of Helena to him in his calamity extended to his memory, which made him extremely wonder at the hidden virtues of Philoclea's letters for working so great a cure in his understanding: therefore now assuring himself the Gods had destined Helena to be his spouse, in pursuance of their pleasure and of his own happiness, he sent to her in an humble manner to entreat her company. Which message, poor Queen, she heard as joyfully as she could have done had Mercury posted from Heaven to bring her tidings of her transporting thither: but yet trembling possessed her delicate body, and would not leave her before she had presented her self to Amphialus, who (taking her by the white, yet shaking, hand) gratefully thanked her for her many favors, and then telling her he should study a requital, besought her to hear the letter that his cousin Philoclea had honored him with. But Helena answered with blushes, whilst he read the letter, thus:

900

For her highly-esteemed Cousin, the Lord AMPHIALUS.

Worthy Cousin,
Might I partake with the Gods in their interest in you, I would not be kept in such ignorance and amazement as I am at this present; but I would thoroughly search what just occasions I have ever given you to hazard your person with such sad apprehensions of my anger, as I hear without speedy remedy will deprive you of all future felicity. But laying by all that ambitious thought, in earnest, Cousin, I must needs tell you how without comparison it troubles me that you should think

910

Line 899. **Mercury**: in Roman mythology, the messenger of the gods.

Lines 914–15. **laying by…ambitious thought**: laying aside…roundabout(?) thought. The exact meaning of "ambitious" is obscure; among the meanings in the *OED* are: eager, aspiring, towering, pretentious, circumlocutory, circuitous, and (by way of the adverb) fawning. A number of the meanings of "ambitious" suggest its Latin origins in *ambire*, to go around, hence "roundabout," in which case Philoclea may be suggesting that Amphialus's worry about her anger misses the point. Other meanings are variants of the modern sense of "desirous of honor," in which case Philoclea may be complimenting Amphialus for his honorable thought but urging him to lay it aside.

me so severe and unnatural to torment you with a second death for that fault which you have by so many evident signs manifested your self to be innocent of, and if you had been guilty (as you are not) I should rather choose to mitigate your crime than any way to heighten it. But yet I will not profusely let slip that advantage, which you have so freely left to my discretion, but will use it as an ornament to make you happy, yet not in way of authority, but as a petitioner I humbly crave of you not to refuse Beauty and Honor when it is so virtuously presented to you by the famous Queen Helena, whose love-lines surpasses all others.

Therefore if you esteem of me, prove it by entirely loving of her, who, I am sure, will endow you with all such blessings as may enrich your contentment. And now with full satisfaction that you will grant me my request, I close up these abrupt lines, and am immovably,

Your faithful cousin and Servant,
PHILOCLEA.

Here the sweet Philoclea ended, and Amphialus with a low congee began to speak to Helena in this manner: "Fair Queen, what excuse I shall make for my long incivility to your singular self, I know not, nor can I imagine with what confidence to beg of you the perfecting of these compassionate lines; therefore for pity sake accept of my cast-down eyes for my solicitors, and let your goodness plead for my backwardness in submitting to that duty of love to you, when the greatest Princes tremble at your sight, and worship you as their image. Madam, suffer your answer may be pitiful, since I acknowledge mine error."

"My Lord," replied Helena, "there is no cause given here to induce you to renew your grief, if my yielding my self to your noble

---

Line 939. **perfecting**: bringing to fulfillment.
Line 943. **image**: idol.   **pitiful**: full of pity.

disposal may be valued as a sufficient satisfactory argument to ease you, that hath ever been my endeavor in all virtuous ways to compass."

"The more may be imputed to my unworthiness," answered Amphialus; "now I am surprised with shame in having so dull an apprehension, such a stony heart to refuse so rare a person as your divine self; but the Gods are just, for now the wheel of Fortune is turned, and if you please to revenge your wrong upon me the instrument, you cannot stab me with a sharper spear than your denial."

"Why," said Helena, "do you force me to repeat my real affections to you so often? is it your jealousy of my constancy? if it be that, with thanks to my Goddess Diana, I avouch that I never harbored the least unchaste thought to scandalize or blemish my purity."

"Now I may challenge you," replied Amphialus, "for searching out new sorrows to your self; but pardon me, dear Madam, for my rash presumption with chiding you for one fault, when I my self am burdened with so many, and believe me, my highest ambition is to hear your heavenly voice sound out the harmony of your love within mine ears; and when you vouchsafe me that, none can parallel with me in happiness."

Thus they passed away the day with these and, afterwards, more fond expressions; and amongst them they concluded to make a journey into Arcadia and, for the greater triumph, to celebrate their nuptials with the other renowned Princes, now in the height of their superfluous complements. The news of the happy success of Philoclea's letter had so spread about that such abundance of the city flocked to the palace to see Amphialus that Helena was forced to command the officers not to let any have admission until some important business they were to consult upon might be accomplished; and then she promised free passage to all. This caused every

950

960

970

Line 957. **jealousy**: mistrust.   Line 959. **scandalize**: disgrace.

Line 971. **superfluous complements**: (overflowingly) numerous ceremonies.

one to retire to their houses, and Helena and Amphialus after a while spared some time to advise with Clytifon to consider of the probablest way for them to go into Arcadia, the people of Corinth-being in great expectation of their solemnizing the wedding there. Then Clytifon counselled them on this manner:

"The surest way that I can think on is to lay open your real intentions to the peers of your land, that by degrees it may be published to the vulgar; also declare that you will not yield to any thing that may prove to their prejudice; but if they will not receive that as satisfactory, but argue that it is a disparagement for their country to suffer their princess to depart from thence and be transported in to another to have her marriage finished, you may easily prevent their future dislike of that particular; since the dishonor of your country concerns you most (and in all reason you should have the most especial care to preserve it) you may please them with telling them, you do intend to make your kingdom famous by the splendor of those Princes that now reside in Arcadia; and then you will solemnize your wedding with the same points that you use when you are there: and I am persuaded their dissensions will be quieted."

The counsel of Clytifon was no way rejected but very well esteemed by the royal lovers, who shewed their thankfulness by the large themes they made of their judgments to him: and then telling him that they must still be more obliged to him, they entreated him to let his return to Arcadia be a little sooner than theirs to give the princely family intelligence of their following after; because they were yet in their private lodge, it would not be commodious for them to come unto them unawares. Clytifon replied that none should do that service but himself; then Amphialus told him it was high time for him to make good his words, for Queen Helena and his own intention was to be at Matenia suddenly; thus after a few

---

Line 979. **probablest**: most credible or persuasive (to the Corinthians).   Line 981. **on**: in.
Line 985. **prejudice**: detriment.   Line 986. **disparagement**: offence.
Line 988. **finished**: solemnized. Line 994. **points**: attributes. Line 998. **themes**: discourses.

more speeches passed, Clytifon took his leave and dispatched away with all expedition.

In the meantime Helena gallantly played her game; for at the immediate time of Clytifon's departure from Corinth, she pro- 1010 claimed free liberty for all her subjects' access unto her: then Amphi-alus and she, being arrayed in glorious apparel, removed from their with-drawing rooms into the presence, and there seated themselves in the throne: their nobles, coming to them in their ranks and kiss-ing both their hands, rendered in all lowly manner their joy for their Queen's careful choice in making so brave a Prince their high Lord. Then Helena declared her mind to them as Clytifon advised her, which at first startled them, but she argued in her own defence so wisely that she quickly confuted and pacified those disturbers. But after them came knights, gentlemen, citizens, in such abundance, 1020 that they confined the Princess to their patience for a week together. Besides, the country peasants, and all sorts of mechanics, that with admiration pressed to gaze upon them. But when their tedious task was over, they spent some time in pleasing their fancies with the contrivance of stately curiosities for the honor of their nuptials, Amphialus and Helena concurring so well together that nothing was commended by the one but instantly it was highly approved of and valued by the other. Which combining of these was a rare example for the under-workmen: they, endeavoring to follow their superiors' rule, delighting in these fellows' judgments, did (to the lovers' joy) 1030 unexpectedly finish their art.

Then all accommodations being prepared in a readiness, they departed from Corinth, their pomp being thus ordered: three chari-ots drawn by six horses apiece came whirling to the gate. The first

---

Line 1021. **to their patience**: i.e., to patient endurance of them.

Line 1022. **mechanics**: workmen.

Line 1025. **contrivance…curiosities**: designing artistic objects or constructions.

Line 1031. **unexpectedly finish their art**: complete their work (or, possibly, perfect their artistry or craft) beyond expectation.

was for six noble men being of Amphialus's bedchamber. That chariot was lined with green figgered-velvet, richly fringed, signifying the
Princes' loves. The horses were black to manifest their mourning for
being so long exiled from their loves. The next chariot was lined
with white satin embroidered with gold; that was to witness their
innocency, their love being virtuous: in that went six ladies, attendants upon Helena. The third and last was for Helena and Amphialus; that was lined with blue, embroidered with pearls and precious
stones; the horses wore plumes of feathers; the coachman, postilion,
and six footmen's liveries were blue, as an emblem of their constancy,
and embroidered as the chariot was. On this triumphant manner
they went to Arcadia, besides an innumerable company of coaches
and horsemen that belonged to the court; which keeping on a moderate pace, in short time safely set footing there: and the flying
report, that would not be stopped for any man's pleasure, quickly
gave notice to the Princes of Helena's and Amphialus's being come.

But they had before removed to their palace, being in perpetual
expectation of their company: and to shew how glad they were to
enjoy it, Musidorus and Pamela, with Pyrocles, going altogether in a
coach, went out a good distance from the city to meet them: which
they could hardly compass to do (by reason of the multitudes that
went to see that magnificent sight) until they had appointed officers
to beat a lane: so that at last they made a narrow passage. It was an
incomparable sight to see Helena and Amphialus greet Philoclea!
what low congees they made to her, as if she had been their Goddess!
whilst she courteously reverenced them again. Then Helena and she
stood admiring one another's beauty, till Amphialus had saluted the
other Princes, and yet returned soon enough to break their silence.

Line 1036. **figgered**: ornamented.   Line 1043. **postilion**: the person who rides the left-hand
horse of the lead horses in a horse-drawn carriage.

Line 1045. **on**: in.   Line 1051. **before**: earlier.   Line 1055. **compass**: plan.

Line 1057. **beat a lane**: i.e., make a path through the crowd.   Line 1059. **congees**: bows.

"Ladies," said he, "there is no occasion given to stir up sadness in rebellion against mirth and happiness, for here we may see love coupled together, when we have known by experiments it to have been dispersed by many strange accidents. And most sweet Princess Philoclea, by your gracious lines I am preserved from perpetual misery, to enjoy a crown endowed with all felicity. But yet, Madam, all that I can do or say in requital is to let you know that I am and ever shall be your humble servant."   1070

"I beseech you, Cousin," replied Philoclea, "do not your self that injury to confess you were thrust forward to your contentment. And seriously, when I obtained a sight of this rare Queen, I was astonished at your former backwardness. But since Cupid did play his part so cunningly as to make you blind, I am extreme glad that I could be an instrument worthy to recover your decayed eyes and languishing spirits; and I am beholding to your goodness in obeying my request." Here Philoclea ended; and Amphialus was furnished with a reply.

Musidorus brought in Pamela to Helena, whom she civilly wel-   1080
comed to Arcadia; but upon Amphialus she looked aloft, as not deserving to be regarded by her. Which Musidorus perceiving, he secretly persuaded her to look favorably upon him. Whose advice was received by her as a command that she durst not withstand. So she, altering her disdainfulness into cheerfulness, bent her discourse to Amphialus, that at last they grew excellent company for one another, and so continued till their thoughts were taken up with amazement at sight of Clytifon, who came hallowing to them and with signs pointed to them to haste into their chariots. But they, not understanding his meaning, delayed their speed till he came nearer,   1090

Line 1074. **backwardness**: bashfulness.

Line 1080. **Musidorus...Helena**: "When" prefaces this clause in the original text, but has been deleted here for clarity.   **she**: i.e., Pamela.

Line 1088. **hallowing**: shouting.

and certified them that there was a messenger come from Plangus to Evarchus, but he would not be persuaded to deliver his business before Musidorus and Pyrocles were present.

This news strook Pamela and Philoclea into an extremity of sadness; for then Plangus's story was renewed into their memory, which made them suspect it was some envious errand to separate their affections; but their beloved Princes used all persuasions that might comfort them, and then led them to Amphialus's chariot, that being the largest and in that regard the most convenient; they, being too full of perplexity to mind matters of state, went altogether that they might the better pass away the time with company.

Then in a distracted manner they went to Matenia, and quietly passed through the streets till they came to the palace, where they had much ado to enter by reason of the throng that was there making inquiries after the Armenian messenger; yet at last the Princes obtained entrance where Helena and Amphialus were with all respect welcomed by Basilius and Genecea: and when many compliments were consummate, they all went to the presence, where Evarchus and the messenger were. Then Evarchus told them there was a business of consequence to discover, and he wished them to give audience to it; then all noise being appeased, the messenger turning to Evarchus, said these following words:

"Most renowned King: Prince Plangus, general of your forces in Armenia, hath sent me to recount unto Your Majesty the truth of his proceedings since his departure from Macedon; which if Your Majesty please to hear, I shall in a little time bring it about to his present condition. Know then, gracious Sir, Prince Plangus had hardly set footing in the Armenian land before he was surprised by the unfortunate news of his Lady Erona's being delivered up into the power of her tyrannical enemies. You may imagine what discouragement this

---

Line 1091. **certified**: informed.   Line 1096. **envious errand**: invidious message.
Line 1108. **consummate**: concluded.

was to him at his first entrance, to be almost deprived of his chiefest
victory: but yet he hid his grief, showing his undaunted spirit to his
army; he doubled their march and at length overtook the forces of
the deceitful Plaxirtus, and with loss of a few men, he so disordered
them that he and all his army marched through the midst of our
adversaries, whilst they like frighted men stood gazing on us; yet we,
not altogether trusting to our safeties, to their amazement placed a
reasonable company in ambush to hold them play if they should
venture to fall on us; and we (having intelligence that Plaxirtus himself was but a mile before us, attended by a small guard, because of   1130
his confidence in his forces that were behind him) pursued him: and
he, not doubting but that we were of his confederacy, turned back
his horse and stayed that we might overtake him, thinking thereby
to do us a favor: but Prince Plangus, not having patience to see him
so well pleased, galloped towards him; which Plaxirtus seeing, and
knowing his own guilt, began to distrust that then he should receive
a due reward; and then he cried out, "Are we friends? Are we
friends?" but Prince Plangus, riding to him, clasped him about the
waist and gallantly threw him off his horse, and then answered him
that he should be always his friend to do him such courtesies as they   1140
were; which the guard hearing, they shewed us that they were expert
in running, though not in fighting, for in a moment they were all
fled away: then Prince Plangus having his greatest adversary at his
feet, and studying the most convenient way to fulfill your Majesty's
desire to preserve him alive till he might be more openly put to
death, just then a trumpeter came to him from Artaxia, with a paper
in his hand, which he delivered to Plaxirtus, wherein Artaxia
declared that her cousin Plangus, whom she entertained civilly in
her court, was risen in arms against her and had brought foreigners

---

Lines 1127–28. **placed…play**: i.e., Plangus placed a moderate number of troops lying in wait
in order to keep Plaxirtus's forces occupied, should they attack.   Line 1139. **gallantly**: bravely,
heroically.

1150 to invade her land, and that he had not only forgotten her former kindness to him, but also broken the laws of Nature, she being his near kinswoman, and not only with her but also with her dear and lawful husband Plaxirtus, whom he had taken and made a prisoner; and she further declared that whatsoever cruelty be inflicted upon Plaxirtus, she would do the like or worse to Erona. And if he did not quickly send her a satisfactory answer, she would begin with Erona first and make her endure the greatest torments that she could possibly, and live.

"This put Prince Plangus into a world of confused cogitations, for
1160 very unwilling he was to let go unrevenged the bloody contriver of these Princes' supposed murder: and if he did not in some degree yield to that, then his beloved lady Erona must suffer those intolerable tortures. But when he was in the height of passion, to think that from a victor he must become slave, we might perceive a traveller guided to us by some of the soldiers. At that sight Prince Plangus entreated the trumpeter to stay till he had known the meaning of the stranger's coming. He was your happy messenger, O King, that delivered the Queen Erona from misery. He it was that brought the joyful news of the safety of these famous Princes to perplexed Prince
1170 Plangus. And that so well revived him, that after he had worshipped Apollo for such an unlooked for blessing, he cheerfully dispatched away the trumpeter with his answer, that now the treachery of Plaxirtus was brought to nought, for Pyrocles and Musidorus were miraculously preserved and lived to be examples of virtue: and if she would stand to the former articles, Plaxirtus should be set at liberty.

"Now the renowned Princes want your assistance in defence of the lady Erona, whose life is now in your power; for by me Plaxirtus and Anaxius challenge you to answer them in a combat for the dis-

---

Line 1176. **Princes**: This may be a misprint for "Prince" (i.e., Plangus), or the text may be garbled, and "renowned Princes" would refer to Pyrocles and Musidorus, whom the messenger is addressing.

tressed Queen, and if you prove victorious over them, the same day Erona shall be freed from her imprisonment: but if the contrary side prevail, at that time Erona must be put to death. These are the articles before agreed upon, and now the second time resolved on. If you will hazard your persons in the quarrel, the whole kingdom of Armenia being in expectation of your valor, that may end the differences." 1180

Thus the messenger concluded, and Pyrocles and Musidorus sent him back to Armenia, with promise of their speedy following after him. It would have made a rock, had it been by, burst out in tears in reference to the company. And had Narcissus been never ravished with his own conceited beauty, yet had he been there, he would have wept into fountains to see the best of Princes turmoiled in waves of affections: and Fortune, deluding them, persuaded them they were near refreshment, when they were environed with their chiefest calamities. Here you might see Pamela with her arms wreathed about Musidorus, as if she intended there should be her rest till he had granted her request, and her cast-down eyes and weepings that bedewed her pure cheeks did witness her abundant sorrow. But at last, wiping them away, she contested with Musidorus and her self on this manner: 1190

"Dear Musidorus, do not part from her to whom you have so often plighted your faith. If you love me, as you vow you do, why will you abandon my presence? oh, do not break my heart with your inconstancy, nor stain your other virtues with such a crime, as never can be washed away; therefore stay, or else confute me with your reason, and then I shall hate my passion, and contemn my self for valuing my interest in your affections above the main treasure, so accounted by the heavenly and earthly society, in keeping an honorable and unblemished reputation; which if you can do, and yet leave 1200

Line 1189. **Narcissus**: in classical mythology, a young man who fell in love with his own reflection in a pool and wasted away from longing.

me, I will never shew my self such a ridiculous lover as to be your
hindrance." "My thrice dearer than my self," replied Musidorus, "do
not afflict me with the word 'inconstancy'; if I were guilty, then
might you justly tax me with it. But far be the thought of infidelity
from me: and believe me, lady, Plaxirtus cannot pierce his sword
deeper into my heart than these sharp words, which proceeded from
your sweet lips, have done. But for my combat in Armenia, that is so
necessary, that none can decide the quarrel, unless it be my cousin
Pyrocles and my self, by reason of Artaxia and Plaxirtus thirsting for
our lives; they will never suffer Erona to be released from prison
before they have vented their malice upon us in as great a measure as
their ability can give them leave. And besides, should I refuse, it
would redound so extremely upon my renown that every one would
be ready to object that since a woman prevailed over me, I am
directly cowardized. And now, dear lady, I dare presume you will
rather let me venture my life in defence of so just a cause than to let
it go unrevenged to my deserved infamy."

Poor Pamela all this while seemed like one in a trance, not having
power to contradict Musidorus in his pleadings, nor yet able to submit her yielding to them, but made her tears and sighs her advocates
when he with all persuasions sought to comfort her. And in the
meantime the sweet Philoclea, who lay grovelling at her Pyrocles's
feet, and would not be removed, expressed her grief in these mournful complaints:

"Ah me!" said she, "that I should be born under such an unfortunate planet of unhappy events that daily afflict me! Tell me, my
Pyrocles, the cause that makes you so willingly hazard your person in
such dangerous attempts. If you can tax me with any errors, to my
self unknown, that might work your displeasure, O tell me what
they are that I may mend, and study some easier way to punish me
than by your intended death. But if nothing else may reconcile me

---

Line 1223. **directly cowardized**: made to look completely cowardly.

to you, yet shew your clemency, and let your own blessed hand first 1240
end my misery."

Here she stopped, and perceiving Pyrocles to be in as amazed condition as she her self was, not knowing what to do or say to appease
her sorrow, she premeditated that now or never was her time to keep
him with her in safety, and then she suddenly arose from the
ground, and standing a while in great devotion, at last she cried out:

"Now am I ready to receive thy harmless spear into my heart; now
shew thy love and pity to me quickly, and preserve me not alive to
endure such terror as cannot be charmed away, unless you will
promise me the enjoyment of your company." But Pyrocles started 1250
up, and catching her in his arms, advised her not to give way to sorrow, the hater of beauty, to rule over her, nor yet to mistrust she ever
offended him, but that she was more precious to him than the world
could be, and that he made no question but that he should return
again from Armenia to enjoy her with peace and happiness.

With these and many more such expressions, he strived to cheer
her up. But she still kept on bewailing her ill fortune, and would not
be pacified until Musidorus came to her and entreated her to go to
her sister Pamela and to shew her discretion by moderating her passion, that she might be a motive to reduce her sister to follow her 1260
example, who now lay weltering in her tears. These tidings persuaded her to defer her own cares, that she might in some measure
work a cure in her sister, whom she valued, next to her Pyrocles,
above all the world. And then she would not delay the time with
bemoaning herself, but hastily went her way supported by the two
illustrious branches of the forest, Pyrocles and Musidorus.

But as she went, there represented to her view the two ancient
Kings, Evarchus and Basilius, walking to and fro like shadows, and
looked as they would have done, had one come out of the grave to
warn them to prepare themselves in short time to come to them. 1270
This doleful sight had like to have prevailed over her and made her
fall into a relapse of passion; but the remembrance of the task she

was going about suppressed those vapors. And being come within the sight of Pamela (whose deluge was stayed a little to pause, that it might issue more freshly and eagerly at Philoclea's presence) whom as soon as she espied, she perceived her hidden discontent and rebuked on this manner:

"Sister, think not your dissembling smiles can entice me to follow your example, for I can as perfectly see through you into your grieved heart as if you were transparent, and know your pain that now you endeavor to conceal. Oh! leave these counterfeits, and you will be a far more acceptable comforter unto me."

Poor Philoclea could no longer withstand the batteries of Pamela, but confessed her forced mirth, and then instead of assuaging they augmented one another's sorrows with such lamentable moans that Pyrocles and Musidorus were forced to give way to sighs, till their thoughts were surprised by the coming of Clytifon, who brought them word that the two Kings stayed at the door to speak with them. Then they softly went out of the chamber and were received by Basilius and Evarchus, who told them that since it stood so much upon their honors to endeavour to redeem that distressed lady, they advised them not to linger in the performance of it, for nothing was in their way to cause any delay, and the sooner they went, the sooner by Apollo's assistance they might return: to whose mercy they recommended them and commanded them that when they had obtained a prosperous journey, and had vanquished their enemies, not to be negligent in sending them word of it, that they might be sharers in their joy as well as their sorrow. Then after both the Kings had made them happy with their blessings, they sent them away.

Though first Pyrocles and Musidorus would needs take a review of their ladies' pavilion, but not of their persons, out of consideration that it would but double their affliction: and then reverencing

---

Line 1277. **on**: in.   Line 1300. **though**: then, next.

Line 1302. **reverencing**: showing respect by bowing or kneeling.

the carpet on which they used to tread, they took their leave of the desolate chamber and did resolve to travel alone, had not Kalodolus (Musidorus's faithful servant) made a vow that no occasions should persuade him to leave his master again; so that Musidorus, seeing there was no remedy, yielded to his desires. Nor could Amphialus's noble heart well brook to stay behind, for oftentimes he entreated them that he might go a second for them, or else a servant to them. But they answered him that he could not do them better service than to accompany his cousins and make much of them in their absence. Then, after they had accomplished some more compliments, they parted, Amphialus to his charge, and the Princes committed themselves into the hands of wavering Fortune: who, having already shewed them her frowns, would now pleasure them with her smiles, which first she discovered by conveying them safely to Armenia, where they were welcomed unanimously by all, but especially by Plangus, who could hardly confine his joy within the bounds of reason. But the Princes, being mindful of his business, desired Plangus to hasten their combat, because their ladies were in a despairing condition of ever seeing them again, and they assured him they did not fear to enter within the compass of Plaxirtus, so long as it was by the public agreement, and not by secret practices. Plangus certified them that all things were prepared for their accommodation, and that they might (if they pleased) exercise their valor upon their enemies the next morning, and that two scaffolds were erected, the one for Artaxia, she intending to be a beholder, the other for Erona, who is to be brought thither guarded as a prisoner, and in her sight there is a stake in readiness to consume her, if they be overcome. This last he uttered in such mournful expressions that Pyrocles and Musidorus vowed to spend their heart's blood, but that they would release and deliver Erona from the power of Artaxia.

Line 1309. **go a second**: go as their representative or attendant in battle.
Lines 1312–13. **compliments**: courtesies.   Line 1323. **certified**: assured.

And before they would refresh themselves with Plangus's entertainments, they dispatched a trumpeter to Plaxirtus and Anaxius to
certify them they were come to answer their challenge and had set
apart the next morning for that purpose: the trumpeter soon
returned with this reply, that the sooner it was, the more advanta-
geous it would prove to them, and they would not fail to meet them
at the place and time appointed. Thus they agreed upon the next
1340   morning; and when the Prince had partaked of Plangus's supper,
they yielded to sleep, which forsook them not till the promised time
was near at hand.

Early in the morning Plaxirtus and Anaxius, puffed up with pride
and not questioning but that they should be conquerors, put on
their armor, and mounting their steeds, galloped to the list. And
Artaxia, thinking to vent her spleen with gazing at the overthrow of
the Princes, came to the scaffold attired in all her costly and glorious
apparel, and with as great a train as she would have had, were she to
have been spectator of her husband's coronation, King of Armenia.

1350   Within a while was Erona brought guarded by a band of soldiers
to her scaffold, where she might see the end of her misery by the fire,
or otherwise by Pyrocles's and Musidorus's victory: but she, being
wearied out of her life by sundry afflictions, looked as gladly upon
the fiery stake as she did upon her famous champions who were then
entered the list and waving their swords about their heads; Pyrocles
encountered Anaxius, and Musidorus Plaxirtus. Then entered they
into so fierce a fight that it goes beyond my memory to declare all
the passages thereof: but both parties shewed such magnanimity of
courage that for a long time none could discern who should be vic-
1360   tors, till at length Musidorus gave a fatal thrust to Plaxirtus, who
being before faint with loss of blood, fell from his steed, and in the
fall clashed his armor in pieces; and then his steed, for joy that he
was eased of such a wicked burden, pranced over his disgraced

Line 1345. **the list**: the scene of combat.
Line 1346. **spleen**: anger, ill-humor, spite.

master, and not suffering him to die such an honorable death as by Musidorus's sword, trampled out his guts, while Plaxirtus, with curses in his mouth, ended his hateful life.

Then Pyrocles redoubled his blows so eagerly upon Anaxius that he could no longer withstand them, but gnashing his teeth for anger, he fell at Pyrocles's feet and died. Thus pride and treachery received their just reward.

But then Artaxia's glory was turned into mourning and her rich attire into rags as soon as she perceived Plaxirtus wounded, his blood gushing out, his horse treading on him, and he himself dying with bitter groans and frantic speeches, which he breathed out at his last moment for fear of further torments: she tare off her hair, and rent her clothes in so enraged a manner that she drew all eyes from the corpse in wonder and amazement on her. Nor could anything regulate her fury, but she violently run down to the corpse, and there breathed out her complaints.

In which time Plangus called his soldiers together and went up to the other scaffold to release Erona, though at first he was forced to make a way with his sword, the guard resolving not to surrender her till they had received a further command from Artaxia: but Plangus made them repent their strictness and ask Erona's pardon for it. And after he was revived with a warm kiss from her hand, he led her down to Pyrocles and Musidorus, who having forgot the former injuries Artaxia had done them, courteously persuaded her not to bemoan him, whose memory was reproachful to all the world for valuing his one deceitfulness above virtue; and then they told her it would be more for her renown to solemnize for him such obsequies as are seeming for a Prince (he being of the race, although he learned not to follow their example) and then to proclaim her sorrow for joining with him in his mischief. Many more speeches they used to her, some to abate her grief and others to assuage her malice; but at first she would listen to none; yet afterwards being better advised,

1370

1380

1390

Line 1388. **him**: i.e., her husband, Plaxirtus.   Line 1389. **one**: own.

she sent for two magnificent hearses, and before she would suffer Plaxirtus's corpse to be laid in, she pronounced her resolution on this manner:

"Since it hath pleased Apollo, who hath the government of all things on earth, to suffer Plaxirtus to fall by your prowess, I do here by this dead body vow to you to end my life in widowhood. And you, cousin Plangus, whom I have so infinitely wronged with this fair lady Erona, to you I do resign up the authority of my kingdom, being, after my decease, the lawful successor. I shall desire only a competency to keep me from famishment: but if these, your valiant champions, will have you go to Arcadia to finish your marriage there, in that time I will be your trusty deputy to order your affairs here in Armenia until you return from thence." Then she commanded the corpse to be laid in the hearse, and taking leave of the royal company, she went along with it.

Now the Princes had time to take notice of Erona's sadness. And Plangus, who had been all this time courting her to be his mistress, could obtain no favor from her but far-fetched sighs and now and then crystal drops distilling from their fountains. These apparent signs of her disconsolate mind grounded a great deal of cares in the hearts of the Princes, who bending all their endeavors to insinuate Plangus into her affections, they first sifted her with these questions: whether her being preserved from the cruelty of Plaxirtus was the cause of her discontentment, or whether she grieved for her deliverance and therefore hated them for fighting in her defense. These questions put Erona into such quandaries that she could not, for a while, determine what to answer. But at last she pitched upon true sincerity, and freely displayed her griefs to them, in these terms:

"Do not, I beseech you, plead ignorance of that which is so palpable. Have you not heard how they tortured my husband Antifalus to death? why then do you renew it in my memory? which might have

Line 1405. **competency:** sufficient income.

been prevented if you, Prince Plangus, had shewed your reality to me (as you protested you would) by policy set him at liberty, but all was neglected and Antifalus was barbarously murdered, and yet you are not ashamed to presume upon my weakness in pretending you   1430
are my servant that you may the second time deceive me." Longer she would have chidden Plangus; but that he, falling down, humbly begged she would have consideration upon him and hear him. Then with silence she admitted him, and he declared how that according to his promise made to her sacred self, he did prosecute so faithfully that he brought all things to a readiness, and might have been perfected, but that the timorous Antifalus discovered the whole plot the same night it was to be put in execution. And this without any scruple, he would take his oath was true. Erona considered very much of this saying of Plangus: and Pyrocles and Musidorus watching their   1440
opportunity, just as she was replying, interrupted her, and told her they were confident she might give credit to what Plangus had spoken; and if she durst rely upon their advice, they would recommend him to her for her husband as soon as the greatest monarch in the world. These Princes, seconding Plangus in his excuses, mitigated Erona's pensiveness, so that cheerfully she yielded her self to be at Pyrocles's and Musidorus's disposing: for, said she, "I am bound by so many obligations to you that I cannot suffer my requital to be a refusal. Only I desire that Prince Plangus may approve the truth of his words with an oath, as he himself hath propounded." Which he   1450
willingly did upon that condition, and she accepted of him as her betrothed husband. And Cupid by degrees so skillfully drew her affection to him that she was as firmly Plangus's as ever she was Antifalus's, to the abundant joy of all their friends.

Line 1427. **reality**: devotion.

Lines 1425–31. **Antifalus...deceive me**: Erona is alluding to Plangus's effort to rescue Antiphilus from Artaxia—an effort that failed, unbeknownst to her, because of his cowardice (1593 *Arcadia*, II.29). See Appendix 3A (Narrative Sources).   Line 1428. **policy**: stratagem.

Line 1434. **admitted**: acknowledged.   Line 1437. **discovered**: revealed.

Now Pyrocles's and Musidorus's employments being in every particular accomplished as well as could be wished, they remembering the charge of Evarchus to them, together with the cares of their sorrowful ladies, they presently sent a post to Arcadia to signify the news of their safety: but yet there remained the care of dispatching 1460 their army into their native country, Macedon. And as they were conferring which way they might compass that matter of such consequence quickly, Kalodolus being at the counsel put in his verdict, which was liked very well and instantly put in practice; for he having a special friend in whom he very much confided, he advised that he might be trusted to be general in Plangus's room that they might orderly go home, and after they were paid their due, to dismiss them and let them go to their own houses.

When all this was performed, they commanded all conveniences to be prepared for their own accommodation about their return to 1470 Arcadia; but for curiosities they would not stay for them, but limited a day for their departure. In which time Erona employed her inventions about a present for Pamela and Philoclea, which she was very ambitious of, they being the mistresses of Musidorus and Pyrocles, to whom she acknowledged her self infinitely engaged; and without delayance, she set all her maids to work the story of their love, from the fountain to the happy conclusion: which by her busy fancy she shadowed so artificially that when it was perfected, and she had shewed it to the Princes, they vowed that had they not known by experience those passages to have been gone and past, they should 1480 have believed they were then in acting in that piece of workmanship.

Line 1458. **post**: dispatch.   Line 1461. **compass**: accomplish.   Line 1465. **room**: stead.

Line 1465. **they**: i.e., the soldiers.   Line 1468. **they**: i.e., Pyrocles and Musidorus.

Line 1470. **curiosities**: the ceremonial artifacts they had earlier commissioned.

Line 1470. **limited**: set.   Lines 1471–72. **inventions**: inventiveness.

Line 1473. **ambitious of**: eager to (invent something special).

Line 1477. **shadowed so artificially**: represented so skillfully.   **perfected**: finished.

Line 1480. **in acting**: enacting.

Now all the work was ended, their necessaries were in a readiness, fair and temperate weather bespake their fuller happiness. All these, so well concurring, enticed the Princes to begin their journey. And Fortune, dealing favorably, conducted them safely and speedily to the Arcadian court, where they were received with such joy by their consorts and parents especially, and by all in general, as it would make too large a story to recount all their discourses with their affectionate expressions that passed between the royal lovers. Passing by all other, give me leave to tell you, it was a pretty sight to see the four ladies, Pamela and Philoclea, with Helena and Erona, admiring one another's perfections, all of them having the worst opinions of themselves, and the better of their neighbors. Therefore to decide the controversy, Philoclea entreated her Pyrocles to make a motion to Musidorus, Plangus, and Amphialus to spend their judgments upon them. Pyrocles immediately obeyed her; but [each of the Princes] esteemed best of their own mistresses.

Pyrocles liked Philoclea best because her sparkling eyes, pure complexion, and sweet features were crowned with such modest courtesy that she ravished all her beholders, and persuaded them they were in paradise, when they were in her heavenly angel-like company, earth not affording her fellow.

Musidorus avouched his fair Pamela was always clad with such a majesty, as bespake her a Queen in spite of the Destinies; yet that majesty was so well composed with humility that it seemed but an out case to a more excellent inward virtue.

Then came Plangus's turn, who said that in his judgement Erona deserved to be extolled in the highest measure, for though her splendor was something darkened by her sadness and sufferings, yet under that veil her brightness did appear to shoot forth beams of goodness to every one that did approach her presence.

Amphialus was last, who protested there could not be a lovelier creature than Helena was, so adorned with all gifts of nature that he

1490

1500

1510

Line 1501. **fellow**: equal.   Line 1505. **out case**: outer covering.

verily believed if she had tempted Adonis, as Venus did, he could not in the least have denied her. And he assured himself that by the determination of the Gods, they being in love with her themselves, Cupid had strook him blind that in the meantime they might pursue their love; but seeing she was resolved to accept of no other but him, they for pity sake opened his eyes: and now he was amazed at his former perverseness. This conceit of Amphialus made the ladies exceeding merry, till Evarchus came to them and spake thus:

"Young Princes, I came now to remember you how often you have been by several accidents frustrated of your desired felicity: you see a little blast alters your happiness into a world of sorrows. Therefore harken to my counsel, whose gray hairs witness my better experience of the world than your green years. Do not linger away the time in courtship: that is as bad as to be carelessly rash. Finish therefore the knot, that no crosses or calamities can unfinish, without further deferrings."

This command of Evarchus did not at all displease the four bridegrooms. Nothing hindered now but their agreeing about the day; and that made no long disputation neither, for two days following happened to be Pamela's birthday, and that they concluded should be the bridal day.

Now the night before these happy nuptials, Erona presented Pamela and Philoclea with her rare piece of work, which they received with thanks and admiration; and for the honor of Erona (she being the inventor of it) they caused it to be hung up by the image of Cupid in the Temple, and after passed the night in quietness.

Early in the morning the sun shot forth his glorious beams and awakened the lovers. But when they were up, he hid himself a while within the watery clouds, weeping that they were brighter suns than he: yet when they were guarded with their nuptial robes, he dis-

Line 1513. **Adonis**: a beautiful youth, who was pursued by Venus, and killed by a boar.

Line 1516. **strook**: struck.   Line 1519. **conceit**: witty thought.

persed the clouds again, and cleared his eyes, that he might with envy gaze upon their luster; and the brides without disdain yielded their beauties to his perusal. When the middle-day had almost run his course to the afternoon, the four bridegrooms, imitating one another in their apparel, were all in gray cloth embroidered with gold, richly clad yet not fantastic; in their left hands they held their swords, but in their right their brides.

First went Musidorus leading his fair Princess Pamela, whose comely behavior and sweet sympathy manifested her joy that then Musidorus and she should be so united to live and die together. Upon her head she bare an imperial diadem, which agreed comparatively to her stately mind. Her garments were cloth of tissue that in a careless fashion hanged loose about her. And round her neck she wore a chain of orient pearl. Upon her alabaster shoulders a blue scarf was cast that, being whirled sometimes with the wind, did seem to blow her to Hymen's Temple. Six virgin nymphs attired in white attended on her. The two foremost perfumed the air as they went with their odoriferous sweets; but that was superfluous, for Pamela's breath left a far more fragrant scent than the artificial curiosities could do; next to them followed two other virgins with holy water in their hands, which they sprinkled as they went to purify all sinful vapors; but that also was needless, for no harm durst come near the virtuous Pamela, whose looks could charm even wicked fiends: then the two last followed Pamela, bearing up her train. Thus was she guarded to the Temple with her beloved Musidorus; and after them went Pyrocles and Philoclea, Plangus and his Erona, and Amphialus with his Helena, all in the same order as Musidorus and Pamela:

Line 1548. **fantastic**: foppish, extravagant.
Line 1554. **tissue**: a delicate fabric, often interwoven with gold or silver.
Line 1558. **Hymen**: god of marriage in classical mythology.
Line 1560. **odoriferous sweets**: perfumes.
Line 1561. **artificial curiosities**: i.e., the perfumes ("odoriferous sweets") of the two foremost virgin nymphs.

1570 then the priest united their hands, and as their hands, so their hearts together; and the former cruelty of fortune was ever after turned into pity.

The Temple, where these nuptial rites were thus celebrated, was situate in a garden, or rather a paradise for its delightfulness; the murmuring of the waters that flowed from a fountain at first entrance dividing themselves into four streams, seeming to threaten, and yet enticing the comers to venter further; the fountains bedecked with the images of Diana and her maids, the Goddess figured with an austere countenance, pointing to the lustful Venus,
1580 whose statue at a little distance stood, as she with lascivious actions endeavored to entrap the modest boy Adonis, but Hymen on the other side disputes, those whom his priests unite cannot be styled Venus's, but Diana's. The perfumed flowers grew so thick in the direct way to the Temple that they served for carpets to consecrate the mortals' feet before they approached into it: the Temple was built of marble, the outsides adorned with portraitures of the gods. Fortune was seated at the frontier of it, which at the least motion of the beholder represented a several gesture. And all the Gods, in their degrees, sat presidents to the observers.
1590 The inside was not so uniform as artificial, it winding into several circles in the passage to the sacred place; and all the way were emblems in marble of the calamities of lovers before they can be set in Hymen's Temple, many of them representing the Princes' suffer-

---

Line 1574. **situate**: situated.

Line 1577. **venter**: venture.

Line 1583. **Venus's...Diana's**: i.e., worshippers of the goddess of chastity (or chaste love) rather than the goddess of sensual lust.

Line 1587. **frontier**: front side.   Line 1588. **several**: different.

Line 1589. **sat presidents to**: sat in front of [Latin *praesidere*, presiding over], i.e., sat [as] presidents to or presiders over (?).

Line 1590. **not so uniform as artificial**: not so plain as elaborate.

Line 1592. **emblems**: images expressing an allegory or moral fable.

ings. The middle of the Temple is not so gorgeous as decent, where there met with the Princes some of Hymen's officers attired in white robes trailing on the ground. These presented the bridegrooms with swords and balances, and their brides with laurel; and when they had here sounded a sweet harmony to Hymen, they went back from the Temple to the court, where you may conjecture with what joy they were received by Evarchus, Basilius, and Genecea, they all pouring   1600 out their blessings upon them. Then passed they away the remainder of the day with all sorts of music, dancing, and other varieties of mirth.

Whilst a famous masque was presenting in the greatest glory to the view of the Prince and an innumerable company of noble personages, Mopsa (sole heir to Dametas, who was by Basilius's favor, the Princess Pamela's governor when she resided in the lodge) went to Philoclea, and wrying her neck one way and her mouth another, she squeezed out these ensuing words: "Fair Princess, I intend not to forget the promise you made me when I told you a part of a curious   1610 tale, how you assured me your wedding gown if I would afford to finish my story on that welcome day: but now the greatest part of the day is run away, and you are raised so high on your tiptoes that you do not vouchsafe me to be in your books, but choose rather to gaze upon these strange sights than to remember me or your gown." The sweet Philoclea could not forbear blushing to hear Mopsa reprove her so sharply; but to make her silent for the present, she renewed her promise, and Mopsa very impatiently stayed out the

---

Line 1594. **not so gorgeous as decent**: not so magnificent, but in more restrained good taste.

Line 1604. **a famous masque was presenting**: a splendid masque was being presented.

Line 1608. **wrying**: twisting.

Line 1610. **the promise**: made by Philoclea in recompense for her interrupting Mopsa's tale (1593 *Arcadia*, II.14). Lines 1634–47 paraphrase the part of the tale told in Sidney. The remaining part of the tale is Weamys's invention. For the Sidneian background, see the entries for Mopsa in Appendix 2 (List of Characters) and Appendix 3c (Narrative Sources).

Line 1610. **curious**: skillfully told, elaborate in construction, perhaps with the modern sense of "exciting curiosity" or "odd."

vanishing of their scenes; which when Philoclea perceived, she
1620 smilingly led Mopsa by her hand into the midst of the royal company, where she left her to exercise her discretion; and withdrawing
at a distance from her, she discovered to her paramour Pyrocles
Mopsa's ambition, who immediately caused all noises to be hushed
that he might with the greater attention harken to Mopsa and
observe all her actions, though never so absurd. But Mopsa valued
not the laughter of her beholders; her little apprehension had already
seized on Philoclea's glittering gown, and she imagined it hung upon
her mothy carcass; and in that firm persuasion she stood looking
upon her self like a peacock, until Pyrocles called to her, which made
1630 her skip and rub her eyes before she could discern her self to be yet
in her rusty feathers. Yet afterwards, playing with her hands for the
more grace, she brake forth into these ensuing words:

"It seemeth best to my liking to rehearse the first part of my story
in brief, that so ye may the better relish the latter. There was a King
(the chiefest man in all his country) who had a pretty daughter, who
as she was sitting at a window, a sprightly knight came to her and
with his dilly phrases won her to be his own, and stealing out of her
father's castle, with many honey kisses he conjured her not to
inquire after his name, for that the water nymphs would then snatch
1640 him from her: howbeit one time, in a darksome wood, her teeth
were set so on edge that she asked, and he presently with a piteous
howling vanished away. Then she, after she had endured such hardship as she never had endured in all her lifetime, went back to one of
her aunts, who gave her a nut, charging her not to open it before she
fell into extremity; from her, she went to another aunt, and she gave
her another nut, counselling her (said Mopsa) in the same words

---

Line 1619. **vanishing of their scenes**: the removal, or changing, of the scenes of the masque.

Line 1623. **ambition**: desire.

Line 1628. **mothy**: moth-infested. Also, a possible misprint for "mothery" (foul, moldy).

Line 1631. **rusty feathers**: shabby clothes.   Line 1637. **dilly**: amorously trifling.

Line 1640. **howbeit**: nevertheless.   Line 1645. **extremity**: extreme adversity.

that her first aunt had done before her, and so sent her packing: but she, one day being as weary as my father's black horse is when he hath rode a good journey on him, sat her down upon a mole-hill, and making huge complaints for her mishaps, a grisly old woman came to her, commanding her to open one of the nuts; and she considering that of a little meddling cometh great ease, broke it open, for nothing venter, nothing have, which proverb she found wondrous true; for within the shell she found a paper, which discovered that her knight was chained in an ugly hole under ground in the same wood where she lost him. But one swallow makes no summer; wherefore she cracked her other nut, from whence there flew out gold and silver in such abundance that the old woman, falling down upon her stumps, scrambled up her lap full, and yet left the joyful maid her load: need makes the old wife trot; nay, it made both the old and young to trot, and to lug away their bags of money: and when they came to a lane with twenty several paths, the old woman took her leave of the king's dainty daughter, bidding her lay down the money, and it should guide her to her knight: with that she laid it down, and the money tumbled the direct way before her."

At this passage Mopsa, conceiting that she saw Mammon's treasure so near her, opened her mouth, which was of a sufficient wideness, and waddled along as if she had been practicing to catch flies there: which if she had, the prisoners might have recreated their wings within their prison walls, they were so large. The princely society could not forbear simpering at Mopsa's ravishment and had burst out into a public mirth, had they not been surprised with a better object.

Which at first view appeared to be the goddess Flora and her nymphs, their adorning imitating hers, but when they drew near,

---

Line 1650. **complaints**: laments.
Line 1653. **venter**: venture.   Line 1666. **conceiting**: imagining.
Line 1666. **Mammon**: traditional personification of riches and avarice.
Line 1674. **Flora**: Roman goddess of flowers.

they discerned their errors, it being Urania, a fair shepherdess, who might be very well taken for Flora; for although it was impossible for her to excel the Goddess in beauty, yet without controlment, in Pamela's and Philoclea's absence she might parallel the most tran-
1680 scendent: on either side of this Urania, there walked the two shepherds, Strephon and Claius, with their eyes fixed on her in celestial admiration: their countenances resembled despair more than hope, and earnestness more than confidence: these addressed themselves unto the Princes, leaving the pretty shepherdess at a short distance with her companions, who in troops attended her; and prostrating themselves at their feet, they burst out into bitter tears.

Musidorus, who was then raised to the height of temporal blessings, disdained not to acknowledge them to have been the founders of his happiness, repeating in public how they had preserved him
1690 from the dangers of the seas: but Claius and Strephon could not suborn their weepings, but continued weltering in their tears, which astonished and strook a sadness into the least relenting spirits, all being ignorant of the accident except Musidorus, who surmised the truth.

Now whilst they expected the issue, Mopsa laid hold on Philoclea, and with many a vinegar look besought her to hear out her tale: and for fear she should be deprived of her gown without depending on a reply, she pursued her story in these her accustomed expressions.

Line 1676. **Urania**: Urania takes her name from the classical muse of astronomy, but in the Renaissance Urania became a "heavenly" muse in a larger sense, associated with "Eternal Wisdom" (see, e.g., *Paradise Lost*, VII. 1–40). Urania's name is traditionally attached to Aphrodite or Venus, the Venus Urania (celestial or virtuous love), who is commonly contrasted with Venus Pandemos or Vulgaris (carnal desire). See Introduction, page xlviii.

Line 1678. **without controlment**: freely, unrestrainedly.

Lines 1680–89. **Urania...Strephon and Claius...how they had preserved him**: Weamys thus begins her continuation of Sidney's Uranian narrative by reuniting Urania with her two shepherd-lovers. As the *New Arcadia* (I.i) opens, Urania has departed for the island of Cithera, and Strephon and Claius are staring longingly out into the distance. At this point they discover and rescue the shipwrecked Musidorus. For a summary of Sidney's Uranian narrative, see Appendix 3D (Narrative Sources).

"Leading her," said Mopsa, "to the very cave's mouth where her knight vented a thousand grievous groans then in her hearing, she   1700
might then joyfully sing, 'Fast bind, fast find,' for there the witches bound him, and there his sweetheart found him, where they plea-sured one another with their sugar-kisses; and after a good while, she unchained him and then they lovingly set them down and slept all night in the cave, because haste maketh waste; but the next morn-ing, she shewed him her monstrous vast sums of money, which so affrighted him that he, clinging his eyes fast together, was not able to say, 'Boo to a goose,' hardly: yet at last she persuaded him, and he peeped up and waxed the merriest man upon earth when he had got himself free, and his mistress again with such store of riches: for then   1710
the old woman that had advised the king's daughter to open her nuts and to lay down the money, appeared to him and released him of his bondage by witchcraft forever after: wherefore the knight and his own sweet darling went back to the king's court as jocundly as could be, and with some of their money they bought them a brave coach and horses, just such as are in my father's stable at home, and in such pomp they went to the King their father, who entertained them bravely, pleasing them with delicate sights, as puppet plays and stately fairs; and their riches increased daily, and they lived gallantly, as long as they had a jot of breath in their bodies."   1720

Thus finished Mopsa her tedious tale, which though it was very ridiculous, yet wanted it not applauses from all the auditors: and Philoclea in requital presented her with her bridal robes, telling her she deserved larger encouragements to elevate her wit; and more speeches she used in Mopsa's commendation, whose partial senses were subject to believe all such rare realities; in which blind opinion I will leave her.

To return to the disconsolate shepherds Claius and Strephon, who when they had wept their passionate fountains dry, they looked

Line 1725. **partial**: biased.

1730   about with adoration upon the pretty Urania as the reviver of their languishing hopes, and Strephon yielding to Claius the pre-eminence by reason of his years, he with great reverence to Basilius with the bridegrooms and brides thus spake:

"Dread Sovereign, and most illustrious Princes, we beseech you not to reckon it among the number of misdemeanors that we shadow the brightness of this nuptial day with our cloudy fortunes, since our aim is to disperse our envious mists and to make it the more glorious by celebrating a feast; and though our triumph cannot amount to such splendor as the four great Monarchs' doth, whose

1740   flourishing dominions can only satisfy their gladness by their Princes' pomp, yet harbor the belief (pardon me if I say amiss) that our bride may equal yours in beauty, though not in rich attire, and in noble virtues, though not in courtly accoutrements; her soul, the impartial diadem of her delicate body, is certainly incomparable to all other of her sex, though heavenly. This mistress of perfections is Urania the shepherdess; she it is that causes my eyes to ebb and flow, my joints to tremble at her looks, and my self to perish at her frowns; but I will not insist too much (upon Your Highness's patience) on this subject; her self is an evident witness of all, and

1750   more than I have charactered: and gracious Sirs, as I am bound by all duty and allegiance to live under the servitude of my Lord Basilius, as well as under his protection, so am I not confined from grateful-ness to such as will oblige me in this my prostrate condition, or in any extremity; for the Destinies have allotted such cruel fates to my friend Claius and me, whose entire affections are never to be severed, that we both are slaves to Urania's piercing eyes! Oh, we both are vas-sals to her devoted graces; yet so much do we esteem of our unfeigned friendship that we will rather abandon all happiness than to cause a discontent or suspicion of our real wishes of one another's

1760   prosperity; out of which intention, we submit to be ruled by the

---

Line 1744. **impartial**: without parts, i.e., complete, entire (like a circle).

judgement of you, renowned bridegrooms, whose prudence and justice is not to be swayed by any partiality; to you it is that we do humbly petition to distinguish which of us two may best deserve to be admitted into Urania's spotless thoughts, as her lawful husband."

Claius had not ceased his suit so suddenly, but that Strephon interrupted him thus abruptly:

"Good Claius, bar the passage of thy tongue, and grant me liberty to speak and ease my fierce torment: the reverence I bear to your age, and my sincerity to your person, permitted you to disburden your fancy first, but not to deprive me of the same privilege. Know then, most excellent Princes, that this incomparable Urania (O, her virtues cannot be expressed by humane creatures! for at the very mentioning of her name my tongue faltered, and my self condemns my self for being too presumptuous, but yet this once we strive against her powers that thus possess me, and will not be persuaded from telling you that), she is compounded so artificially as she cannot be paralleled nor described; for believe it, she is above the capacity of the most studious philosopher: and do not harbor, I beseech you, a prejudicial opinion of her under the notion of her entertaining two lovers at one instant, since it hath been always contrary to her chaste disposition to accept of the least motion concerning a married life; and for Platonic courtiers, her heavenly modesty is a palpable witness of her innocency. Besides the many dolorous hours that my friend Claius and I have passed away, our only recreation we enjoyed being in recounting the careless actions she used when we declared our passions and commending our choice though she was cruel. But when this your happy day was prefixed, she shot forth beams of goodness on us, and in charity she concluded that her intentions were far from

1770

1780

Line 1772. **humane**: human.

Line 1776. **she is compounded so artificially**: i.e., the elements of her beauty are compounded according to the best rules of art.

Line 1785. **careless**: indifferent, without interest or concern.

our destructions; and since now she perceived our lives were in jeop-
1790 ardy, and we depended only upon her reply, she would no longer
keep us in suspense, but was resolved her nuptials should be solemnized on this day, following the example of the two royal sisters,
whom she ever adored. And because she would not be an instrument
to disturb that knot of friendship between Claius and me, she
referred her choice to your wisdoms, worthy Sirs, the excellent sisters' bridegrooms; you it is whom she desires to pronounce either
my felicity or my overthrow."

Then Strephon, closing his speech with an innumerable company
of long-fetched sighs, departed to his goddess Urania, who was envi-
1800 roned by her fellow shepherdesses, which in admiration, love, or
envy stood gazing on her; but he pressed through the thickest of
them to do homage to her sweet self, she looking on him carelessly,
without either respecting or disdaining him.

But aged Claius had cast himself at the Princes' feet, where he
pleaded for his own felicity on this manner:

"Consider my ancient years, and in compassion think how easily
grief may cut off the term of my life; when youthful Strephon may
baffle with love, and court some other dame, I'll find him one who
shall be as pleasing to his eyes, as Urania is in mine, unless the fates
1810 have raised him to be my victorious rival. But alas, O tell me Strephon! did I ever injure thee, that thou seekest my untimely death?
Hast not thou ever been in my sight as a jewel of an unvalued rate?
why dost thou then recompense me so unkindly? I know thou wilt
argue that the passion of love with a woman, and with such an one
as Urania is, cannot be contradicted by the nearest relations. But I
pray thee, Strephon, cannot the importunities of me, thy foster-
friend, regulate, nay assuage thy passions to keep me from perishing?" Now Strephon, when he had revived his drooping heart with
perusing the delicate Urania, and fearing that Claius was supplicat-

---

Line 1802. **carelessly**: indifferently.   Line 1805. **on**: in.   Line 1808. **baffle**: struggle.

ing to Pyrocles and Musidorus for her, he returned back, happening   1820
to come at the minute when Claius questioned him, to whom he
thus replied: "What the Gods have appointed cannot be prevented,
nor quenched by the powerfullest persuasions of any mortal: and let
that suffice." Claius, being so fully answered to his conjecture, rested
silent to hear his sentence. Strephon, who was of a more sprightly
constitution, recreated himself sometimes with glozing upon Urania, and then to observe the looks of the Princes (as they were conferring together about what to determine on concerning them),
besides his pastoral songs that he sounded in Urania's praise.

But the Princes, who were then in serious consultation, listened to   1830
Basilius, who advised them in this manner:

"Despise not Claius his complaints though he be afflicted with
the infirmities of old age; youthful Strephon may seem more real
and pleasing to the eye, yet Claius's heart, I am confident, is the
firmest settled; youth is wavering, age is constant; youth admires
novelties, age antiquities. Claius hath learned experience by age to
delight Urania with such fancies as may be suitable to her disposition; Strephon's tender years cannot attain to any knowledge but as
his own genius leads him. Wherefore consider before you denounce
your sentence, whether Urania may not be Claius's spouse better   1840
than Strephon's."

Pyrocles, knowing that Basilius's aim was to plead in defence of
dotage, refrained to make any other reply than, "What you command, Sir, we must and will obey." For as he was both by birth and
education a Prince, so had he not neglected to be instructed in the
duty of a subject. Not that he was forced to acknowledge it to Basilius as his due, any otherwise than as his goodness induced him to,
that he might be a pattern to draw the Arcadians to follow his

---

Line 1826. **recreated himself…with glozing upon**: diverted himself with flattering.

Line 1839. **genius**: inclination, temperament.   **Wherefore**: therefore.

Line 1839. **denounce**: proclaim.   Line 1848. **that**: in order that.

example, they wholly determining to be ruled that day by Pyrocles
1850 and Musidorus, who after Basilius's decease was to be their
successive King. And they were not ignorant of the intimacy
between his cousin Pyrocles and him; wherefore they reverenced and
observed both their actions. But the Princes Musidorus and Pyrocles, to avoid the rumors of the people that thronged about them to
overhear their resolution concerning the shepherds, retired to an
arbor-walk, where none but the sweet society of birds attended
them: there Pyrocles ripped open his supposition to Musidorus,
which was to this effect:

"My dear cousin," said he, "for of that honored title my memory
1860 shall never be frustrated, dost thou not imagine Basilius's guiltiness
when he pleads for dotage so extremely? he hath not unburdened his
conscience yet of his amorousness of me in my Amazon's metamorphosis: I know it stings him by the arguments he supports. However,
he may cease his fears of my discovering his courtship, for I have
always persevered in allegiance and duty to my father, my King; nor
do I doubt my failing now in those principles, since I have you, my
worthy cousin so near me." Musidorus, embracing his cousin, protested that he harbored the same fancy and, said he, "The stammering of his words declared the certainty: but did you not admire the
1870 heavenly behavior of my Pamela today when she ascended into the
Temple, how her soul seemed to fly with her body to that sanctified

Line 1851. **successive**: succeeding by inheritance.

Line 1863. **it**: Pyrocles's pronoun may refer to Basilius's guilty "conscience" for his doting
desire for him (as Zelmane) in the 1593 *Arcadia*, but it may refer to Basilius's (persisting)
"amorousness."

Line 1864. **my discovering his courtship**: Pyrocles seems to imply that he suspects Basilius
fears he will make a public disclosure ("discovering") of Basilius's courtship of him. However,
in the 1593 *Arcadia* (V.5), Pyrocles has already made a disclosure to the Arcadian court sitting
in judgment of him. Weamys may be ignoring this, or she may be assuming that his disclosure
was at most equivocal (Pyrocles reveals only that "I bare no more love to the chaste Philoclea
than Basilius (deceived in my sex) showed to me") or that Basilius, still under the effects of a
sleeping potion at the time of Pyrocles's disclosure, did not hear it. See Appendix 1 (Synopsis).

Line 1869. **his words**: Basilius's words.

place, as transported with entering into so holy an habitation which was too sacred for any other but her self." And replied Pyrocles, "Philoclea might be admitted with her, whose humility did seem to guard her, or else sure she had stumbled, so lightly did she set her feet upon the pavement, lest she should profane it. And sometimes dropping agonies did so surprise her that she seemed to contemplate with divine mystery, and then to look down upon her own unworthiness with such humbleness as made her most into tears, as it were for soaring above her elements." 1880

Whilst the Princes were discoursing in commendations of their brides, Claius in the presence of Basilius and the remaining Princes fell down and fainted. Strephon stood thumping his breast and crying, "O Musidorus! think upon us who succored you, and let not a third rival deprive us of the incomparable Urania." This unexpected passion of the shepherd's astonished the senses of all the beholders, yet none were so stupid as to neglect their serviceable care: yea Urania her self, though just before (when Pamela and Philoclea sent and entreated her company) she had returned a modest refusal, yet now perceiving Strephon's and Claius's distress, she tarried not to hear the 1890 news by harbingers but went the foremost to relieve them. Upon distracted Strephon she smiled, saying, "Is Fortune thine enemy, Strephon?" but her voice sounded so harmoniously in his ears that he disclaimed all sadness, promising himself the victory. She then absented from him that she might work as effectual and sudden a cure upon aged Claius, who ghastfully lay foaming on the ground, yet that terrible sight was not so obnoxious to her as to oversway her compassion; she pinched and pulled him, endeavoring to restore his

---

Line 1877. **dropping**: desultory or, perhaps, drooping (depressed, dispirited).
Line 1879. **most**: moist, moisten, soften, melt.
Line 1880. **elements**: element, basic condition.
Line 1887. **stupid**: stunned, amazed.   **serviceable**: attentive.
Line 1896. **ghastfully**: frightfully.

life again; but nothing would recover him, until she breathed on

1900 him with stooping near him and pronouncing these words:

"Unhappy Claius, whose life depends upon a woman! this once look up, and speak me blameless. Have not I ever abhorred the thought of Strephon or your ruins? yes sure, I have, and have dallied with you both, apprehending either's danger if I should forsake one and resign my self up to the other's disposal; neither have I regarded the piping of the shepherds, nor the songs of the shepherdesses: and on festival days, when they have elected me Queen of their triumphs, I have excused my self and retired into solitary groves, where I have spent the day in musing upon my lovers' desperate conditions

1910 and studying for the probablest antidotes that might cure their distempers without blemishing mine own reputation. But that was so hard a task that I could never accomplish it. Claius's age could not endure such a penalty as my denial without miscarriage: and Strephon's working brain would not receive it without practicing a tragedy upon himself. Wherefore I made patience my friend, and coyness my favorite, neither slighting nor esteeming their large allusions of my beauty and their passion, which they oft repeated, until the reports of the consummating of the Princesses' nuptials were confirmed. And then I resolved that as I abhorred murder, so I

1920 would no longer admit them into my company, before the priest of Pan hath united me to one of them, that then I might, without derogating from my honor by censorious suspicions, enjoy the society of him whom the Princes shall select to be my wedded husband. So indifferent is my choice of these two constant friends and unmoveable servants."

Line 1904. **apprehending**: apprehensive of.

Line 1916. **coyness**: reserve, aloofness (probably not, as modern usage can have it, coquettish).

Lines 1916–17. **large allusions of**: copious references to.

Line 1924. **indifferent**: without a preference.

Before Urania had finished these words, Claius in a rapture of joy roused up his drowned spirits. And then Urania retired back to her fellow shepherdesses; but the Princes were so inquisitive to know what accident had brought Claius and Strephon into such despairing agonies that they would not permit them to tender their service 1930
to Urania at her present departure for desire of questioning them. Strephon made this quick reply, that a stranger presumed to gaze upon Urania; and his feet going as nimbly as his tongue, he tripped after her, not asking leave of the concourse of people that thronged about him.

But aged Claius, whose tongue was livelier than his feet, spake after this manner:

"My greedy eyes," said he, "being dazzled with looking too long upon Urania (who is adorned with as glorious beams as Phoebus can boast in his brightest day), I yielded them respite, giving them leave 1940
to take a view of mortals, clearing their dimness with their equal light; but there I did espy an haughty youth, who scoffingly stared upon me, seeming to call me insolent for striving to purchase Urania, and conceiting himself to be worthier of her, he did so amorously seal his eyes upon her that sundry times he made her paint her cheeks with harmless blushes: and my jealous fancy comprehending no other reason than that as he obtained free access with his eyes, so he might with his person, I rendering myself into the hands of cruel death."

The Princes could no longer tolerate Claius in his ungrounded 1950
mistrusts, but interrupted him by informing him that Basilius had sent for Musidorus and Pyrocles, the messenger happening to come at the immediate time when they were extolling their mistresses; but then they left off that subject till a more convenient hour and applied their answer to the intelligencer, promising to follow

---

Line 1933. **his feet**: Strephon's feet.

speedily: yet contrary to their resolutions, they lingered in the way, a doleful voice persuading them to stand and harken, which sounded out these words:

"Fair Titan, why dost thou deride me with thy smiles, when I do homage to thy resplendent beams! and you pleasant bells, why do ye not compel your notes to ring me to my funeral? for since she is tyrannous, why should I live to endure her torments? my superiors triumph in their loves: my fellow shepherds can boast of theirs: it is wretched Philisides, oh, it is I that am singularly miserable, made so by a beautiful, yet cruel mistress." The Princes knew him to be Philisides, the despairing shepherd, by his sorrowful subject; and he, rising from under an hedge, discovered himself to be the same: there the Princes, leaving him in a forlorn posture, hastened to their other company to execute their office, which they had agreed upon as they went: Claius and Strephon were amazed at their sight, their fear commanding them to give way to sorrow, but their hopes bade them both to bury sadness in the lake of oblivion: in this unsettled condition they continued not long, the division of their thoughts being suppressed by the sentence which Musidorus uttered thus:

"An oration might be acceptable to the ears of these auditors, but that the evening desires me not to be tedious, especially to these expecting lovers: in compassion to you both, oh Claius and Strephon, I do heartily wish there were two Uranias, and should be exceeding well content if some others were to decide this business than my cousin Pyrocles and my self, he for my sake being equally obliged with me to you for your unspeakable courtesy to me when I was a distressed stranger and encompassed by the frowns of Fortune;

1960

1970

1980

Line 1959. **Titan**: in classical mythology, Helios, or Sol, the sun.

Line 1964. **Philisides**: Sidney's pseudonym in the *New Arcadia*. See Appendix 2 (List of Characters).

Line 1972. **lake of oblivion**: perhaps an allusion to Lethe, in classical mythology a river in the underworld whose waters caused those who drank of them to forget the past.

Line 1981. **unspeakable**: indescribable.

our affections to you both may be evenly balanced, but your activity cannot be justly summoned together: Claius's age manifests a dullness, and Strephon's youth his lightsomeness; or else your worthiest exploits, without disputing, might conquer Urania." At this Claius, as if he had been revived, ventured to jump, but his heels served him a trick, teaching him to kiss his mother Earth, as more suitable to his ancient years than a young shepherdess was: but he vexing at so public a disaster, fell in a rage upon Strephon, who   1990 esteemed it more nobleness to hold his hands than to recompense his blows. Claius, holding in disdain his backwardness, left his eagerness, and turning to the princes with tears in his eyes, he beseeched them if it should be his unhappiness to be deprived of Urania, to grant him the privilege of her presence, though at as great a distance as possibly he could discern her. Strephon, not knowing the subtlety of Fortune and doubting the worst, desisted not from craving the like favor. The Princes mercifully yielded to their requests, and Musidorus proceeded in his sentence:

"Urania deserves to possess the first lodgings of the wisest hearts,   2000 she is too pure to be a second; out of which consideration, we have resolved that you shall both swear by the sacred name of Pan whether you have ever been defiled with another object or have been afflicted with Cupid's dart, though in a virtuous way; which if you both can protest against, we will prohibit this invention and determine on some other; and if but one can clear himself, he shall be acknowledged the fittest husband for her."

Strephon without scruple offered to take his oath; Claius, though he was enticed by the force of beauty, yet his conscience withdrew

---

Line 1985. **dullness**: sluggishness, tiresomeness.   **lightsomeness**: lightheartedness, frivolity.

Lines 1992–93. **Claius…eagerness**: i.e., Claius, holding in disdain Strephon's holding himself back ("backwardness"), left off his fierceness ("eagerness").

Line 2001. **a second**: i.e., a second love.   Line 2004. **though**: even if.

Line 2005. **prohibit this invention**: abandon this method (for weighing Strephon's and Claius's claims).   Lines 2009–10. **withdrew him**: drew him back.

2010 him from perjuring himself, persuading him to defer the time. The Princes, perceiving his slowness, guessed the matter, and lest he should be surprised with the vanities of this world, they commanded him and Strephon to convey Urania to the Temple: Musidorus and Pyrocles, with Pamela and Philoclea, and the other royal bride-grooms and brides, besides the resort of shepherds and shepherdesses attending on them: where being come, Claius and Strephon ascended to the altar, and with great reverence Strephon professed his innocence from female creatures and withal his chaste affection, which he constantly bare to Urania: and Claius with jealous devo-
2020 tion affirmed that Urania was a precious jewel, locked up in the trea-sury of his heart, which none could bereave him of unless they murdered him; neither spared he room for any other to abide there but her divine self: yet he could not deny but that in his younger days his indulgent fantasy had seized upon a shepherdess, though not with any other entire affection than as her pretty songs inveigled him; and since he had wholly abandoned her and cleaved to Urania, the severest justice could not make that a sufficient pretense to give away his elected spouse.

Thus Claius advocated for himself; but Pyrocles and Musidorus
2030 caused silence to be made, and then Musidorus said:

"For as much as you have referred your selves, before evident wit-ness, to the judgement of Prince Pyrocles and my self (who, without any expulsion to your side, have sincerely bestowed it upon you), we will admit of no addresses to recall our judgements, for that were to accuse ourselves of infidelity; but we will not see it put in execution:

Line 2010. **defer the time**: stall.

Line 2012. **surprised with the vanities of this world**: i.e., overcome by a vain desire for romantic success at the expense of truth.

Line 2033. **expulsion to your side**: refusal or demurral from you(?).

Line 2035. **not see it put in execution**: not see it (our "infidelity") put into action, i.e., not break our word (?). It is possible that "not" may be a misprint for "now," so that the meaning is "now see it ['our judgment'] put in execution."

and Strephon shall enjoy his first love, the shepherdess Urania, and Claius may dwell in the view of her to save him from perishing."

Strephon, as a man who newly embraced a life ransomed from the power of hateful death to inhabit a glorious paradise, snatched Urania from out of the hands of amazed Claius, and in a ravishment ran for the priest of Pan, who, in the midst of the throng, consummated their union. This last couple wanted not applauses, though they were inferior to the other in dignity; for Strephon's comeliness and Urania's gracefulness seemed to adorn their harmless robes: their becoming modesty enthralled the hearts of their observers, their courtesy conquered the eyes of their profession, that beheld in what estimation they were with the Princes, and their happiness equalled the greatest personages.

But alas, in Strephon's felicity consists Claius's misery, his grief being so infinite that his passages of tears was stopped, and a frantic brain possessed him more than a womanish sorrow; against this life he exclaimed; Strephon and himself he abhorred; and endeavouring to set a period to his afflictions, he brake out into these words: "Proud love, who gloriest in tormenting mortals, this once moderate thy rage by dispatching me quickly from under thy tyranny; for in what have I displeased thee, you cannot signify, I have so faithfully served to your cruelty. But now to gratify me, you plunder me of my only blessing, and yet in derision you make me to live. But O Cupid! if any pity or remorse dares harbor in thee, as thou hast deeply wounded me, so directly slay me, and I shall entitle thee merciful. But if thou fliest from such a compassionate act, then Prince

2040

2050

2060

Line 2040. **ravishment**: ecstasy.

Line 2041. **Pan**: the ancient Greek god of shepherds and woodlands.

Line 2041. **consummated**: solemnized.

Line 2043. **other**: others.   Line 2044. **harmless**: innocent.

Lines 2045–47. **their courtesy…Princes**: The exact meaning of "profession" and the antecedent of "that" are uncertain, but the sense seems to be that the observers are won over by the pastoral couple's courtesy and by the approbation given them by the Princes.

Musidorus and Pyrocles, whose fame is enriched with goodness, replenish it more by my speedy destruction and make me breathless. And shepherds and shepherdesses, let not the dreadful name of tragedy affright you, my death will be the obsequies of a comedy; therefore if any spleen reign victor in you, revenge your self upon me that am the most contemptible wretch."

2070 This speech he uttered with such distracted actions that terrified the women and afflicted the men. But at appointment of the Princes they conveyed him to some private habitation, where he had attendants who oftentimes prevented him from mischieving himself. But for Strephon and Urania, the Princes solemnly invited them to their society for that evening, where at Pamela's and Philoclea's entreaties, they retiring to a pleasant summer house, Strephon rehearsed these passages concerning Urania, Claius, and himself, on this manner:

"To recollect Urania's virtues, or what surpassing beauty engaged Claius and me to be her servants, would be superfluous, since her divine self is present to merit divine praises from the dullest spectators. Only first her pretty innocence withdrew our eyes from gazing
2080 on the stars to salute her heavenly spheres that reflected upon us as she passed by. For Claius and I, having separated our flocks from our neighboring shepherds into a fresh and sweet pasture, where none frequented or trode the pleasant grass but savage satyrs and dancing fairies, we espied a tree, whose flourishing branches seemed to fortify themselves against the heat of the sun, and we, enticed by the shadow, repaired to it: there we lay down, purposing to try our skill in describing the pitiful decorums of the shepherds that were enchanted by Cupid's quiver to adore the fair beauty of mortals: but the wonderful justice of the highest powers taught us to acknowl-

---

Lines 2076–2219. This section of Strephon's account of his and Claius's love for Urania is taken from Lamon's account in the First Eclogues of the 1593 *Arcadia*. See Appendix 3D (Narrative Sources).

Line 2086. **shadow**: shade.   Line 2087. **pitiful decorums**: pitiable behavior.

edge our frailty by inflicting the like punishment upon us: for as we   2090
were reproaching their lovesick infirmities, fair Urania, induced by a
sparrow that flew from her when she had courteously bred it up,
pursued after it to take it prisoner, her course bending towards us:
but when she had surprised it, she confined it to a paradise, putting
it between the pillows of her breast, and checking it no otherwise
than with her harmless kisses, she went away, leaving Claius and my
carcass behind her, but our souls cleaved immovably unto her; and
fixing our eyes upon one another, as ashamed of our prodigious censoriousness of our neighbors, we suffered not our lips to open till we
were acquainted with the subject that did triumph over us; but   2100
sounding our bell, we secured our flocks and hastened to repose our
selves upon our beds, but our memory of the most divine Urania
taught us a more watchful lesson than drowsiness: her image, which
was engraven in our fancy, disdained to be blurred by our forgetfulness, wherefore the restless night we passed over with sighs, reviling
the Fates for burying our felicity in the depth of adversity, so hard
and explete did we account it ever to obtain Urania; and though
Claius and I were one another's rivals, both aiming at one, yet did it
not any way mitigate our friendship, I applauding Claius's choice,
and he mine; neither did we ignorantly admire our judgments, but   2110
did inquire, and receive, the approbation of a multitude of swains,
who with abundant devotion extolled Urania's worth: yet Fortune,
that favors not the purest souls, knit her brows, frowning upon our
goddess Urania, who mildly strived to wash them away with her
crystal tears: the occasion I heard her whisper out one time (when
she imagined little and I resided so near her) in these sweetly

Line 2092. **when**: even though.

Line 2097. **carcass**: the living body (but without the soul, which still cleaves to Urania).

Line 2098. **as ashamed of**: as though ashamed of, or being so ashamed of.

Lines 2106–7. **so hard and explete**: so hard an exploit(?). "And" may be a misprint for "an"; "explete" is "in some examples perhaps a variant of 'exploit'" (*OED*).

expressed yet dolorous words: 'Too great a burden for me to bear oppresses me; Antaxius is too officious in his love, I wish he were more calm; my parents' rigor is too too intolerable, unless my dis-
2120 obedience had been palpable; I have never offended them wilfully, no, not in this their desired match, except they interpret my silence for a refusal, that being the only symptom of my discontent; nor do I reveal my affection to any but to thee, my sparrow, who canst not discover it with thy chirping, and that note of thine is to me condoling and cheerful, my disconsolate heart not knowing how to value any other melodious sounds: but alas, my incredulity of the divine Providence may justly reprove and punish me; yet since I do humbly acknowledge thy all-sufficiency, let thy Mercy chastise me, and deliver me from the thraldom of Antaxius.'

2130   "Then wiping her bedewed eyes, she arose, as confident her devout prayers had conjured the Gods to pity her distress, and [I,] beseeching the Deities to make me their instrument, called after her: 'Fair creature, pardon me if I profane your sacred title with a feeble one, since your humility vouchsafes earthly troubles to perplex you; and believe me, the fabric of this world is built upon diverse motions, it can boast of no firm foundation; the rarest beauties in their age seldom escape adverse billows and boisterous winds, and without relying on a rock their perishing is sure: wherefore, sweet nymph, accept of me to be your rock, and questionless you shall be
2140 preserved from all tempestuous weathers.'

"Urania, trusting in no other power than what was celestial, looked up to the element, where seeing no heavenly object, she cast her eyes down, fixing them upon me with such blessedness as strook

---

Line 2118. **Antaxius**: the rich herdsman whom Urania's parents insist she marry.
Line 2118. **officious**: zealously forward.   Line 2128. **thy**: Providence's.
Line 2134. **since your humility vouchsafes**: since your meekness (or low estate) permits.
Line 2142. **the element**: the heavens.   Line 2143. **strook**: struck.

me to the ground, not being capable of assisting my self; however, I
fed upon her voice, which she displayed in this language: 'What a
presumptuous mortal art thou to frame thy self to be a God, that by
such a pretense thou mayst insult over me? For better powers cannot
support me from furious storms.' This spoken, she went away, as
loathing the sight of such a blasphemous serpent as she thought me
to be. Which I perceiving, and rousing my self from out of a trance,   2150
I began to cry, 'O stay, stay, stay'; but she, deaf to my persuasions,
hastened beyond the limits of mine eyes; but the rebounding of my
words sounded in the ears of the pastor Claius, who was with his and
my flock at a little distance from me. He harkening to my voice, and
discerning me to wander out of the close, his jealous brain supposed
the reason, and walking as swiftly as his aged legs would suffer him,
he found me out, his inquisitiveness enforcing me not to be niggardly in my answers, which were so tedious that the sun vanished
from our horizon (as tired with our unnecessary speeches) and took
his farewell, highing him to his eastern home. But at length Claius   2160
and I yield[ed] our selves to silence, though not to rest: experience
had taught us to despair of sleeping until Cupid's wounds were curable. And early in the morning when the shepherdesses had driven
their flocks into the pastures, we lingering with ours that we might
see the place made happy with Urania's abiding there, her enemy
Antaxius, the wealthy herdsman, driven by a flattering current of his
success, approached near us, not scrupulous in asking Urania's harbor: we making much of our opportunity directed him the contrary
way from her, to the island of Citherea, her parents dwelling there;
only they had trusted her with the flock on this side the river to feed   2170

Line 2158. **tedious**: long.   Line 2160. **highing**: hying, with a possible play on "high."
Line 2161. **yield[ed]**: "yielding" in the original text.
Line 2167. **scrupulous**: chary, distrustful.   Lines 2167–68. **harbor**: dwelling.
Line 2169. **Citherea**: Cithera, an island off the Greek coast, associated with Aphrodite.

them with a livelier pasture. But we protested to him that in the morning we saw the grass to weep for her departure, and the seas dance with joy that she relied on their mildness. Antaxius easily believed our intelligence, and thanking us for it, he hastened to overtake her: and we pleased with our prosperous subtlety, drove our flocks to a pasture adjoining to Urania's, and entreating Pan to be their guardian, we left them to try Fortune's courtesy.

"Urania, blushing at our presence, at mine especially, who had before abruptly assaulted her, seemed to rebuke me with it, as in earnest so it did; my trembling witnessed my guiltiness, and my tears and sighs my repentance: my slowness to utterance allowed Claius a convenient time to discover his passion to Urania. The policy used to Antaxius he forbore to repeat, until my repentance had obtained a pardon, and then he related in what expedition we sent away her undesired suitor; which at first vanished the red from her face, her fears usurping in her tender breast, lest her parents should doubt her safety at Antaxius's report. Yet when she remembered her absence might extinguish Antaxius's lust, her vermilion came back to mixture and adorned her, as detesting to be deprived of such an alabaster shelter.

"Claius made poesies in her praise to please her, dedicating to her service all his studies. My art in framing of garlands (shewing the flowers' natural curiosity in their variety of shades, a device that sets them forth most perfectly) I did teach her; oftentimes presenting her with the choicest of my flock, when she would accept of them; and if wolves or other ravenous beasts had happened to lurk that way, I never left hunting them till their hands evidenced me their con-

Line 2171. **livelier**: fresher.

Lines 2188–89. **vermilion…mixture**: i.e., Urania's skin returned to its usual blend of red and white.

Line 2192. **framing**: fashioning.   Line 2193. **curiosity**: artistry.   Line 2197. **hands**: paws.

queror, which I used to lay at Urania's feet; other tricks I invented to be admitted into her society."

Here Strephon stopped: but the Princes entreated him to go on. "Which happiness of mine," saith he, "continued not long without interruption. Antaxius, learning that Claius and I pretended affection to Urania, he proudly landed at our haven, rudely carrying her away without resistance. Her commands, that could not be disobeyed, ordained the contrary. Then it was, most gracious Prince Musidorus, that you escaped the seas. O then it was that Urania floated on them, and we bitterly bemoaned our loss. Certainly by the appointment of the Gods the ocean waxed so calm, yet about where she was embarked, the waters murmured, and the winds sweetly whistled, combining their voices so harmoniously that she might really believe they conspired to crown her with some unexpected blessing; as indeed so they had: for when we had conducted you to my lord Kaleander's house, we received a letter from our adored goddess. We might have been justly taxed of incredulity at the first view of it, our remembrance of her uncivil carrier demolishing all hopeful thoughts; but when we had more believingly read over and saluted those heavenly lines, we taking a short farewell of Your Highness, conformed our pace to our eagerest disposition and came to the sands against the island of Citherea; where not caring for any other passage but Charon's boat, we committed ourselves to

2200

2210

2220

Lines 2201–2531. This section of the Uranian narrative is, with the exception of a few details, Weamys's invention. See Introduction, page li, on Weamys's rewriting of Sidney's account of Urania's departure, and Appendix 3D (Narrative Sources).

Lines 2212–14. **when…goddess**: In the 1593 *Arcadia* (I.2), Strephon and Claius escort Palladius (Musidorus) to Kalander's house after rescuing him on the shore; and soon after their arrival, they receive a letter from Urania.

Line 2215. **carrier**: abductor (i.e., Antaxius).   Line 2219. **against**: opposite.

Lines 2219–20. **not caring for**: not caring about, indifferent to. **but**: than, except.

Line 2220. **Charon**: in Greek mythology, the ferryman who conveyed the dead across the river Styx to Hades (the underworld realm of the dead).

heaven's protection and fixed our eyes upon Urania's island. Leaping into the sea, there we had like to have participated of Leander's entertainment, but our lucky stars preserved us to better fortune. The waves growing turbulent, the winds roared, the skies thickened, and all tempestuous weather threatened to combine against us. My friend Claius's faint limbs I was glad to support with my tired ones, and we both had perished and resigned our breaths to the Giver, but that the storm forced a bark to cast anchor and harbor in our coast, from whence we had not swom far (though the billows had thrown us up and down, as contemning us for our presumption in pursuing our loves to Urania); but the company in the bark, weighing our calamities (and their own, too, should they neglect so charitable an act as endeavouring to help us, imagining the Gods would be deaf to their prayers if they were careless of ours), they let their sails fly towards us, and lengthening the cord of their cockboat, they sent it to us; we, skilled in their meaning, laid hold on it, and by degrees we purchased the insides for our security; they, pulling us to the bark, helped us in, where we were gazed on with astonishment by all; neither were our eyes indebted to theirs, so many of Urania's associates did we espy in the bark to look upon; and amongst the rest there was Antaxius: O, Claius, hadst thou been here, thou wouldst have justified thy paleness, and my choleric flushes, that with zeal strove for victory over our haughty rival, who (being vexed at the sight of us, and minding nothing so much as our fatal ruin) stretched his voice,

2230

2240

Lines 2222–23. **participated of Leander's entertainment**: partaken of Leander's fate (with perhaps an ironic glance at Neptune's "entertainment" or hospitality).   **Leander**: in classical mythology, Leander was a youth who drowned while swimming across the Hellespont to see his beloved, Hero.

Line 2234. **careless**: uncaring.   Line 2236. **skilled in**: having grasped.

Line 2237. **purchased the insides for our security**: i.e., climbed inside for our safety.

Line 2239. **our eyes indebted to theirs**: i.e., we gazed at them with equal amazement.

Line 2241. **Claius**: an aside to the absent Claius, who was earlier conveyed to "some private habitation" (86).

Lines 2241–42. **justified**: confirmed, corroborated as true.   Line 2244. **stretched**: strained.

which was most hideous, to condemn us. 'What monsters are these,' said he, 'that you have had pity upon? their physiognomies resemble ours, but the shape is different; therefore hurl them overboard, lest they do drown us with their enchantment.' The gulf of salt water that flew out of our mouths, and our wet garments that hung confusedly, with his aggravations, pierced into the stupid senses of the 2250 company, who doubted whether we were very Claius and Strephon or no, yet dreaded to question us: my anger for Antaxius's unworthy affronting us could not be moderated, but acting the fierceness of a tiger, I fell upon him and flung him into the sea, where he deservedly tasted of such pleasures as he had allotted for us: such is the wisdom of the higher powers to recompense what is due.

"The affrighted people fled into their cabins; the pilot and sailors, forsaking their employments, hid themselves under the decks: but all this time I never ceased to pray for Urania's safeguard, being ignorant of the chance that brought Antaxius thither, or where she 2260 resided (her letters signifying only how much she wished to see us, our vowed friendship obliging her in all virtuous ways to honor us): but having quelled the courage of the sailors, the storm assuaging, we shewed our authority, commanding them to strike their sail to the island of Citherea: and giving a visit to our prisoners in the cabins, we entreated them to suppress all prejudicial conceit of us, who never intended to injure them, though we had revenged our selves upon Antaxius for scandalizing us and persuading them barbarously to murder us under the pretense of sea monsters: nor did we neglect to tell them how infinitely they would favor us in relating what acci- 2270 dent had enticed Antaxius to that bark without his mistress Urania, who was reported to be his only delight.

Line 2246. **physiognomies**: faces.

Line 2250. **with his aggravations**: along with his accusations.

Line 2268. **scandalizing**: slandering.

Lines 2270–71. **accident**: event.

"The young shepherd Lalus, being present, interrupted me thus: 'Urania disdains to be the mistress of so base a fellow, though his importunity both to her nearest relations and to her divine self forced her to grant him the privilege of charactering her perfections in poetry, amongst which he had declared his lust, shadowing it with the title of love (when he might as well transform a dove to a kite, or a wolf to a lamb, as lust to love); Urania, abhorring him for it, charged me (who am bound to obey her charge) to be urgent with Antaxius to come this voyage with me. I assaulted him with the question; he thought it no ways requisite for his proceedings, but at her persuasions he ceased to argue. This voyage we intended for a cheerful one, but it hath proved a fatal one to him, though a fortunate one to Urania; for she as far excels Antaxius in desert, as our Princess Pamela does Mopsa, master Dametas's daughter.'"

At this passage the princess smiled, and Strephon blushed at his true, yet blunt expression: but longing to be freed from tautalogizing, his modesty not suffering him to court Urania there, he persisted in his rehearsal.

"It afflicted me to reckon (O, I could not reckon) the number of rivals that waited to frustrate me of my felicity. All that ever beheld her commended her; few they were that did not court her, but most lived in hopes to enjoy her; however I dissembled my grief and congratulated with Lalus for his courteous relation, telling him I had seen that paragon and did as much admire her as I could any of her sex, though my delight consisted chiefly in other recreations than to extol a woman. This drift of mine enticed him earnestly to better my opinion, and in his highest rhetoric, he labored to inform me concerning the passion of love, that though it were mixed with bitterness (in consideration of some griefs that follow it) yet seldom it is

---

Line 2276. **charactering**: describing.   Line 2280. **be urgent with**: urge.

Lines 2288–89. **tautalogizing**: repeating himself (?).

Lines 2294–95. **congratulated with**: rejoiced along with.

but that the conclusion is happy. I, making as though I listened not to his discourse, sung a song, the subject whereof tended against love and women: he, increasing his desires to work my conversion, determined to bring me to Urania. I willingly seemed to yield to his request; Claius wondered at my disguised heart, yet held his peace, trusting to my poor discretion.

"Now the seamen bringing us news of our safe arrival in the ports of Citherea, we landed, releasing the bark; I could hardly confine my joy within so small a compass as my heart when I went upon the ground where she had trode, and not reveal it; but I restrained it as much as possibly I could, slighting his description of Urania's worth. But alas, my hopes of the success my designment might have was frustrated; upon so tottering a climate do we mortals restless live that when we think we have escaped the dangerousest storms, our feet stand upon the brims, ready to be blown down at every flirt of wind to the depth of misery. 2310

"For Urania, my secret jewel (and Lalus that reveiled me), was missing, not to public pastorals, nor yet solitary retirements, but by the soul practices of a knight named Lacemon, who violently carried her away from her sheep whilst she was complaining of Claius's and my tedious absence. 2320

"The reporter of this doleful news lay hid under a hedge, the glistering of rude Lacemon's armor advising him to conceal himself; such was the cowardliness of the simple swain. Lalus would have murdered him, had not we by force withheld him; yet I made him feel the stroke of my cudgel to make him repent his folly, a poor

Line 2307. **discretion**: judgment.

Line 2312. **slighting**: ignoring.   Line 2313. **designment**: plan.

Line 2314. **tottering**: changeable, unsteady.   **climate**: weather(?), region or zone of the earth(?), firmament (?).   Line 2316. **brims**: banks, shores.

Line 2318. **reveiled me**: revealed her presence to me.   Line 2320. **soul**: sole.

Line 2323. **The reporter**: presumably "the simple swain" of line 2324, but the narrative is somewhat obscure.

revenge for so heinous a trespass, yet that disburdened me of a greater, so subject are we in affliction to double our error with a crime more odious: Urania was lost, yet the memory of her name, virtue or beauty could never be expired: neither did we linger in pursuance of Lacemon, nor in her search, whose heavenly soul, as we imagined, must needs perfume and leave a scent where it had breathed, which was the sign that we besought the sacred powers to grant, might be our convoy to her. Then Lalus departed from us, choosing his path; Claius and I would not be separated, if possibly we could avoid it. I know not whether this unwillingness to part with me proceeded from a jealous humor, his nature being always inclinable to it; but I am sure mine was real, doubting not but what the divine Providence had agreed on should be accomplished whate'er it were.

"The byest ways, as we conceived, might be the likeliest to find Urania, Lacemon having many: […] his felicity, since he had deprived the land of its goddess; and we (as deeply engaged against him, our presumptuous rival, as any other) searched the most suspicious corners; but no tidings could be heard of Urania up the island, where we had wandered, except profane ones; for ask the swains that sluggishly sat nodding by some of their scattered sheep (whose fellows had been devoured by wolves through the carelessness of their shepherds), when we examined them concerning Urania (whom we described by her prayers and tears made to a knight accoutered in a martial habit), their reply would be so absurd, nay between sleeping and waking, divers did affirm they saw her, directing us to unseemly mortals, who indeed had usurped Urania's name, though they came

Line 2342. **byest**: least travelled.   Line 2343. **many**: i.e., many ways he might have taken.

Line 2343. **[…]**: Some words from Weamys's manuscript seem to have been omitted by the typesetter, either here or possibly between "his" and "felicity."

Line 2347. **profane**: irreverent.   **ask**: i.e., when we asked.   Line 2351. **knight**: Lacemon.

short of her perfections. I can not judge which was victor in me of rage and sorrow; furious I was at the counterfeit Uranias, and desperate, despairing of ever finding the real one."

At this passage Strephon burst out into floods of tears, which he endeavored to conceal, excusing his too large rehearsal, and desired to break off; but the Princes' earnestness to hear Urania rescued from the power of Lacemon induced him to proceed on this manner: "My choleric passion I vented upon the stupid men, instructing them to entitle their dames with some meaner name than Urania, under penalty of their lives, which they dearly valued: and then Claius and I renewed our languishing travels.

"When we had passed through the public and remote places of the island, meeting with no obstacles in the way, either by friends or enemies, we crossed the ocean, landing at the sands over against the island; we continued not there, though we could not determine where we had best continue, but a pilgrim's life we resolved on, unless Urania's unexpected security should forbid it; when therefore we had traced about the confines of Arcadia without any comfortable reports of her, we rose with the sun to take a longer journey, but the tiredness of our legs prolonged the time, and so proved faithful instruments to further our felicity by delaying our haste. Upon a bank we sat down, chafing at the grass for looking fresh and green in Urania's absence; and Claius, folding his arms and casting his eyes on the ground as a fit object for him to view (especially when he pitched on such a subject as deserved opposition, as he then did), uttering these words: 'Seldom it is but the fairest physiognomies harbor the foulest souls; all reason proves it so; nay the Gods abhor partiality; why then should they adorn a creature so richly surpassing

2360

2370

2380

Line 2368. **the ocean**: the high sea, possibly a rustic exaggeration of the Gulf of Laconia between the Greek mainland and Cithera.   Line 2372. **confines**: borders.

Line 2376. **chafing at**: scolding.   Line 2382. **partiality**: incompleteness, imbalance of parts.

above the rest visibly, and yet give her a soul answerable? Urania! O Urania! I will not, no I durst not say unchaste, though the summers mourn not for her exilement, nor the birds cease from their various notes, which comfort we heretofore apprehended they made to invite Urania to reside altogether in the woods; nor yet the shepherds refrain from their pleasant sports; nor do the shepherdesses neglect their care of medicining their tender lambs to celebrate a day in their bewailings.'

"Age we reckon stands at the gate of death: yet Claius's years was a target to defend him from it, otherwise I should not have thought a reply a sufficient revenge, which I did in these terms: 'A suspicious head is as great a torment as I could wish to light upon Lacemon; besides the unjustness of it, your uncharitable censures may too soon redound upon you, when repentance hath lost its opportunity to crave and receive a pardon: expose not your self to that crime which never can be purged away, should it damage the reputation of those that imitate Diana's qualities in as great a measure as her beauty; for if the Gods have bestowed on them reasonable souls, why should we pine at their industry to make them admirable? You argue that the summer keeps its natural course though Urania is missing: which is a manifest testimony of her virtues, boisterous and cold weather being a foe to travellers, but the warm sun is delightful, and the birds proudly chant their tunes, for I am confident they ravish her far above the lofty expressions of Lacemon. Neither wonder at the mirth and employments of the shepherds and shepherdesses, for the virgins are glad to exercise their inventions to charm back the belief of Urania's loss, so darksome and odious is it to them, the shepherds (their paramours) fostering, though with sadness, their busy fancies.'

Line 2383. **answerable**: corresponding (to her beauty).
Line 2384. **the summers**: the summer.
Line 2399. **Diana's qualities**: i.e., chastity.   Line 2405. **ravish**: delight.
Line 2408. **back**: away.

"Claius, fixing his eyes on the ground, as convinced of his error, sought not to frame an excuse, yet to shew that age had not deprived him of his senses, he thus spake: 'An odoriferous scent seems to command me to rest silent and to bear the blame without controlment, and dreadfulness mixed with hope possess me. O Strephon, Strephon, faithfully conceal my folly, I beseech thee.'

"At this sudden alarm, I gazed about me, an happy sight, though an amazed one, approaching near me; Urania it was, with her arms spread, and cries in her mouth, which mentioned murder, her hair contemptibly hung about her, though delicate; and patience and anger seemed to combat in her rosy cheeks for the victory; but at last, abundance of crystal tears became the arbiter, which when she had vented, she distributed to us these words: 'Never was I yet in the turret of felicity, but I have stumbled, and fell to the pit of adversity: Antaxius, in the island of Citherea, lustfully expects me; and here, if I continue, the Fury Lacemon will overtake me; O whither shall I fly for safety?' 2420

"My pity would not suffer me to retain her in ignorance, wherefore I related Antaxius's death: her silence seemed to condemn me of rashness for granting him no time of repentance; but my excuse was prevented by the rageful coming of Lacemon, who with eyes sparkling and armor stained with blood (an emblem of the tragedy he had committed), holding in his right hand a spear and a shield in his left, he mustered up to us; we, nothing dreading but Urania's trembling, with our staves (weak instruments, as he imagined) to resist him, made towards him: he, disdaining Claius's age and my youth, exercised neither vigilance to withstand our blows nor strength to 2430

Line 2414. **without controlment**: freely, without resistance or complaint.
Line 2415. **dreadfulness**: dread.
Line 2419. **mentioned**: bespoke.
Line 2420. **contemptibly**: as if an object of her scorn or disregard.
Line 2420. **delicate**: graceful to behold, elegant.   Line 2425. **expects**: awaits.

repay them: I, vexed at his so slight regard of my valor, and persuading Claius to retire to Urania (who willingly yielded to my counsel),
2440   I renewed the encounter, and with such fierceness that Lacemon was forced to stand on his own defense; his want of experience might be the cause of his overthrow; for I am certain I can boast but of little that caused it, though the fortune of my blows proved fatal to him, thrusting him off his horse and beating out his brains: his life was so hateful that his death was welcomed by most, and commiserated of none: Urania highly commended my action, too large a recompense for so poor a desert, yet I thanked the Gods for giving me such success as she thought worthy of her acceptance; and waiting upon her to the island of Citherea, by the way she yielded to our request,
2450   gracefully delivering these words:

"'The motions of this world I cannot comprehend but with confusion, so unexpectedly do they surprise me. Antaxius by Lalus's instigations trusted to the sea's fidelity, your compulsion forcing them to deceive him, in whose banishment I sent a letter to you, wherein I acknowledged your sincere affection, and by all the ties of virtuous friendship conjured you not to deny me your counsel or company in my extremity; and happening to repose my self upon the clifts, my harmless sparrow I set down at a little distance from me, learning it to come at my inducement; the pretty fool, with
2460   shivering wings aspired to mount towards me; but the tiger Lacemon (or monster, for his disposition could never pretend to humanity, being prepared in a readiness to commit such a treacherous act), came from a darksome hole, suitable to his practices, and seized on me and my sparrow for prisoners, and conveying us to his provided

---

Line 2448. **waiting upon her**: while accompanying her back.

Lines 2452–54. **Antaxius...him**: them=the seas(?) him=Antaxius(?) The sense of Urania's periphrasis seems to be that Antaxius went to sea ("trusted to the seas' fidelity"), but Strephon's throwing him overboard (Strephon's "compulsion") forced the seas to be unfaithful by drowning him ("to deceive him").

Line 2454. **in whose banishment**: probably a euphemism for Antaxius's enforced absence by drowning.   Line 2459. **learning**: teaching.

boat, we were sailed over, and by him conducted, to this country of Arcadia, where in a cave he hath enclosed me: and perceiving that I consorted with my bird and delighted in its innocency, a virtue which he mortally detested, he unmercifully murdered it, lingeringly tormenting it to death, whilst my sparrow with its dying looks seemed to check me for enduring its sufferance without resistance: thus he endeavored to terrify me with his cruelty, but if it were possible, it made me more inflamed to withstand his assaults; neither threats nor entreaties were wanting to tempt me to his base desires, but I absolutely refused him, till necessity persuaded me to try the effect of policy.

"'His own reports signifying Phalantus's (Helena, the Queen of Corinth's brother's) defiance to the Arcadian knights, his lance willing to defend his mistress Sortesia's beauty against other champions, I counterfeited earnestness to Lacemon in exercising his skill to purchase my glory: he, puffed up with hopes of future success (considering it was the first time that I had employed him, and so publicly), with all expedition hasted to the lodge with my picture, where by a thrust from off his horse he was made to leave my picture to reverence Sortesia's surpassing one; with a cloudy soul, he returned to me, I being compassed to stay within his bounds, so many bars and bolts frustrating my escape; but by his muttering I discerned his discontent, an humor that best suited his condition: I strictly examined concerning my picture's triumph and his fortune; he, studying to delude me, replied that business of importance had enforced Basilius to defer the challenge for a while, out of which regard he, by the example of other noble personages, resigned up my picture to the

Line 2470. **check**: rebuke.

Lines 2476–78. **Phalantus's...defiance...against other champions**: In the 1593 *Arcadia* (I.15–17), Phalantus defends the picture of his mistress Artesia (Weamys's Sortesia) against all challengers. See the entry for Artesia, Appendix 2 (List of Characters).

Line 2490. **defer the challenge**: Lacemon was lying to Urania. In the 1593 *Arcadia* (I.16), in Artesia's triumphal procession of the pictures of women whose knights have lost to Phalantus, Lacemon is alluded to as "a rich knight called Lacemon, far in love with [Urania], [who] had unluckily defended" her picture.

custody of the governor of Basilius's lodge, and should be extremely well pleased if I would vouchsafe him my company into the fresh air. Few persuasions served to remove me from that stifling cave besides the hopes that I relied upon of your encountering Lacemon; but [I] little imagined the shepherd Lalus would be the first. Kind Lalus! it was the least of my thoughts of thy so cheerfully losing thy life for the preservation of mine; for when Lacemon had (with boastings for not being overcome by any of his subjected rivals) brought me near the confines of Arcadia (swelling with pride, his rough arms rudely striving with me), then it was that Lalus succored me with his own fatal ruin: for though I was by Lacemon disguised, by his suggestion, I knowing no other sign, he discovered me to be Urania: his desire to rescue me from Lacemon extinguished the reprehension of his own eminent danger; his courage though exceeding Lacemon's, yet his strength and shield was far inferior to him in the heat of the blows. Before conquest was decided on either side, I fled from dreadful Lacemon.

"'His speedy pursuance after me might be a means to preserve Lalus's life, yet I doubt it, Lacemon's bloody armor prenominating his wicked action. But I protest that I had rather my skin should imitate Pan's, and my complexion Vulcan's, than that any one tragedy should be committed in its defence.'

"Fountains running from Urania's sparkling eyes stopped the remainder of her speech. Lalus's being my assured rival mitigated very much my sorrow for him. However, lest I should forfeit Urania's favor, I seemed sad, yet strived with it that I might be a more acceptable instrument to moderate hers. Neither was Claius negligent in his love, but with rhetorical speeches he sought to win on her

---

Line 2500. **confines**: borders.   Line 2504. **reprehension of**: apprehension over.

Line 2510. **prenominating**: specifying beforehand, announcing.

Lines 2511–12. **my skin should imitate Pan's, and my complexion Vulcan's**: i.e., my skin would be rough and hairy like Pan's (traditionally represented as half-goat) and dark and sooty like Vulcan's (Roman god of fire and patron of smiths).

Lines 2519–20. **win on her affections**: gain advantage over, win over.

affections; and the island of Citherea in a while flourished with her 2520
adored goddess. Her parents in heavenly raptures welcomed home
their dearest daughter, keeping her watchfully under their eyes, and
jealous of our depriving them of her the second time, though we had
safely delivered her into their hands. And Urania her self, suspecting
our often resorting to her might redound to her prejudice, made
excuses to abandon our company. But death in a short time
appeared in his visage to Urania's parents, carrying them to the Elysian Fields: she then having the liberty to dispose of her self, which
she with confinement did (not delighting in the pastorals, nor yet in
our society, until this happy day was nominated). And now, great 2530
Princes, I humbly beseech you to pardon this my tedious relation."

The Princes courteously declared Strephon to be worthiest of
Urania, the particulars of his exploits witnessing it. Basilius on that
day preferring him in his court, honoring him with knighthood, and
both he and his lady Urania lived in great reputation with all,
obtaining love and esteem from the stateliest cedar to lowest shrub.

But when Cynthia drew her curtains, commanding the Princes to
hide themselves within their pavilions, and they retiring to obey her,
just then an unusual voice sounded to them, and close behind it
rushed in Lalus the shepherd. Anger composed with reverence beset 2540
him: both being so officious that reverence environed passion within
the compass of civility, and passion allowed reverence to shew a
pretty decent behavior (though not affected); both dying cheeks
with ruddiness, whilst he (applying his speech to Pyrocles and Musidorus) spake to this purpose:

Line 2525. **prejudice**: detriment.

Lines 2527–28. **Elysian Fields**: in classical mythology, the abode of the blessed dead.

Line 2530. **nominated**: appointed (for the marriages of the Princes).

Line 2537. **Cynthia**: in classical mythology, Diana, goddess of the moon; hence, the moon.

Line 2539. **unusual**: unfamiliar.   Line 2541. **both being so officious that**: i.e., both emotions (anger and reverence) performing their office so well that, etc.

Line 2543. **affected**: emotionally overwrought.   **both**: i.e., both passion (anger) and reverence.

"Great Princes, I will not presume to question your justice, but your knowledge. It was I that gave Lacemon his death's wound. Strephon did but lessen his torments by quick dispatching him when he fled from me, pretending Urania was his only happiness that he 2550 desired to enjoy, and not my blood."

The Princes certifying Lalus that other arguments enjoined them to bestow Urania on Strephon, they left him, but not so disconsolate for Urania's loss as to keep his eloquence from courting other shepherdesses in as high a degree as ever he did her. But aged Claius, having wrestled with death all the night, not that he desired to live, but unwilling to leave off calling on Urania, blessed Urania! yet in the morning he was overcome, resigning up his breath with her name in his mouth. Basilius had him sumptuously buried, and Musidorus caused a famous monument to be built in his memory. On the top 2560 of it, before the sun had fully dried it, there was found Philisides the despairing shepherd dead, yet not by other practices than a deep melancholy that overpressed his heart. These lines were engraven on a stone that lay by him: *Judge not uncharitably, but believe the expression of a dying man: no poisonous draught have I tasted of, nor any self-murdering instruments have I used to shorten my miserable life: for by the authority of the Gods, the time of my end was concealed from all but my self. I am sure it came not unwished for, for why should I live to be despised of her whom above all the world I honored? I will forbear to name her, because my rival shall not triumph in my death, nor yet con-* 2570 *demn me for coveting so rare a person. My ambition is to have the tears of the Arcadian beauties shed at my funeral and sprinkled on my hearse; and when my body is so magnificently embalmed, let it be interred with Claius's: two lovers, both finishing their lives for their mistresses' sakes. His is publicly known to be Urania; my breast is the cabinet where mine is fixed, and if you rip that open, you will find it (though perhaps not so*

Line 2551. **certifying**: assuring.   Line 2570. **ambition**: desire.

Line 2574. **cabinet**: private chamber, treasure chest.

Line 2575. **fixed**: held fast.

perfect as I could wish it were, the cabinet melting into tears for its unkindness). And now farewell all the world; and I beseech the Divine Powers to bind Cupid's hands from wounding, unless he have a certain salve to cure them.

Thus died Philisides, his will being faithfully performed by the Princes and the beauteous Princesses, with Urania and other pretty shepherdesses, needing no imprecations, faithfully bemoan[ing] his death, burying him with plenty of tears.

Thus were their nuptials finished with sadness. But before the solemnities were quite over, there came more Princes that had partaken of the benefit of Musidorus's and Pyrocles's valor, with presents of gratitude for their brides, Pamela and Philoclea. Then after all ceremonies accomplished, they retired severally to their flourishing kingdoms of Thassalia and Macedon, and Armenia with Corinth, where they increased in riches, and were fruitful in their renowned families. And when they had sufficiently participated of the pleasures of this world, they resigned their crowns to their lawful successors, and ended their days in peace and quietness.

Line 2577. **unkindness:** unkind treatment.

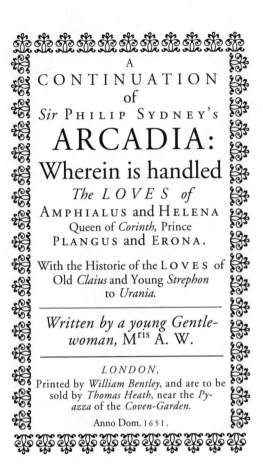

A

CONTINUATION

of

Sir PHILIP SYDNEY'S

ARCADIA:

Wherein is handled

The LOVES of

AMPHIALUS and HELENA
Queen of *Corinth*, Prince
PLANGUS and ERONA.

With the Historie of the LOVES of
Old *Claius* and Young *Strephon*
to *Urania.*

---

*Written by a young Gentle-
woman,* Mris A. W.

LONDON,

Printed by *William Bentley*, and are to be
sold by *Thomas Heath*, near the *Py-
azza* of the *Coven-Garden.*

Anno Dom. 1651.

A CONTINUATION. This page and the following dedicatory poems are approximations of the layout of the original pages in the 1651 edition.

To the two unparalleld
S I S T E R S,
and Patterns of Virtue,

The Ladie } Anne }
and } } Perpoint,
The Ladie } Grace }

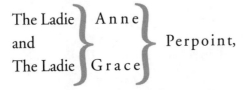

Daughters to the Right Honour-
able the Marquess of
DORCHESTER.

IF I had not observed that the greatest humilitie, reigns in the bosoms of the Noblest Personages, I should not presume to Dedicate this most unworthie Fabrick to your Honours; especially when I consider the poorness of my endeavours, and admire the Learned *Sidney's* Pastimes; Whereof I beseech you charitably to believe, that my ambition was not raised to so high a pitch, as the Title now manifests it to be, until I received Commands from those that cannot be disobeyed. But however, if your Ladiships will graciously vouchsafe to peruse such a confused Theam, I shall harbour the better opinion of it, and shall acknowledge my self, as in all Gratefulness,

10

Your Honours devoted
Servant,

A. W.

The
STATIONER
to the ingenious
READER.

MArvel not to find Heroick Sidney's renowned Fansie pursued to a close by a Feminine Pen: Rather admire his prophetical spirit now as much, as his Heroical before. Lo here Pigmalion's breathing statue, Sir Philip's fantasie incarnate: both Pamela's Majestie, and Philoclea's Humilitie exprest to the life, in the person and style of this Virago. In brief, no other than the lively Ghost of Sydney, by a happie transmigration, speaks through the organs of this inspired Minerva. If any Critical ear, disrealish the shrilness of the Note; let it be tuned to Apollo's Lyre, and the harmonie will soon be perceived to be much better; and the Ladie appeare much more delightfull to her Musidorus: So wisheth

Thine and Her servant,

T. H.

NO thing doth greater disadvantage bring
Than by too great commending of a thing;
Thus Beauty's injur'd, when the searching eye
Deceiv'd by others over flatterie:
Finding that less, was magnify'd before,   5
Thinks there is none, because there is no more.
Art suffers too by this, for too great praise
Withers the greenness of the Poets Bays:
For when mens expectations rise too high,
Ther's nothing seen or read will satisfie.   10
This fault is epidemical, do but ore-look
The Stationers Stall, 'tis spoke in ev'ry book:
Where some are so voluminous become
With Prefaces of this kind, as scarce a room
Is left for th' Authours self. But I can quit   15
My self of this, till now I never writ:
Nor had I done it now, but that a She
Did tempt my pressing for her companie;
From whence when she's return'd, pray use her wel,
She's young, but yet ingeniously will tell   20
You prettie Stories, and handsomly will set

111

An end to what great *Sydney* did beget,
But never perfected, these Embryons she
Doth Mid-wife forth in full maturitie.
Nor is't, where things are left undone, a sin, 25
To seek to end what greater ones begin.
Therefore who ere reads their ingenious style,
Not with a Frown compare them, but a Smile.
She does not write for Criticks, for who ere
Loves for to be censorious, forbear. 30
Then this of both, let nothing else be said,
This *Sydney's* self did write, but this a *Maid.*

H. P. M.

To the Ingenious *L A D I E* , the
Authour of the *Continuation* of
Sir *Philip Sydney's*
ARCADIA.

FAir Authour! though your Sex secure you so,
That all your Dictates will for Classick go:
Yet to be lik'd thus onely, will sound less
Our Approbation, than our Tenderness.
Because the Civil World will judgement spend,   5
That we are bound in Manhood to commend.
Taking our praises level from that sight
Of what you are, more than from what you write.
Whence Critick-wits this nice pretence will find,
That we our Courtship speak, but not our Mind.   10

    But when they single each respect apart,
Viewing the Virgin there, and here the Art:
Their Prejudice will then to Wonder reach,
Not spent on both United, but on Each.
For though the Stars shine in a Beauteous Sphere,   15
Yet are they not more Stars, for shining there:
But would boast lustre of as great a force,
Though their containing Orbs were dim and course.

F. L.

On the *Continuation* of Sir *Philip Sydney's* A R C A D I A.

By Mistress *A.W.*

M *Uch of the Terrene Globe conceal'd doth lie,*
Cheating the Searchers curious industrie:
A R C A D I A too, till now, but partly was discri'd;
Sydney *her beautie view'd, fell Love-sick and dy'd*
Ere he could show the world her perfect state   5
And glorie, interrupted by his Fate.
Amazement at her Frame did him betray,
In each rare Feature too too long a stay:
Till being, benighted, left imperfect this
Earth's Paradise, to possess one perfect is,   10
In pitie o'th' loss, and to repair't, believe
His gallant generous spirit, a reprieve
From's sleeping dust hath purchas't, Deaths malice
Defying with a timely Metempsychosis.
He breathes through female Organs, yet retains   15
His masculine vigour in Heroick strains.
Who hears't may some brave Amazon *seem to be,*
Not Mars *but* Mercury's *Champion,* Zelmane.
And well he may: for doubtless such is she,
Perfection gives t' Arcadia's Geographie.   20
Arcadia *thus henceforth disputed is,*
Whether Sir Philip's *or the* Countesses.

F. W

114

To Mistress A. W.
Upon her *ADDITIONALS* to
Sir PHILIP SYDNEY'S
ARCADIA.

IF *a* Male *Soul, by Transmigration, can*
Pass to a Female, *and Her spirits Man,*
Then sure some sparks *of* Sydney's *soul have flown*
Into your breast, which may in time be blown
To flames, *for 'tis the course of* Enthean *fire*   5
To warm by degrees, and brains to inspire,
As Buds to Blossoms, Blossoms turn to Fruit,
So Wits ask time to ripen, and recruit;
    But Yours gives Time the start, as all may see
By these smooth strains of early Poesie,   10
Which like Rays of one kind may well aspire,
If Phœbus *please to a* Sydneyan *fire.*

JAM. HOWEL.

On the *Continuation* of Sir *Philip Sydney*'s A R C A D I A ;

By Mistress *A. W.*

L*Ay by your Needles Ladies, take the Pen,*
The onely difference 'twixt you and Men.
'Tis Tyrannie to keep your Sex in aw,
And make wit suffer by a Salick *Law.*
Good Wine does need no Bush, pure Wit no Beard;   5
Since all Souls equal are, let all be heard.

    That the great World might nere decay, the Main,
What in this Coast is lost, in that doth gain:
So when in Sydney*'s death Wit ebb'd in Men,*
It hath its Spring-tide in a Female Pen.   10
A single Bough shall other Works approve,
Thine shall be crown'd with all DODONA*'s-Grove.*

F. VAUGHAN.

CONTINUATION
of
Sʳ PHILIP SYDNEY's
ARCADIA.
Wherein is handled the

Loves of *Amphialus* and *Helen*
Queen of *Corinth,* Prince *Plangus* and
Erona : With the Historie of
the Loves of old *Claius* and
young *Strephon* to
Urania.

In the time that *Basilius* King of *Arcadia,* with *Genecea* his Queen, and his two renowned daughters, the Paragons of the World, *Pamela* and *Philoclea,* were retired from the Court to a private lodge amongst the shepherds, there to refresh themselves with their pleasant & harmless sports. In the time that *Pyrocles,* son and heir to the good *Evarchus* King of *Macedon,* disguised himself to an Amazonian Ladie, for the love of his Venus, the sweet *Philoclea.* And *Musidorus* Prince of *Thassalia* disrobed himself of his glorious rayment, and put on Shepherds weeds, for the sight of the stately *Pamela.* And when *Cupid* displayed his quivers throughout his circle, and brought the famousest Princes in the world to adore his mothers beautie: Then Prince *Plangus,* son to the King of *Iberia,* at the first view of *Erona,* a Queen in *Lydia,* was made a Prisoner to her who was a Prisoner. And he whose resolutions were altogether fixed on the rare beautie of

10

Erona, resolved with himself, either to release his incomparable Jewel out of a dolefull Prison, or else to loose his life in the enterprise.

Then he became an humble suitor to *Artaxia*, Queen of *Armenia*, under whose custodie the fair Ladie was, telling her his life was bound up in *Erona's*. And then would he vow it was pitie so sweet a creature should pass by the pleasures of her life in so solitarie a place. And sometimes he would pray for her, and then again he would praise her. But *Artaxia* would no ways be perswaded to any compassion: the more he desired, the more she denied, which he perceiving, with a soft voice and deep sigh, he brake out into these words,

Great Queen, if my grief and groans cannot mollifie your heart, nor the rememberance that once I was your beloved Kinsman, nor yet the beautie of *Erona* can be a sufficient remedie to cure your anger; yet call to mind she was your royal Brothers Mistress; and can you imagin that he would have endured the thought that *Eronas* bloud should so innocently be shed! no, but assure your self, that whensoever a drop of it is spilt, out of his ashes there will rise a Revenger to root you out of your Kingdom.

But *Artaxia* arose out of her throne with a gracefull Majestie, and did protest she would be revenged on her brothers murderers: for, said she, although my brother did love and honour *Erona* too well, yet her hate of him was the cause of his being slain, and of his subjects overthrow. And Prince *Plangus*, if your affections be never so extreamly set upon *Erona*, yet I am resolved to keep her lie in my power. But because you shall have no occasion given you, to brand me with the title of Tyrant Queen, in the word of a Princess I do promise you, that if within two years after the day of my brothers death, you can procure Prince *Pyrocles* and *Musidorus* to accept of a combat against two others of my choosing, to obtain the libertie of *Erona;* if they overcome those Knights of my electing, that day shall *Erona* be at her own disposal: but if my Champions manifest their valour to that height, as to receive the victorie, the same day *Eronas* bodie shall be consumed to ashes, and I shall endeavour to gratifie their courage.

Plangus joyfully accepted of this proposition, since he could obtain no better. And well he knew the Princes cared not for their proud looks, nor feared the glittering of their swords; yet little did he know the craftiness of *Artaxia*. But such subtile Policie seldom ends with an happie conclusion.

And now in hopes of a prosperous journey, he bends his course towards *Greece*, there to deliver his message, upon which his life depended. But he had not travelled many days, before he had surprised a Letter, the superscription was to *Plaxirtus*, brother to *Leonatus* King of *Paphlagonia;* he without fear or dread, brake it open, and read it. He had no sooner perused it over, but that he wished it closed again. Then cried he out aloud, Can it be possible? is *Artaxia* such a deceitfull Politician? can her lips utter that which is so far at distance from her heart? and can flattering make her seem the lesse cruel? No sure, her very name will be hatefull to all Posteritie.

See here, saith he to some of his servants that were with him, see here a Letter from *Artaxia* to *Plexirtus*, how she praises him for a treacherous act, how she condoles with him for the death of *Pyrocles* and *Musidorus*, the two gloriousest Princes that ever lived in the world; how she promises him to end the Tragedie with a Comedie; she tels him the Gods set to their help to revenge her brothers death; and then she acknoledges her self and her Kingdom his, according to her proclamation.

Thus *Plangus* was breathing out his griefs, but had not altogether eased himself, before he was interrupted by a messenger, who not being accustomed to complements, came to him, and certified him that he came from *Armenia*, and that he was servant to that Nobleman, to whom *Artaxia* and he reposed so much confidence in, to intrust *Erona* to be under his charge; and that now, contrarie to the Articles agreed upon between them, *Plaxirtus* had brought the news to *Artaxia* of the death of *Pyrocles* and *Musidorus*, which had been procured by his contrivance; and said he, she hath married him in requital. And by this time he hath besieged my Lords Castle where *Erona* is confined. Then my Lord having intelligence of it, immediately sent me after you, to let you understand that he was not furnished with conveniences well enough to hold out long: therefore as you love *Erona*, so come with speed to relieve her. Now I have finished my message, and I must be gone. So with less reverence than he used when he came, he hastily went his way. *Plangus* being cast into such an astonishment, that he let him go at his pleasure, without so much as inquiring after *Eronas* welfare. But at length, he rouzed himself out of his amazement, and then would have poured out his soul in complaints, had he not espied his news-monger galloping almost out of his sight, then sending his eyes after him, he made a virtue of necessitie, and contented themselves that they were spectatours of the nimble Nag, which shewed his unwillingness to rest his foot upon the ground, before he entered his native soil. This tempted *Plangus* to discover his fancie, which he did in these terms, certainly said he,

There is a charm in Beautie, that Beast do homage to, and must obey; that now makes the Nag to trip so fast away to do *Erona* service. Shall I then be worse than a beast? no, although I cannot pass along with thee; yet my heart shall always keep before thee. And dear *Erona*, though now I turn my face from thee, yet my deeds shall always declare to be for thee, and shall endeavour to clear the clouds that now obscure thy brightness.

Thus, between hope and despair, he mounted his horse, and commanding his servants to follow him, he resolved to go into *Macedon*, to report the news to *Evarchus*, of his sons and nephews death. For he was perswaded, that *Evarchus* would not be backward from bringing to due punishment the causers of his unspeakable loss. And by that means he thought he might handsomly shew his valour, and prove it upon his Ladies enemies. Yet sometimes fears would make conspiracies within him, and almost overwhelm him, untill he recalled his sences, and considered, that it was not a daunted spirit that could serve *Erona*. Then setting spurs to his horse, he travelled in a night and a day without once opening his lips; silence, in his opinion being the best companion to a troubled mind.

But at last he entered into the pleasant countrey of *Arcadia*, which was adorned with stately woods: No cries were heard there but of the lambs, and they in sport too sounded their voices to make their play-fellow lambs answer them again in imitation of the like. And the abundance of shadie trees that were there, were so beautifull with the sweet melodie of birds, that any one, save love-sick *Plangus*, might think it a sufficient harmonie to draw away their delight from any other vanitie of the world. Besides, there were the Shepherds piping to their prettie Shepherdesses, whilest they chearfully sang to pleasure them again. In this sweet place, he sat himself down, with an intention to rest his wearied limbs under a branched tree, whilest his servants refreshed themselves, & baited their horses, but no ease could be harboured in his disquieted heart, his eys being no sooner closed, but that he imagined he saw *Erona* burning in their unmercifull fire: at which sight he staringly opened them, and determined with himself, that since sleep would procure no comfort to him, other then Tragical scenes, he would never enjoy any contentment before he had settled *Erona* in her throne in safetie.

He had not been long in this perplexitie, before he was kindly examined the cause of his sadness. *Plangus* hearing the question, and musing extreamly who it should be that to his thinking should ask so strange an one, heaved up his head, which before he had carelesly held down, and seeing onely an ancient man attended by his two Daughters, and hoping he would be a companion suitable to his disposition, he courteously answered him, that it would be but a trouble to him to understand the occasion of his grief, for, said he, it will be too melancholly a storie to rehearse to you, unless you were in a capacitie to help me.

It is possible I might do you service, replied the old man; for now you are in *Arcadia*, where I am King, and having retired from my Court to a private Lodge, which is seated in a Grove hardby, I with my two daughters, happening now to walk for recreation into this

120

130

140

pleasant place, and I perceiving you being a stranger, lying in such a
150 forlorn posture, I must confess it was incivilitie in me to disturb you,
but my compassion would submit to no causalities that could hinder
my desired knowledge. And now I hope it will be no inconvenience
to you to relate your own Historie to me.

But *Plangus*, with humble reverence excused his denial, and
beseeched *Basilius* first to grant him his pardon, since it was a fault
of ignorance, and not of perversness. And that he promised himself,
that he would chuse rather to be his Chyrurgian to heal his wounds,
than in the least to marr or make them.

Basilius would suffer him no longer to go on with his frivolous
160 civilities, and telling him they should serve his turn, made him sit
down. Then *Plangus* related all circumstances in the same manner,
that afterward the divine *Philoclea* sweetly declared to her lover, the
admirable *Pyrocles*. And believe me, she told it with more liveliness
and quickness of wit, than *Plangus* did himself: For oftentimes his
thought was strayed from his storie, to sigh, with gazing upon the
splendor of *Pamela* and *Philoclea*, for he conceited that in their beauties he might see *Eronas*. But alas poor Prince! *Cupid* in that had
blinded him, for although *Erona* might deserve a large share of
praises, yet the two Sisters could not be paralelled. But when he had
170 concluded his passionate relation, he earnestly craved release of *Basilius:* who answered him, that he governed a quiet and a peaceable
Countrey, and that he should very unwillingly teach his people the
way of dissention; but yet he would command a Guard of *Arcadians*
to conduct him safe into *Macedon.*

Plangus, in lowly submission, congratulated with *Basilius* for that
favour, believing that time and entreatie would amplifie his goodness, according to his abilitie. Then as he was appointing a place
where the *Arcadians* should meet him, his servants presented themselves to him, and certified him, that the day was far spent, and that
180 it would be necessarie for him to go to the next town, and there to
lodge that night. *Plangus*, very well liked of their advice, that he

might have the more freedom to contrive his best way to act his part
he had alreadie begun to play. Then after they had ended their sundrie discourses, he parted from *Basilius* and the two surpassing sisters.

Now *Eronas* beautie had grounded such an impression in his
heart, that no other thought, but of her perfections, could enter into
his. She was his Image, her he worshipped, and her he would for ever
magnifie. And untill he came near the Citie, he busied his fancie in
extolling his Ladie. But there he was received by the governour of
the Town with as great gallantrie as could be expected, considering   190
the short warning *Basilius* gave them, there wanting no cost that
might be pleasing either to his eye or tast. A stately supper being
provided, which was garnished with a royal banquet, sent from *Basilius;* and all was finished in so gorgeous a manner, that *Plangus* did
assure himself he was no ordinarie, nor yet unwelcom Guest. But all
the sweet musick with the plentie of delicates was no more to *Plangus*, than the rememberance of his own misfortune. Yet having a
Princely care not to show himself unthankfull to the meanest supporter of his undeserved Festivals, he would oftentimes praise them
for their bountie to him a stranger, and one that was no way able to   200
make them the least requital, but they replied, that his acceptance
was as much, and more than they deserved or expected. Then after
they had a good while parlied together upon several occasions, the
Citizens returned to their houses, and *Plangus* went to his lodging,
then prostrating himself before *Cupid* for his happie success in fulfilling of his own desires, beseeched him to unite *Erona*s affection as
firmly to him, as his was unmoveable to her; and that both might be
so well preserved, that at length they might enjoy the happie fruition
of real friendship between him and *Erona*, at whose name he ended;
and as if he received his life from thence, he fell into a little slumber,   210
which continued for so short a time, that when he awaked, the
clouds were not separated to give way to the approaching day, that
was then extreamly wisht for by him, who determined to spend the
hour-glass of his life in defence of his esteemed mistress.

By that time he had run over his thoughts to the end of his intended enterprises, *Phebus* spread his beams over his curtains, which cast so great a reflection upon him, that though his eyes were still dissembling sleep, yet the Suns brightness made him gaze about him, and seeing it so sweet a morning, he believed it to be an emblem of his prosperous success. In this perswasion he arose, and charging his servants to be in a readiness, he walked into a Gallerie, where multitudes stood waiting for his presence, he kindly saluting them, and repeating his former speeches of courtesie and gratitude, he commanded his man to bring out his Steed; and then taking his leave of the *Arcadians*, saving the residue which *Basilius* appointed to wait on him, he raised himself upon the beast, which gently received him, as willing to bear so loved a burden, and sprightly ambled along: but *Plangus* was forced to hold his bridle, and teach his Nag his bounds were no further than his Commission, by reason of a calling from a young Shepherd, who speedily running to *Plangus*, and in a breathless manner he certified him that he was sent by his Lord *Basilius* to excuse his absence, the occasion being his retiredness to so private a place, that with no conveniencie he could entertain him there agreeable to his greatness, nor yet to remove so far so suddenly.

Plangus requested the Shepherd to return his thanks and obedience to his Sovereign, and seeing it was a matter of no greater importance, he would endure no longer hinderances, but set spurs to his horse and gallopped away with all expedition: but not without some turbulent passages that he was fain to endure, before he could attain to his desired haven: yet at last he arrived under the Dominions of *Evarchus* in *Macedon*, where he was welcomed by a companie of dolorous persons, who without entreatie would participate with him in his sorrows: but alas! there were few comforters, all the people seeming like shadows, in regard of the miss they had of their young Prince, who after he had brought so many Kings in subjection under his prowess and valour, should now himself be lost, none knowing where or how; but perpetually hearkening to several relations, which put them into more fears and doubts every day than they were in before. 250

Musidorus wanted not bewailing neither; for well they knew *Pyrocles* life was bound up in his, and that he loved & respected the *Macedonians* as much for *Pyrocles* sake, as he did the *Thessalians* for his own sake, and that they learned one another virtuous qualities, which were equally distributed between them; therefore the whole Kingdom groaned under burthensom calamities for their witnessed loss: but by the enterance of *Plangus*, who was a stranger to them, their complaints were turned into whisperings, and their sighs into listenings, all being earnest to know who he was, and the cause of his Posting from citie to citie towards the Court. Some would believe 260 the worst, and then would swear they did see sadness in his face; others would perswade themselves, it was his hastie travelling that made him seem careful But *Plangus* not staying to hearken to their mistrustfull uncertainties, kept on his former pace, till he was come within a mile of the Palace, where he was stopped by one *Kalodolus*, an ancient servant belonging to *Musidorus*, who hearing of the coming of a Foreigner, and infinitely longing to hear from his dear Master, and meeting *Plangus*, he fell down at his feet, and besought him to have commiseration upon him, and tell him of the safetie of *Musidorus*. 270

This request silenced *Plangus* for a while, who could not imagin what reply to make to him: but having considered a little better of it, he brake his silence on this fashion. Sir, it grieves me extreamly that I cannot give you such satisfactorie answer as I wish I could: however do not afflict your self, for I dare assure you that he is happie, being a more glorious Prince, and far greater than all the Kingdoms of the World could make him.

Why? is he dead? said *Kalodolus;* then all virtue is fled away: but I will follow thee *Musidorus*, where ere thou beest, I will not stay behind. Then snatching out a Rapier from him that was nearest him, 280 he would have sent his soul to *Pluto*, had it not been prevented by the quick eye of *Plangus*, who apprehending his danger, leaped upon him, and with violence wrung the Rapier out of his hand, but yet he would not be pacified for a time, nor perswaded from practising his intended mischief, till reason over-swaying his patience, made him becom a moderator of his own rashness; for said he, What good can my death do to *Musidorus?* shall I my self destroy, and do my Prince the wrong? no, I will live as long as fortune pleases, and guid my steps about the world, till I have found his Tomb, where I will sol-

290   emnize such Obsequies as may be thought worthy to be titled the Funeral of so worthy a Prince. Then I will weep my self to tears upon his grave, to water that illustrious Plant, that certainly must needs spring up & flourish; for it is impossible so rare a thing can be obscured in the earth.

Here *Kalodolus* speech was stopped by a floud, that would endure no longer to be hid within his aged carkass. And the noble *Plangus* answered him with sighs, as if his heart would break: then they both lookt so stedfastly in pitie upon one another, that if a Painter had been present, he could not take, nor have a livelier Master-piece of

300   sorrow than this lover and servant represented, they being both void of comfort, and equally afflicted, until *Plangus* pluckt up his dead spirits, and adviced *Kalodolus* to cease his complaints, and not to suf-fer grief to overrun his patience, for since *Musidorus* was dead, the onely service he could do for him, was to help forward the revenging of the Actors in his death. And then he required him to direct him the way to *Evarchus:* which command *Kalodolus* instantly obeyed. And guiding him through stately Courts, paved all with Marble, and compassed in with Marble pillars, that were adorned with such goodly proportioned Statues, that had not *Plangus* been employed

310   with matters of consequence, he would not so regardlesly have passed by them, without prying into their Storie; which might per-haps have been beneficial unto him, to know the several tricks of warlike *Hercules*, as was there curiously engraven by famous Anti-quaries. But *Plangus* thoughts were higher flown than these Portai-

tures could reach to; those he valued like shadows in comparison of his valiant enterprises, that artificially his invention would lay before him, as if it were accomplished alreadie. And in that unsatisfied perswasion he was brought to *Evarchus*, whose sight awakened him from his fabulous fantasie. And then with a sad reverence he kneeled down.

But the good King would not suffer that, but lifting him up, he entreated him to use no such ceremonies, but to discourse that which he earnestly wisht to know without any delays. So *Plangus* being extream willing to fulfill *Evarchus* charge, though first to bring him by degrees to the hearing of those mournfull tidings, he began with this Prologue:

Most gracious Sir, did I not consider your wisdom in governing your passions, far surmounting other mens, I should not so abruptly presume to be the messenger of such unfortunate news, as now I am. But since my life is hazarded in several respects, I know your goodness will no way persevere against me, for necessitie hath no rule, and that is the reason which now inforces me to manifest that unto you, which I am loth to utter: But I assure my self, that your Majestie will no way despise the sovereign salve called Patience, that is a present Remedie for all afflictions.

Know then, great King, that the mirrours of virtue, the famous *Pyrocles* your son, and *Musidorus* your nephew are treacherously slain by the bloudie plot of *Plaxirtus*, false Brother to *Leonatus* King of *Paphlagonia*, and revealed to me by the surprisal of a letter of congratulation from *Artaxia* Queen of *Armenia*, under whose power *Erona* Queen of *Lydia* is a prisoner; and without speedie succour, she will be put to death in the cruellest way that can be imagined, by the same instruments that exposed her Champions to theirs: But yet Sir, they have left behind them so pretious a name, that their adversaries cannot blemish: and so long as their better part flourishes on earth, all the realitie that can be shewed for the lesser, is to go on couragiously, and revenge your loss, and to give *Apollo* thanks for their leaving so glorious a memorie behind them.

Thus *Plangus* ended, without further mentioning *Erona*, until
350   *Evarchus* grief was somewhat digested: which he did perceive
extreamly to over-sway him, by the changing of bloud in his face,
that perpetually going and coming, would sometime wax pale and
wan; and then would flush, as if he threatened to make *Plaxirtus*
smart for all his villanie. And in this conflict of sorrow and anger he
continued a great space: but at last they both yielded to reason, and
Evarchus wisely became the Judge of the Sessions; for said he,

It is Justice to bring murderers to their deserved punishments.
And because you Prince *Plangus* testifie your self to be such an affectionate Friend to my dear Children, shew your self one in their
360   revenge; you I will entrust to be the General of my Armie; prove as
valiant now as you have ever done; let all your aim be at *Plaxirtus;*
and if possible, convey him hither alive, that he may die a publick
spectacle of shame and terror before all the People. And I give you
free libertie to use your power in the release of that distressed Ladie
you spake of, for certainly their hearts are infinitely hardened for any
mischief: but for *Artaxia*, remember she is a woman, and subject to
degrees of Passion as well as man. But alas! she desired the destruction of *Pyrocles* and *Musidorus*, and now she hath rendered her recompence to *Plaxirtus* for that abominable deed. O the thought of
370   that Action reaches further than my compassion: but I will resign
my power to you, therefore though you grow Victorious, yet
strengthen your self with discretion, and let not rashness nor faintheartedness prevail over you. Now go on with your intentions, and
prosper, whilst I end my days in solitariness.

Evarchus had no sooner done, but he bowed to the earth, as if he
wisht to be there quickly; and then after he had signed a Commission for raising of an Armie, he withdrew into his chamber, and
Plangus waited upon him to the enterance, and so they parted; one
to temperate melancholly, the other to Hope intermixt with cares:
380   for though *Plangus* was loaded with troublesom imployments, yet
those he took for refreshments, because the foundation of them was
laid for *Erona*'s sake. But *Evarchus* grieved, as he had too just cause,

to think that he should never more behold the joy of his heart again; and so he continued without the least show of a contented mind, yet not with a desperate rage. A large and rare Theme might be Chronicled of his wisely governed Passions; but that is too pregnant a virtue for my dull capacity to go on with.

Therefore surrendering that to sharp wits, I will onely mention *Plangus* happie success that he obtained in *Macedon;* for in short time he levied an Armie, sufficient to conquer all *Armenia,* every one being desirous to revenge their Princes quarrel, and thought it a preferment to be the meanest Souldier; then being all in a readiness, they march away. But *Plangus* before he went, sent his Ambassadors to *Delphos,* to know of the Oracle his Destinie, and just as he was managing his Armie, in their march they returned with this answer;

That he should be Victorious over his Enemies, if so be he would be vigilant in guiding his Forces in a way of deliberation; and not to venture to shew his Valour, in over-rash attempts in a Bravado before his Mistress, which oftentimes hath been the cause of the Routing a magnificent Armie: but he must remember the eyes of all the World were upon him as their Defence and Shield, whose wisdom must preserve them from their furious enemies.

This Oracle infinitely comforted *Plangus;* and when he had given thanks to *Apollo* for his proclaimed prosperous Fortune, he kept on his march to *Armenia;* whom we will leave for a time.

Now I will discover some Passages that passed between *Amphialus* Nephew to *Basileus* the King of *Arcadia,* and *Helena* Queen of *Corinth,* how that after she had carried him away in a Lighter from *Arcadia,* what bitter complaints she made for him, untill she had brought him to *Corinth,* that would be to pitifull a subject to stay on; therefore leaving that to several conjectures, I will onely rehearse those particulars that united those rare Persons together to both their abundant felicitie.

When *Helena* had conveyed her beloved *Amphialus* to her renowned Citie *Corinth,* and lodged him in the richest furnished Chamber that could be devised, yet all she thought too mean for

such an imcomparable Guest: then she advised with her skilfull
Chyrurgeons how she might have his wounds healed; and had
always an especial care to see the salves applied to them her self; and
420   when all was finished, she passed away the day with sighs by sence-
less *Amphialus*, who lay so quietly, that for a great time none could
perceive the least motion of life in him: but at last the Chyrurgeons
avouched they could find warm bloud strive for life in his (now in all
likelihood) curable wounds. Which speech of theirs did make *Helena* wash her fair face with her tears for joy, when before it had not
touched a drop of water, from the time that she found *Amphialus* in
so wofull a condition. Then began she to discourse with him, as if he
could mind her what she said.

Tell me dear *Amphialus*, said she, what occasion have I given you
430   to make you hate me? have I not ever honoured and loved you far
above my self? O yes! and if I had a thousand lives to lose, I would
venture them all for your sake. But since that is an impossible thing,
propound to me the most probable way for me to purchase you, and
I dare undertake it, be it never so dangerous: But if it be the Princess
Philoclea that lies as a block in my way, so that I must either continue where I am, or else stumble over it and be made quite hopeless,
yet let me counsel you as a faithfull friend, not to engage your affections to one that is so negligent of it, but rather bestow it upon me
that will accept of it. Oh hear me, and have pitie on me, O *Amphi-*
440   *alus, Amphialus!*

Then she flung her self down upon his bed, with a resolution not
to stir before she had discerned some sign of life in outward appearance. And as she was earnestly looking upon him, she espied his eyes
a stealing open; but immediately, with a long fetcht sigh, he closed
them up again, as grieving for their tenderness they could not gaze
upon beautie. But *Helena* replying with twentie to his one, went on
with her love-sick speeches.

Alas poor Prince! said she, is it thy hard fortune to receive thy life
again in sighs? hath such il-favoured spleens no place to settle in, but

in thy noble breast, which shines in goodness? Chear up, dear   450
Prince, and let not thy greatest Foe find cause to tax thee with the
least blemish.

Longer she would have proceeded in her bemoaning of *Amphi-*
alus, had she not been interrupted by the Chyrurgeons that were in
the chamber, and hearing her voice, came instantly to her, and
kneeling down, intreated her to abandon the chamber, for as much
as her presence and complaints caused disturbance in *Amphialus*,
and procured nothing but that which was hurtfull to her own person: and then they assured her, that if she would forbear his companie, they could perfect the cure in half the time, that otherwise   460
they should be constrained to be tedious in, by reason that her sad
speeches would ground such an impression in him in his weakness,
that it would be as much as their skill could reach unto, to keep his
wounds from growing worser than better. These perswasions of the
Chyrurgeons had a very great influence over *Helena*, and she forsaking her former passions, guarded her self with a long Robe of wise
considerations, and departed his chamber without any shew of fondness, to the admiration of all beholders. Yet she never neglected the
care of *Amphialus*, but diligently enquired after his amendment, that
she might know all passages as punctually, as if she had been with   470
him. In this golden mean of Patience she continued so long, till
Amphialus had revived somewhat his decayed spirits, & the Chyrurgeons had so well overcome his wounds, that by degrees he was
brought to walk about his chamber; but always he would be crossing
his Arms, knocking his Breast, and breathing speeches to himself in
so wofull a manner, as would make the hardest heart burst into a
deluge of tears. Yet all this time he never examined by what means he
was conveyed thither, nor any other question that concerned *Hel-*
*end*s or his own condition. And so for a great while he imprisoned
himself in such ignorance, till by the coming of a young Gentleman,   480
named *Clytiphon*, son to *Kaleander*, a Noble man of *Arcadia*, his
concealed estate, and all other circumstances that had happened in

Arcadia from his departure from thence, were declared to *Amphialus* wonder and astonishment.

For this *Clytifon* was sent as an Ambassadour to *Amphialus* from his uncle the King of *Arcadia*, to congratulate with him for his recoverie, and to certifie him of his Cosins deliverance out of his Castle, by the prowess of Prince *Pyrocles* and *Musidorus;* and how they disguised themselves for the love of *Pamela* and *Philoclea*, with all the several attempts that they practised to obtain their desired enterprise. (As their bringing *Anaxius* to submit to their mercie, *Pyrocles* having granted him his life on condition he would acknowledge it) and finally to give him notice, that the nuptials of *Pyrocles* and *Philoclea*, with *Musidorus* and *Pamela* were onely deferred for the time they could hear from *Amphialus*. This was the chief of *Clytifons* Ambassage, which he carefully obeyed.

But before he entered into *Corinth*, the Citie swelled with rumour, every one being greedie to know that which nothing concerned them. But *Clytifon* knowing it was not a time of dalliance, hastened to the Palace, where he was waited for by *Helena*, whose watchfull eyes and attentive ears could not pass by any suspitious whisperings, but would always make strict enquirie of the cause of them. So now she believing the credible report, would needs come down her self, attended with a train of Ladies, to welcom the Ambassadour to her Court, when as soon as she perceived a glimpse of him, she perfectly knew him to be that noble *Clytifon*, whom before she had been beholding to for his excellent companie. Then whilst she was shewing her courtesie to him for his former civilities, he with an humble reverence, yet supported with a Garb of Majestie, came to her after the manner of an Ambassadour, and presenting mightie high commendations to her from all the Princes that resided in *Arcadia*, she besought him to accept of such poor entertainment as her abilitie could make him. Then leading him into the Presence (it being in the after-noon) she commanded a delicate Collation to be set before him, which was fulfilled so quickly and so decently, that *Clytifon* could not choose but sit and extol their comely order; and within a while fell to eating those rarities that *Helena* had pro- vided for him; but she would not be perswaded to tast of any, her troubled mind was too full of jealousies and fears, to think of pleas- ing her appetite. Sometime she mistrusted that *Basileus* had sent for 520 *Amphialus* to be tried by the Law for his Mother *Cecropids* stealing away his Daughters, that he might have a fair pretence to take away his life. But quickly she vanquished that doubt by another that she imagined to be most probable, which was, that *Philocleds* heart might be mollified, and that she under-hand had made choice of *Clytifon* to be her Proxie, in wishing *Amphialus* to pursue his former Petition to *Philoclea*, that she with the more modestie might grant him his request. This fancie of *Helena* made such a wound within her breast, that a thousand of sighs had free passage there, and in silence she did think out her complaints; until *Clytifon* had disor- 530 dered the artificial curiosities with tasting of their goodness, and had sufficed his natural hunger. Then *Helena* taking him aside from the companie that came to gaze upon him, with many shews of grief she conjured him, that if ever he had been real to any friend, to shew himself one to her, who vowed faithfulness and secresie: but yet if it were a matter of such weightie importance, as he could not repose so much confidence in her, being a Princes of another Countrey, yet she entreated him to certifie her whether it concerned *Amphialus*, or in his her own ruin.

Clytifon had hardly patience to hear her out, but removed her 540 fears on this manner: Chear up great Queen, said he, those cloudie shadows of discontent and fears never do good but hurt, and wrong your Beautie, that otherwise would be the sweetest, and the singular Flower that could be found in the large Garden of the world. Chear up then and rejoyce at joyfull tidings: for to the amazement of all, the two ever blessed Princes, *Pyrocles* and *Musidorus*, are by many strange accidents found to be alive, though disguised, within my Sovereigns Lodges (from being gallant Souldiers) the one to a

woman, the other to a comely Shepherd, which was brought to pass
by the industrie of blind *Cupid*, who takes pleasure in wounding the
best of undaunted spirits. But yet he hath dealt so favourable with
these incomparable Persons, that he hath equally wounded *Pamela*
and *Philoclea* to them again: so that now *Arcadia* waits onely for the
nuptials finishing, to be made happie in having so glorious a Prince
to reign over them, and that is delayed onely for the time that they
might hear from my Lord *Amphialus*.

Helena's joy at the hearing of this news, was too great for my dull
expression, yet after she had moderated her excessive mirth, and
brought it within the bounds of reason, she feared that *Amphialus*
would be so over come with despairing grief, that nothing but death
could end his miserie. Then fell she at *Clytifon's* feet, and begged of
him not to be over-hastie in declaring his Ambassage to *Amphialus*,
but to compass him in by degrees to the hearing of it. This request of
hers *Clytifon* courteously promised to perform. And she guiding him
to *Amphialus* chamber door, desired him to walk in, and departed.

But *Amphialus* espying *Clytifon*, and leaping upon him, and then
lovingly embracing him, said, How doest thou *Clytifon?* thou lookest as if thou meanedst to chide me; but spare your labour, I will do
that my self, nay, and more if *Philoclea* would command it, let her
desire my heart and she shall have it, and with mine own hand Ile
pluck it out to give her, yet think it all too little to excuse my crime.
But she is gratious and noble, answered *Clytifon*, and will be readier
to forgive, than you can be to begge your pardon of her. But I will
never presume to aske forgiveness, replyed *Amphialus*, since I deserve
all punishments. Though you do, said *Clytifon*, yet if you will
present your self unto her in an humble and submissive way, and
cast off your former Suit, I durst assure you she would not onely
grant your life, but would also receive you to her favour as her near
Kinsman. If I could think so, replied *Amphialus*, I should be highlie
contented far above my deserts or wishes, and said *Clytifon*, would
you be pleased to hear that she were married to another or else likelie

to be so suddainly? Yes with all my soul answered *Amphialus*, but yet upon condition, that it may be to her all flourishing happiness. As for my own particular, that is the least thing I regard or hope for, onely as I said before, that the Princess *Philoclea* may be endowed with all felicity, that will procure to me an uncontrouled blessedness.

Then *Clytifon* asked him if he would accept of him to be the bearer of a letter from him to *Philoclea?* which he promised carefully to deliver, if it were such an one as might be received without scruple. *Amphialus* answered he would gladly write to *Philoclea*, but it should no way be prejudicial to him, he intending onely to manifest his grief for her ill usage in his Castle; and to let her know how readie he was to welcom any punishment she would inflict upon him. Then after more such speeches passed between them, *Clytifon* rehearsed the truth of his message. Which at first *Amphialus* heard with trembling, untill *Clytifon* remembered him of his former discourse, that nothing that could make *Philoclea* happie, should ever make him unhappie. Then rousing up himself, he wished *Clytifon* to leave him to his privacie, that he might have the more libertie to endite a letter worthie of her acceptance; *Clytifon* being to carrie it away the next morning. So he, without the least contradiction, left *Amphialus*, who being alone fell into a passion (as afterward he confessed) that had almost made him senseless, untill time that wears out all things, recaled his memorie back to him again, which first discovered it self thus:

Alas miserable *Amphialus!* thou imployest thy self to extol thy Rival, and meanest to make it thy recreation to do so always. Now I can remember the *Amazon* Ladie that fought so gallantly with me in the *Arcadian* woods, for the Princess *Philoclea*'s Glove; what blows she strook at me, and with what nimbleness she avoided mine, when I aimed at her in mine own defence. I must confess it daunted me to see a woman rant so over me, but yet it made me the more admire her valour, and brought down my former loftiness, to wonder at my timourousness. But since she is discovered to be the noble *Pyrocles*, I shall be so far from hiding that disguised exploit of his, that I shall blazon it about the world in triumph, as an honour for me to be overcome by him; and it shall never be said, that envie of my Rival shall make me obscure his worth, for I shall applaud his wisdom in making so rare a choice. Nor did I ever hear of any that could deserve him better than the divine *Philoclea.* Then grieve no more *Amphialus,* at thy Ladies happiness, since in hers all thine consists; but prepare thy self to obey her commands, be they never so contrary to thy nature.

With these resolutions, although with a shaking hand, he began to write his letters. But *Clytifon,* as soon as he came out of the chamber, was received by *Helena,* to whom he related *Amphialus* and his whole discourse. And she being in hope to make him a fortunate messenger for her proceeding, used him with all the courtesie that could be. And then by her favours she enticed him to her bait, and made him as much her humble servant, as he was *Amphialus:* For then he had promised to be a nimble Post to them both: and he must be conducted to his lodging, and *Helena* to her closet.

Where she began too hard a task for her distracted mind, a letter she did write unto *Philoclea,* but that did no way please her, it was not sufficiently adorned with Rhetorick for so rare a Princess. Another she did like reasonable well, but that was so blured with her tears, that the best of eyes could not read it. More she wrote, and found blemishes in them all. But at last being tired with scribing so long upon one subject, she resolved that the next should go what ere it were, which in earnest proved the worst of all. But yet because you shall understand the enditment of it, it is set down as ensueth. The *Superscription* was,

For the virtuous Princes Philoclea.

Sweet Princess,

Did I not hear in what raptures of happiness your Divine self is involved, or could I in the least comprehend the splendor of your goodness to spread upon your distressed Cosin Amphialus*, I should willingly*

resign up all my claim to felicitie, so that you, of farr worthier endow-
ments, might enjoy it. But since it hath pleased the destinies to place you
in the highest firmament of contentment, that you may with the more 650
ease behold the calamitie of your Admirer, let me therefore intreat you to
shew your compassion to him by mildness, and suffer his punishment,
may be sincere affection to me; and you will infinitely above measure
oblige your devoted servant,

HELENA *of* Corinth.

Often did she peruse this Letter to find out cavils in it, until sleep
would endure no longer to be resisted, nor hindered from seizing on
so pure a soul, which she evidenced by letting her letter fall out of
her delicate proportioned hand that held it: then fell she into slum-
bers, and starts would now and then afright her, but those she ended 660
with sighs, and fell asleep again, and then she passed away the
remainder of the night with varietie of dreams, untill the approching
day roused up her senses, and remembered her it was high time for
Lovers to be stirring. Then she being always mindfull of such observations, took her letter, and making it fortunate with her prayers,
she carried it into the Presence, where she stayed for *Clytifon*, who
was receiving his farewel of *Amphialus*.

For after *Amphialus* had finished his humble suit, as he termed it,
and had endured a tedious night, *Clytifon* must needs be sent for to
prescribe the likeliest medicine for a love-sick remedie. *Clytifon* 670
could not be asked an harder question, for he himself would gladly
have taken Physick, had he been sure of the cure. Tell me *Clytifon*,
said he, is there no help for a troubled mind? no cordial to bring
sleep into these eyes of mine? If you will submit your actions, replied
Clytifon, to my approbation, I will set you in a perfect way of quietness, though it should procure mine own endless miserie. He
deserves no Physician, answered *Amphialus*, that will not accept of
his advice, when it is so freely profered him. Know then, said
Clytifon, your onely way to obtain contentment, is to honour, nay,
and love her who so entirely loves and respects you. O stay there, 680

cried out *Amphialus*, and do not weigh me down with clogs of grief, I am ballanced sufficiently alreadie, why do you with more burdens strive to sink me? nothing but *Philocleas* commands I find can enter into my heart, and they may strike me dead. Flie then *Clytifon*, flie as swiftly as *Phœbus* can, and make a quick return to let me know *Philocleas* censure equal to my deserts. With these words he gave *Clytifon* his letter, and with a sad gesture turned away. But *Clytifon* without deferring went his way; though first he received *Helenas*, and with many protestations vowed to further her undertakings.

690   And now I will leave these two lovers in longing expectation of his return, and will trace along with *Clytifon* to accompanie him, he being destitute almost of any comfort, by reason his affections were so extreamly engaged to *Helenas* beautie, that nothing but envious death could aswage it. This caused such a conflict to arise between *Cupid's* discharged Bowe, and *Clytifons* making his own wounds to gape with contrarying the God of loves commands, and hastening from the Mistress of his desires to gain her to another: that often-times he was turning back to discover his intentions to her. But this design he vanquished by confuting himself.

700   It is true said he, I ride apace towards mine own overthrow; but since it was her charge, how dare I harbour a thought of refusing? no it is her gracious pleasure to vouchsafe me to be her Messenger, and shall I loose her esteemed favours, which I infinitly hazard if I do not manifest my faithfull endeavours in gaining *Amphialus* to be her Husband, but I will choose to be her loyal Servant, rather than to her sweet self an importunate Suiter. And I should account my self ever happie, could it lie in my power to further hers; but I am unworthy to receive such a Title as a poor Instrument to redeem her Majestie to her former felicitie: however I will shew my willingness, 710   by my nimbleness; and then teaching his Steed to give a gallant caper, he speedily rode away, and without the least hinderance he quickly set footing in the Countrey of *Arcadia*, where he was welcomed by Peals of Bels, and Shoutings of People, with varietie of sports contrived by young children: besides the pleasant Shepherds

blowed their pipes, whilest the prettie Shepherdesses chanted out
their praises of their great God Pan. All these harmless pastimes were
ordered so conveniently, that he might have a perfect view of them
as he went by: and all was to declare the joy they conceived for *Clyti-*
fon's safe return, whose stay they heard was the onely delayance of
the Princes Nuptials. And as he rode along, the silly Lambs did wel-   720
come him with leaps, whilest the Fox that lurked in his private corner to catch them, discovered himself to do homage unto *Clytifon,*
and by that means lost his game; yet he chearing himself up with
hopes of a more plentifull prey hereafter, returned to his former
craft, and received that misfortune as a just recompence of his carelesness.

Thus *Clytifon's* thoughts were taken up by sundrie objects, till he
had traced along ground so far as to the Citie of *Matenia:* there he
might see Noble Personages glorie with their imployment, and to
esteem themselves to be regarded were they not set to work. There   730
he might behold the Palace richly furnishing, and all the houses
gaudily decking up. There he might hear of abundance of several
inventions for Masques, & other curious sights that might be
delightfull to the eye. But *Clytifon* passed by all these rare Scenes,
they being in comparison of his fantasie, by him reputed superfluous.

And now his eye was fixed upon the Lodge that shadowed the
wonders of the world, and was seated about two miles distance from
Matenia. Thither with eagerness he goes, where he was onely saluted
by the diligent servants that directed him to the grove adjoyning to   740
the Lodge, where the Princes just before were walked for recreation.
Then as he went gazing about him, he discerned *Evarchus* King of
Macedon, who signified his joy for his Sons and Nephews, to him,
revived lives, by his lifted up hands and eyes, which with great devotion he rendered to the Gods in thankfulness.

For it happened after *Plangus* departure from *Macedon* with an
Armie, *Evarchus* fearing his love-lines would give opportunitie for
sadness to overcome his languishing spirit, made a journey into

Arcadia to visit his antient Friend *Basilius*. And after many strange
accidents had apparently been discovered, as the famous Sir *Philip
Sydney* fully declares, *Pyrocles* and *Musidorus* were found to be alive;
and now he tarried in *Arcadia* to see his blessedness compleated in
their Marriages. And in the mean time he dispatched a messenger to
Plangus to encourage him with those welcom tidings. And then the
good King confined himself wholy to the continual praises of the
Divine providence for his unlooked for comfort. And now straying
from the rest of the Princely companie, he fell to his wonted contemplations, and never moved from his devout posture, till *Clytifon's*
suddain approach into his sight, made him start, and withall raised
him.

Then *Evarchus* examined him how the noble Gentleman *Amphialus* did? but *Clytifon* was so mightily dashed with his disturbing of
Evarchus, that he let silence be both his Answer and Pleader for his
presumption, which *Evarchus* perceiving, brought him into that solitary Arbor where *Pyrocles* in his disguizement had the priviledge to
resort: There sate *Basilius* with *Genecea* his Queen, and he lovingly
condoling with her for her former sufferings that she was then a
sounding in his attentive ears, but at *Evarchus* and *Clytifons* enterance they rose up, and graciously saluting *Clytifon*, they commanded
him to repeat those Adventures that had befallen him at *Corinth*, if
they were remarkable; but *Evarchus* prevailed with them to have
patience, that *Philoclea*, whom it most concerned, might hear as
soon as any; then they all went to the young Princes, and found
them so well imployed, that had they not espied them, they would
in pitie have passed by, and not disturbed them.

Pyrocles and *Musidorus* being seated upon a Fountaines brim,
where in the middle *Cupids* Image was placed, ready the second time
to have wounded them; but they not minding him, strived who
should with the comeliest grace, and highest Rhetorick extoll their
Mistresses; whilst the faire *Pamela*, with lovely *Philoclea* tied the truest Lovers knot in grasse, that ever yet was tied; and now and then

would pick a Flower to shew their Art, to tell the vertue of it; in these harmless pleasures their Parents found them busied.

Then *Basilius* comming to *Philoclea*, told her that *Clytifon* had brought her news of her servant *Amphialus*, & she modestly blushing, replyed, that she should be glad to hear of her Cosins health; then *Basilius* desired them all to sit down, that they might lend the better attention to *Clytifon;* but he in reverence to his Soveraigne, would stand, till *Basilius* lay'd his commands upon him to the contrarie: then *Clytifon* recounted all circumstances saving that about himself, as I have set down; and when he had ended, he presented *Philoclea* with *Helena*s & *Amphialus* Letters, which she courteously received, & when she had broken them open, she read them, but with such Crystall streames all the time droping from her Rosie cheeks, that had *Venus* been by, she would have preserved them in a Glasse to wash her faice withall, to make her the more beautifull; and then her Servant *Pyrocles* gently wiped them away; but seeing them yet distil, he was angry, and shewed it on this manner. It is a hard Riddle to me, said he, that a Lover should write such a regardless Letter, to grieve and mar that face that he so much adored. He would longer have chid *Amphialus*, but that *Evarchus* advised him to take the Letter from his sorrowfull Ladie, which she willingly resigned unto him; and he read as followeth.

For the Incomparable Princess, the Princess *Philoclea*.
Madam,
I am confident, you have heard what affection I have harboured in my heart, your (though unknown to me) most barbarous usage, and that I might clear mine innocence of such an heinous crime, with what a Tragical act I heaped up miserie upon miserie, which hath infinitly overwhelmed my distracted soul; and now I onely rest in expectation of your commands. I beseech you let it be so pitifull, that it may procure eternal ease to my extream perplexity; and nothing can diminish that but Death by your appointment; and that to me shall be most welcom; and I shall

*account my self happy in obeying your desires at the last moment, which
I vow to accomplish what ere it be, with chearfulness; and with this
undaunted resolution, I will ever continue to be,*

Your faithfull, though unworthy Servant,

AMPHIALUS.

Whilest *Pyrocles* was reading this, the sweet *Philoclea* stopt the
remainder of her tears, till she had taken a view of *Helen's*. Then she
entreated her *Pyrocles* to read over her Cousin *Amphialus* lines to her
again. And she attentively listening to his passionate Phrases, the
second time she renewed her weeping deluge: but the stately *Pamela*
said, her Cosin did wisely to cast himself into the Power of her sister,
he knew her clemencie, and considered it was his safest way to do so,
before he set footing in *Arcadia*.

Then they all perswaded *Philoclea* not to grieve for that which she
might remedie, and adviced her to go and write a letter to *Amphialus*, and in it to command him to put in execution *Helen's*
demands. She immediatly arose, and at her rising made the flowers
to hang down their heads for want of her presence: but her breath
being a sweeter perfume than the scent of the choicest Flowers,
made her careless of their sorrow; for she not minding them, went
her way; and *Pyrocles*, who could be as well out of his life, as from
her company, followed after her, and would needs wait upon her to
the lodge; and there he staid till she had written her Letter.

Which she had no sooner ended, and *Pyrocles* perused, but that
ingenious *Clytifon* was readie upon his Horse to receive it, that he
might with speed convey it to *Corinth*. So after abundance of commendations from *Philoclea* to *Helena* and *Amphialus*, he parted, and
without any remarkable Passage, he quickly attained to his journeys
end: where he was received between hope and fear by *Helena*, who
hearing of his return, withdrew into a private room, and then sent
for him; but as soon as he was entred into her sight, she cryed out.

Good Sir, doe not break my heart with delayance; is there any possibility for me to live? if there be none, O speak, that I may die! and end my fears: for if *Amphialus* doom be death; I am resolved not to live one minute after him. But *Clytifon*, as desirous to give her ease, as she could be to ask it of him, answered, That now the joyfull time was near at hand that *Amphialus* and she should be united together, and should flourish with all happiness that could be imagined. I beseech you do not flatter me, said *Helena*, such vain perswasions will do no good, but make my fall the higher and so more dangerous. Madam, replyed *Clytifon*, let me beg the favour of you to believe me, and if I have told you any falshood, say I was never trustie to my Friend, and you cannot punish me more to my vexation: but here is a Letter from my Lord to *Amphialus*, that will verifie me of the truth: Upon this *Helena* was brought to believe that felicitie to her, that she so long hath wished for, and caused vermilion Red to die her cheeks in preparation to receive their welcom Guest: and then her earnestness grew impatient of deferrings, she longing to prie into *Phylocleds* letters, therefore sealing up her lips from further questions, she directed *Clytifon* to *Amphialus*, and then she left him.

Amphialus in the mean time, whose bowels earned for *Clytifon's* return, listened to all whisperings. So then he seeing the Attendants so busie in their private discourses, he enquired whether *Clytifon* was come? just as he entered his presence. Then after due civilities passed between them, *Clytifon* delivered up his charge to *Amphialus*, who used many ceremonies before he would presume to touch it; but when he was better advised, he joyfully imbraced it, and by degrees he intruded upon it, for first he brake the seal, and then he made his protestation.

Now I do vow and promise before *Cupid*, whose dart hath so cruelly wounded me, and before *Venus*, to whose beautie I am so much a slave, never in the least to resist *Philocleds* lines; but I will shew my dutie to her by my willingness to obey her pleasure. And you my Lord *Clytifon*, with this Noble companie are witnesses of this my Protestation.

880   Thus concluded he his solemn vow, and then he carefully unfolded the treasure of his life, with a belief that every fold drew him nearer than other to Paradise: and when he read it, the curiousest eye could not espie the least motion of discontent to reside in him; but he rather seemed as a Conquerour that had suddenly surprised unlookt-for comfort, which much conduced to the joy of the beholders. And when he had fully delighted his eyes with *Philoclea's* gracious lines, he changed his note from admiring her perfections, to blazon his now amorous Phrases of *Helena's* worth; and then the sweet behaviour of *Helena* to him in his calamitie extended to his
890   memorie, which made him extreamly wonder at the hidden virtues of *Philoclea's* letters, for working so great a cure in his understanding: therefore now assuring himself the Gods had destined *Helena* to be his Spouse, in pursuance of their pleasure, and of his own happiness, he sent to her in an humble manner to entreat her companie. Which Message, poor Queen, she heard as joyfully, as she could have done, had *Mercury* posted from Heaven to bring her tidings of her transporting thither: but yet trembling possessed her delicate bodie, and would not leave her, before she had presented her self to *Amphialus;* who taking her by the white, yet shaking, hand, gratefully thanked
900   her for her many favours: and then telling her he should studie a requital, besought her to hear the letter that his Cosin *Philoclea* had honoured him with. But *Helena* answered with blushes, whilest he read the letter, thus,

For her highly-esteemed Cosin, the Lord AMPHIALUS.

Worthie Cosin,
Might I partake with the Gods in their interest in you, I would not be kept in such ignorance and amazement, as I am at this present; but I would throughly search what just occasions I have ever given you, to haz-

ard your person with such sad apprehensions of my anger, as I hear with-
out speedie remedie will deprive you of all future felicitie. But laying by 910
all that ambitious thought, in earnest, Cosin, I must needs tell you, how
without comparison it troubles me, that you should think me so severe
and unnatural, to torment you with a second death, for that fault,
which you have by so many evident signs manifested your self to be inno-
cent of, and if you had been guiltie as you are not, I should rather choose
to mitigate your crime, than any way to heighten it. But yet I will not
profusely let slip that advantage, which you have so freely left to my dis-
cretion, but will use it as an ornament to make you happie, yet not in
way of authoritie, but as a Petitioner I humbly crave of you not to refuse
Beautie and Honor when it is so virtuously presented to you by the 920
famous Queen Helena, *whose love-lines surpasses all others.*

Therefore if you esteem of me, prove it by entirely loving of her, who, I
am sure, will endow you with all such blessings as may enrich your con-
tentment. And now with full satisfaction, that you will grant me my
request, I close up these abrupt lines, and am immoveably,

Your faithfull Cosin and Servant,
PHILOCLEA.

Here the sweet *Philoclea* ended, and *Amphialus* with a low congee
began to speak to *Helena* in this manner: Fair Queen, what excuse I
shall make for my long incivilitie to your singular self, I know not, 930
nor can I imagin with what confidence to beg of you the perfecting
of these compassionate lines; therefore for pitie sake accept of my
cast-down eyes for my Soliciters, and let your goodness plead for my
backwardness in submitting to that duty of love to you, when the
greatest Princes tremble at your sight, and worship you as their
Image. Madam, suffer your Answer may be pitifull, since I acknowledge mine error.

My Lord, replied *Helena*, there is no cause given here to induce
you to renew your grief, if my yielding my self to your noble disposal
may be valued as a sufficient satisfactory Argument to ease you, that 940
hath ever been my endeavor in all virtuous ways to compass.

The more may be imputed to my unworthiness, answered *Amphialus;* now I am surprized with shame in having so dull an apprehension, such a stony heart to refuse so rare a Person as your divine self; but the Gods are just, for now the wheel of Fortune is turned, and if you please to revenge your wrong upon me the instrument, you cannot stab me with a sharper spear, than your denial.

Why, said *Helena,* do you force me to repeat my real affections to you so often? is it your jealousie of my constancie? if it be that, with thanks to my Goddess *Diana,* I avouch, that I never harboured the least unchast thought to scandalize or blemish my puritie.

Now I may challenge you, replied *Amphialus,* for searching out new sorrows to your self; but pardon me dear Madam, for my rash presumption with chiding you for one fault, when I my self am burdened with so many, and beleeve me, my highest ambition is to hear your heavenly voice sound out the Harmonie of your love within mine ears; and when you vouchsafe me that, none can paralel with me in happiness.

Thus they passed away the day with these, and afterwards more fond expressions; and amongst them they concluded to make a journey into *Arcadia,* & for the greater Triumph, to celebrat their nuptials with the other renowned Princes, now in the height of their superfluous complements, the news of the happy success of *Philoclea's* Letter had so spread about, that such abundance of the Citie flocked to the Palace to see *Amphialus,* that *Helena* was forced to command the Officers, not to let any have admission, until some important business, they were to consult upon, might be accomplished; and then she promised free Passage to all: This caused every one to retire to their houses, and *Helena* and *Amphialus* after a while spared some time to advise with *Clytifon* to consider of the probablest way for them to go into *Arcadia;* the people of *Corinth* being in great expectation of their solemnizing the wedding there.

Then *Clytifon* counselled them on this manner. The surest way that I can think on is, to lay open your real intentions to the Peers of your Land, that by degrees, it may be published to the Vulgar; also declare that you will not yield to any thing that may prove to their prejudice; but if they will not receive that as satisfactory, but argue that it is a disparagement for their Country to suffer their Princess to depart from thence, and be transported into another, to have her marriage finished; you may easily prevent their future dislike of that particular; since the dishonour of your Countrey concerns you most; and in all reason you should have the most especial care to preserve it; you may please them with telling them, you do intend to make your Kingdom famous by the splendor of those Princes that now reside in *Arcadia;* and then you will solemnize your wedding with the same points that you use when you are there: and I am perswaded their dissentions will be quieted.

The Counsel of *Clytifon* was no way rejected, but very well esteemed by the Royal lovers, who shewed their thankfulness by the large Theams they made of their judgements to him: and then telling him, that they must still be more obliged to him, they entreated him to let his return to *Arcadia* be a little sooner than theirs, to give the Princely family intelligence of their following after; because they were yet in their private lodge, it would not be commodious for them to come unto them unawares. *Clytifon* replied, That none should do that Service but himself; then *Amphialus* told him it was high time for him to make good his words, for Queen *Helena*, and his own intention was to be at *Matenia* suddenly; thus after a few more speeches passed, *Clytifon* took his leave, and dispatched away with all expedition.

In the mean time *Helena* gallantly played her game; for at the immediate time of *Clytifon's* departure from *Corinth*, she proclaimed free Liberty for her Subjects access unto her: then *Amphialus* and she being arrayed in glorious Apparel, removed from their with-drawing Rooms into the Presence, and there seated themselves in the Throne: their Nobles coming to them in their ranks, and kissing both their hands, rendered in all lowly manner their joy for their Queens

carefull choice, in making so brave a Prince their high Lord. Then
Helena declared her mind to them as *Clytifon* advised her, which at
first startled them, but she argued in her own defence so wisely, that
she quickly confuted and pacified those disturbers. But after them
came Knights, Gentlemen, Citizens, in such abundance, that they
confined the Princess to their patience for a Week together. Besides,
the Countrey Peasants, and all sorts of Mechanicks, that with admiration pressed to gaze upon them. But when their tedious task was
over, they spent some time in pleasing their fancies with the contrivance of stately curiosities, for the honour of their Nuptials. *Amphialus* and *Helena* concurring so well together, that nothing was
commended by the one, but instantly it was highly approved of and
valued by the other. Which combining of these, was a rare example
for the under-workmen, they endeavouring to follow their Supe-
riours Rule, delighting in these fellows judgements, did to the lovers
joy, unexpectedly finish their Art.

Then all accommodations being prepared in a readiness, they
departed from *Corinth*, their pomp being thus ordered, Three Chariots drawn by six horses apiece, came whirling to the gate, the first
was for six Noble men being of *Amphialus* his Bedchamber. That
Chariot was lined with green Figerd-velvet, richly fringed; signifying
the Princes loves. The Horses were black; to manifest their mourning for being so long exiled from their loves. The next Chariot was
lined with white Sattin, embroidered with gold, that was to witness
their innocencie, their love being virtuous: in that went six Ladies,
attendants upon *Helena*. The third and last was for *Helena* and
Amphialus, that was lined with blue, embroidered with Pearls and
pretious Stones, the Horses wore plumes of Feathers; the Coachman, Postilian, and six Footmens liveries were blew, as an Emblem
of their constancie, and embroidered as the Chariot was. On this triumphant manner they went to *Arcadia*, besides an innumerable
companie of Coaches and Hors-men that belonged to the Court;
which keeping on a moderate pace, in short time safely set footing

there: and the flying report, that would not be stoped for any mans pleasure, quickly gave notice to the Princes of *Helenas* and *Amphialus* being come.

But they had before removed to their Palace, being in perpetual expectation of their companie: and to shew how glad they were to enjoy it, *Musidorus* and *Pamela*, with *Pyrocles*, going altogether in a Coach, went out a good distance from the Citie to meet them: which they could hardly compass to do, by reason of the multitudes that went to see that magnificent Sight; until they had appointed Officers to beat a Lane: so that at last they made a narrow passage. It was an incomparable Sight to see *Helena* and *Amphialus* greet *Philoclea?* what low congies they made to her, as if she had been their Goddess! whilest she courteously reverenced them again. Then *Helena* and she stood admiring one anothers Beautie, till *Amphialus* had saluted the other Princes, and yet returned soon enough to break their silence. Ladies, said he, there is no occasion given to stir up sadness in Rebellion against mirth & happiness, for here we may see Love coupled together, when we have known by experiments it to have been dispersed by many strange accidents. And most sweet Princess *Philoclea*, by your gracious lines I am preserved from perpetual miserie, to enjoy a Crown endowed with all felicitie. But yet, Madam, all that I can do or say in requital, is to let you know that I am and ever shall be, your humble Servant.

I beseech you Cosin, replied *Philoclea*, do not your self that injurie, to confess you were thrust forward to your contentment. And seriously, when I obtained a sight of this rare Queen, I was astonished at your former backwardness. But since *Cupid* did play his part so cunningly as to make you blind, I am extream glad that I could be an instrument worthie to recover your decayed eyes and languishing spirits; and I am beholding to your goodness in obeying my request. Here *Philoclea* ended; and *Amphialus* was furnished with a Replie.

When *Musidorus* brought in *Pamela* to *Helena*, whom she civilly welcomed to *Arcadia;* but upon *Amphialus* she looked aloft, as not deserving to be regarded by her. Which *Musidorus* perceiving, he secretly perswaded her to look favourably upon him. Whose advice was received by her as a command that she durst not withstand. So she altering her disdainfulness into chearfulness, bent her discourse to *Amphialus*, that at last they grew excellent companie for one another, and so continued; till their thoughts were taken up with amazement at sight of *Clytifon*, who came hallowing to them; and with signs pointed to them to hast into their Chariots. But they not understanding his meaning, delayed their speed, till he came nearer, and certified them that there was a Messenger come from *Plangus* to *Evarchus*, but he would not be perswaded to deliver his business, before *Musidorus* and *Pyrocles* were present.

This newes strook *Pamela* and *Philoclea* into an extremity of sadness; for then *Plangus* storie was renewed into their memorie, which made them suspect it was some envious errand to separate their affections; but their beloved Princes used all perswasions that might comfort them, and then led them to *Amphialus* Chariot, that being the largest, and in that regard the most convenient; they being too full of perplexity to minde matters of State, went altogether, that they might the better passe away the time with company.

Then in a distracted manner they went to *Matenea*, and quietly passed through the Streets till they came to the Palace, where they had much ado to enter, by reason of the throng that was there making enquiries after the *Armenian* Messenger; yet at last the Princess obtained entrance; where *Helena* and *Amphialus* were with all respect welcomed by *Basilius* and *Genecea:* and when many Complements were consummate, they all went to the Presence, where *Evarchus* and the Messenger were. Then *Evarchus* told them there was a business of consequence to discover, and he wished them to give audience to it; Then all noise being appeased; the Messenger turning to *Evarchus*, said these following words.

Most renowned King; Prince *Plangus*, Generall of your forces in *Armenia*, hath sent me to recount unto your Majestie the truth of his proceedings since his departure from *Macedon;* which if your Majestie please to heare, I shall in a little time bring it about to his present Condition. Know then, Gracious Sir, Prince *Plangus* had hardlie set footing in the *Armenian* Land, before he was surprised by the unfortunate News of his Ladie *Eronds* being delivered up into the power of her Tyrannical enemies. You may imagine what discouragement this was to him at his first entrance, to be almost deprived of his chiefest victory: but yet he hid his grief, shewing his undaunted spirit to his Armie; he doubled their march, and at length overtook the Forces of the deceitfull *Plaxirtus,* and with losse of a few men, he so disordered them, that he and all his Armie marched through the middest of our Adversaries, whilst they like frighted men stood gazing on us; yet we not altogether trusting to our safeties, to their amazement, placed a reasonable company in Ambush to hold them play, if they should venture to fall on us; and we having Intelligence that *Plaxirtus* himself was but a mile before us, attended by a small Guard, because of his Confidence in his forces that were behind him, pursued him: & he not doubting but that we were of his confederacie, turned back his Horse, and staid that we might overtake him, thinking thereby to do us a favour: but Prince *Plangus* not having patience to see him so well pleased, galloped towards him; which *Plaxirtus* seeing, and knowing his own guilt, begain to distrust that then he should receive a due reward; and then he cryed out, Are we freinds? Are we freinds? but Prince *Plangus* riding to him, clasped him about the wast, and gallantly threw him off his horse, and then answered him, That he should be always his freind to do him such courtesies as they were; which the Guard hearing, they shewed us that they were expert in running, though not in fighting, for in a moment they were all fled away: then Prince *Plangus* having his greatest Adversary at his feet, and studying the most convenient way to fulfill your Majesties desire, to preserve him alive, till he might be more openly put to death: just than a Trumpeter came to him from *Artaxia,* with a paper in his hand, which he delivered to *Plaxirtus,*

1110

1120

1130

1140 wherein *Artaxia* declared, That her Cosin *Plangus*, whom she entertained civilly in her Court, was risen in Arms against her, and had
brought Forreigners to invade her Land; and that he had not onely
forgotten her former kindness to him, but also broken the laws of
Nature, she being his neer kinswoman; and not onely with her, but
also with her dear and lawfull Husband *Plaxirtus*, whom he had
taken and made a Prisoner; and she further declared, That whatsoever cruelty be inflicted upon *Plaxirtus*, she would do the like, or
worse to *Erona*. And if he did not quickly send her a satisfactorie
Answer, she would begin with *Erona* first, and make her endure the
1150 greatest torments that she could possibly, and live.

This put Prince *Plangus* into a world of confused cogitations? for
very unwilling he was to let go unrevenged the bloudy contriver of
these Princes supposed murder: and if he did not in some degree
yield to that, then his beloved Lady *Erona* must suffer those intollerable tortures. But when he was in the height of passion, to think that
from a victor he must become Slave, we might perceive a Traveller
guided to us by some of the Souldiers. At that sight Prince *Plangus*
entreated the Trumpeter to stay till he had known the meaning of
the strangers coming. He was your happy Messenger, O King, that
1160 delivered the Queen *Erona* from miserie. He it was that brought the
joyful news of the safetie of these famous Princes to perplexed Prince
Plangus. And that so well revived him, that after he had worshipped
Apollo for such an unlookt-for blessing, he chearfully dispatcht away
the Trumpeter with his answer, that now the Treacherie of *Plaxirtus*
was brought to nought, for *Pyrocles* and *Musidorus* were miraculously preserved, and lived to be examples of virtue: and if she would
stand to the former Articles, *Plaxirtus* should be set at libertie, now
the renowned Princes want your assistance in defence of the Ladie
Erona, whose life is now in your power; for by me *Plaxirtus* and
1170 *Anaxius* challenge you to answer them in a Combat for the distressed
Queen, and if you prove victorious over them, the same day *Erona*
shall be freed from her imprisonment: but if the contrarie side pre-

vail, at that time *Erona* must be put to death. These are the Articles before agreed upon, and now the second time resolved on. If you will hazard your Persons in the Quarell, the whole Kingdom of *Armenia* being in expectation of your valour, that may end the differences.

Thus the Messenger concluded, and *Pyrocles* and *Musidorus* sent him back to *Armenia,* with promise of their speedie following after him. It would have made a Rock, had it been by, burst out in tears in reference to the companie. And had *Narcissus* been never ravished with his own conceited beautie, yet had he been there, he would have wept into fountains, to see the best of Princes turmoiled in waves of affections: And Fortune deluding them, perswaded them they were near refreshment, when they were environed with their chiefest calamities. Here you might see *Pamela* with her Arms wreathed about *Musidorus,* as if she intended there should be her rest, till he had granted her request, & her cast-down eyes and weepings that bedewed her pure cheeks did witness her abundant sorrow. But at last, wiping them away, she contested with *Musidorus* and her self on this manner:

Dear *Musidorus,* do not part from her to whom you have so often plighted your faith. If you love me, as you vow you do, why will you abandon my presence? oh do not break my heart with your inconstancie, nor stain your other virtues with such a crime, as never can be washt away; therefore stay, or else confute me with your reason, and then I shall hate my passion, and contemn my self, for valuing my interest in your affections above the main treasure, so accounted by the heavenly and earthly societie, in keeping an honourable and unblemished reputation; which if you can do, and yet leave me, I will never shew my self such a ridiculous lover as to be your hinderance. My thrice dearer than my self, replied *Musidorus,* do not afflict me with the word Inconstancie; if I were guiltie, then might you justly tax me with it. But far be the thought of infidelitie from me: and believe me Ladie, *Plaxirtus* cannot pierce his sword deeper into my heart, than these sharp words, which proceeded from your sweet lips have done. But for my Combat in *Armenia*, that is so necessarie, that none can decide the Quarrel, unless it be my Cosin *Pyrocles* and my self, by reason of *Artaxia* & *Plaxirtus* thirsting for our lives, they will never suffer *Erona* to be released from prison, before they have vented their malice upon us, in as great a measure as their abilitie can give them leave. And besides, should I refuse, it would redound so extreamly upon my renown, that every one would be readie to object, that since a Woman prevailed over me, I am directly cowardized. And now, dear Ladie, I dare presume you will rather let me venture my life in defence of so just a cause, than to let it go unrevenged to my deserved infamie.

Poor *Pamela* all this while seemed like one in a trance, not having power to contradict *Musidorus* in his pleadings, nor yet able to submit her yielding to them; but made her tears and sighs her advocates, when he with all perswasions sought to comfort her. And in the mean time the sweet *Philoclea*, who lay grovelling at her *Pyrocles* feet, and would not be removed, expressed her grief in these mournfull complaints.

Ah me! said she, that I should be born under such an unfortunate Planet of unhappie events that dayly afflict me! tell me, my *Pyrocles* the cause that makes you so willingly hazard your person in such dangerous attempts? if you can tax me with any errors, to my self unknown, that might work your displeasure, O tell me what they are that I may mend, and studie some easier waw to punish me than by your intended death. But if nothing else may reconcile me to you, yet shew your clemencie, and let your own blessed hand first end my miserie.

Here she stopped, and perceiving *Pyrocles* to be in as amazed condition as she her self was, not knowing what to do or say to appease her sorrow, she premeditated, that now or never was her time to keep him with her in safetie, and then she suddenly arose from the ground, and standing a while in great devotion, at last she cried out;

Now am I readie to receive thy harmless Spear into my heart, now shew thy love & pitie to me quickly, and preserve me not alive to   1240 endure such terrour as cannot be charmed away, unless you will promise me the enjoyment of your companie. But *Pyrocles* started up, and catching her in his arms, adviced her not to give way to sorrow, the hater of Beautie, to rule over her; nor yet to mistrust she ever offended him, but that she was more pretious to him than the world could be; and that he made no question but that he should return again from *Armenia* to enjoy her with peace and happiness.

With these and many more such expressions, he strived to chear her up. But she still kept on bewailing her ill fortune, and would not be pacified: untill *Musidorus* came to her and entreated her to go to   1250 her Sister *Pemela*, and to shew her discretion by moderating her passion, that she might be a motive to reduce her Sister to follow her example, who now lay weltering in her tears. These tidings perswaded her to defer her own cares, that she might in some measure work a cure in her sister, whom she valued, next to her *Pyrocles*, above all the world. And then she would not delay the time with bemoaning herself, but hastily went her way supported by the two illustrious branches of the forest, *Pyrocles* and *Musidorus*.

But as she went there represented to her view the two antient Kings, *Evarchus* and *Basilius* walking to and fro like shadows, and   1260 looked as they would have done, had one come out of the Grave to warn them to prepare themselves in short time to come to them. This doleful sight had like to have prevailed over her, and made her fall into a Relapse of passion; but the rememberance of the task she was going about suppressed those vapours. And being come within the sight of *Pamela*, whose deluge was stayd a little to pause, that it might issue more freshly and eagerly at *Philocleas* presence, whom as soon as she espied, she perceived her hidden discontent, and rebuked one this manner.

1270   Sister, think not your dissembling smiles can entise me to follow your example, for I can as perfectly see through you into your grieved heart, as if you were transparent, and know your pain that now you endeavour to conceal. Oh! leave these counterfeits, and you will be a farr more acceptable comforter unto me.

Poor *Philoclea* could no longer withstand the batteries of *Pamela*, but confessed her forced mirth, and then instead of asswaging, they augmented one anothers sorrows with such lamentable moans, that *Pyrocles* and *Musidorus* were forced to give way to Sighs, till their thoughts were surprised by the coming of *Clytifon*, who brought
1280   them word, that the two Kings stayed at the door to speak with them. Then they softly went out of the Chamber, and were received by *Basileus* and *Evarchus*, who told them, that since it stood so much upon their Honours to endeavour to redeem that distressed Ladie, they advised them not to linger in the performance of it, for nothing was in their way to cause any delay, and the sooner they went, the sooner by *Apollo's* assistance they might return: To whose mercie they recommended them, and commanded them, that when they had obtained a prosperous journey, and had vanquished their ene- mies, not to be negligent in sending them word of it, that they
1290   might be sharers in their joy as well as their sorrow. Then after both the Kings had made them happie with their blessings, they sent them away.

Though first *Pyrocles* and *Musidorus* would needs take a review of their Ladies Pavilion, but not of their Persons, out of consideration that it would but double their affliction: and then reverencing the carpet on which they used to tread, they took their leave of the des- olate Chamber, and did resolve to travel alone. Had not *Kalodolus*, *Musidoru's* faithful Servant, made a vow that no occasions should perswade him to leave his master again; so that *Musidorus*, seeing
1300   there was no remedie, yielded to his desires. Nor could *Amphialus* noble heart well brook to stay behind, for oftentimes he entreated

them that he might go a second for them, or else a servant to them. But they answered him that he could not do them better Service than to accompany his Cosins, and make much of them in their absence: then, after they had accomplished some more Complements, they parted, *Amphialus* to his charge, and the Princes commited themselves into the hands of wavering Fortune. Who having already shewed them her frowns, would now pleasure them with her smiles, which first she discovered by conveying them safely to *Armenia*, where they were wellcomed unanimosly by all, but especially by 1310
Plangus, who could hardly confine his joy within the bounds of reason.

But the Princes being mindfull of his busines, desires *Plangus* to hasten their Combat, because their Ladies were in a despairing condition of ever seeing them again, and they assured him they did not fear to enter within the compass of *Plaxirtus*, so long as it was by the publick agreement, and not by secret practices. *Plangus* certified them that all things were prepared for their accommodation, and that they might, if they pleased, exercise their valour upon their enemies the next morning. And that two Scaffolds were erected, the one 1320
for *Artaxia*, she intending to be a Beholder, the other for *Erona*, who is to be brought thither guarded as a Prisoner, and in her sight there is a Stake in readines to consume her, if they be overcome. This last he uttered in such mournful expressions, that *Pyrocles* and *Musidorus* vowed to spend their hearts bloud, but that they would release & deliver *Erona* from the power of *Artaxia*.

And before they would refresh themselves with *Plangus* entertainments, they dispatched a Trumpeter to *Plexirtus* and *Anaxius* to certifie them, they were come to answer their challenge, and had set apart the next morning for that purpose: the Trumpeter soon 1330
returned with this reply, that the sooner it was, the more advantagious it would prove to them, and they would not fail to meet them at the place and time appointed. Thus they agreed upon the next

morning; and when the Prince had partaked of *Plangus* Supper, they yielded to sleep, which forsook them not till the promised time was near at hand.

Early in the morning *Plaxirtus* and *Anaxius* puffed up with Pride, and not questioning but that they should be Conquerours, put on their Armour, and mounting their steeds, galloped to the List. And 1340 *Artaxia*, thinking to vent her spleen with gazing at the overthrow of the Princes, came to the Scaffold attired in all her costly and glorious apparel, and with as great a Train as she would have had, were she to have been spectator of her Husbands Coronation, King of *Armenia*.

Within awhile was *Erona* brought guarded by a Band of Souldiers to her Scaffold, where she might see the end of her miserie by the Fire, or otherwise by *Pyrocles* and *Musidorus* victorie: but she, being wearied out of her life by sundrie afflictions, looked as gladly upon the fiery Stake, as she did upon her famous Champions who were then entered the list, and waving their swords about their heads; 1350 *Pyrocles* encountred *Anaxius* and *Musidorus Plaxirtus*. Then entered they into so fierce a fight, that it goes beyond my memorie to declare all the passages thereof: but both Parties shewed such magnanimity of Courage, that for a long time none could discern who should be victors. Till at length *Musidorus* gave a fatal thrust to *Plaxirtus*, who being before faint with loss of bloud, fell from his Steed, and in the fall clasht his Armour in pieces; and then his Steed, for joy that he was eased of such a wicked burden, pranced over his disgraced master, and not suffering him to die such an honourable death as by *Musidorus* Sword, trampled out his guts, while *Plaxirtus*, with curses 1360 in his mouth, ended his hateful life.

Then *Pirocles* redoubled his blows so eagerly upon *Anaxius*, that he could no longer withstand them, but gnashing his teeth for anger, he fell at *Pyrocles* feet and died. Thus pride and Treacherie received their just reward.

But then *Artaxia's* glory was turned into mourning, and her rich attire into rags, as soon as she perceived *Plaxirtus* wounded, his bloud gushing out, his Horse treading on him, and he himself dying with bitter groans and frantick speeches, which he breathed out at his last moment for fear of further torments: she tare off her hair, and rent her cloths in so enraged a manner, that she drew all eyes from the corps in wonder and amasement on her. Nor could any thing regulate her furie, but she violently run down to the corps, and there breathed out her complaints.

In which time *Plangus* called his Souldiers together, and went up to the other scaffold to release *Erona;* though at first he was forced to make a way with his sword, the Guard resolving not to surrender her, till they had received a further command from *Artaxia:* but *Plangus* made them repent their strictness, and ask *Erona* pardon for it. And after he was revived with a warm kiss from her hand, he led her down to *Pyrocles* and *Musidorus:* Who having forgot the former injuries *Artaxia* had done them, courteously perswaded her not to bemoan him, whose memorie was reprochfull to all the world, for valuing his one deceitfulness above virtue; and then they told her, it would be more for her renown, to solemnize for him such obsequies as are seeming for a Prince, he being of the race, although he learned not to follow their example; and then to proclaim her sorrow for joyning with him in his mischief. Many more speeches they used to her, some to abate her grief, & others to asswage her malice; but at first she would listen to none; yet afterwards being better advised, she sent for two magnificent Hearses, and before she would suffer *Plaxirtus* his corps to be laid in, she pronounced her resolution on this manner:

Since it hath pleased *Apollo*, who hath the Government of all things on earth, to suffer *Plaxirtus* to fall by your prowess, I do here by this dead bodie vow to you, to end my life in Widowhood. And you Cosin *Plangus*, whom I have so infinitely wronged with this fair Ladie *Erona*, to you I do resign up the Authoritie of my Kingdom, being, after my decease, the lawfull Successour. I shall desire only a competencie to keep me from famishment: but if these your valiant

1370

1380

1390

1400 Champions will have you go to *Arcadia*, to finish your Marriage there, in that time I will be your trustie Deputie, to order your affairs here in *Armenia*, until you return from thence. Then she commanded the corps to be laid in the Hearse, and taking leave of the Royal companie, she went along with it.

Now the Princes had time to take notice of *Erond's* sadness. And *Plangus*, who had been all this time courting her to be his Mistress, could obtain no favour from her, but far-fetcht sighs, and now and then Chrystal drops distilling from their fountains. These apparent signs of her disconsolate mind, grounded a great deal of cares in the 1410 hearts of the Princes, who bending all their endeavours to insinuate *Plangus* into her affections, they first sifted her with these Questions; Whether her being preserved from the crueltie of *Plaxirtus*, was the cause of her discontentment? or whether, she grieved for her deliverance? and therefore hated them for fighting in her defence? These Questions put *Erona* into such Quondaries, that she could not, for a while, determin what to answer. But at last she pitcht upon true sinceritie, and freely displayed her griefs to them, in these terms:

Do not, I beseech you, plead ignorance of that which is so palpable. Have you not heard how they tortured my Husband *Antifalus* to 1420 death? why then do you renew it in my memorie? which might have been prevented if you, Prince *Plangus*, had shewed your realitie to me, as you protested you would by Policie set him at liberty, but all was neglected and *Antifalus* was barbarously murdered, and yet you are not ashamed to presume upon my weakness, in pretending you are my Servant, that you may the second time deceive me. Longer she would have chidden *Plangus;* but that he falling down humbly begged she would have consideration upon him, and heare him. Then with silence she admitted him, and he declared, how that according to his promise made to her Sacred self, he did prosecute so 1430 faithfully, that he brought all things to a readiness, and might have been perfected, but that the timorous *Antifalus* discovered the whole Plot the same night it was to be put in execution. And this without

any scruple, he would take his oath was true. *Erona* considered very much of this saying of *Plangus:* and *Pyrocles* and *Musidorus* watching their opportunity, just as she was replying, interrupted her, and told her they were confident she might give credit to what *Plangus* had spoken; and if she durst rely upon their advice, they would recommend him to her for her Husband, as soon as the greatest Monarch in the world. These Princes seconding *Plangus* in his excuses, mitigated *Erona's* pensivenes, so that cheerfully she yielded her self to be   1440
at *Pyrocles* and *Musidorus* disposing: for, said she, I am bound by so many Obligations to you, that I cannot suffer my requitall to be a refusall. Onely I desire that Prince *Plangus* may approve the truth of his words with an Oath, as he himself hath propounded. Which he willingly did upon that condition, and she accepted of him as her betrothed Husband. And *Cupid* by degrees so skillfully drew her affection to him, that she was as firmly *Planguses*, as ever she was *Antifaluses* to the abundant joy of all their friends.

Now *Pyrocles* and *Musidorus* imployments being in every particular accomplished as well as could be wished, They remembring the   1450
charge of *Evarchus* to them; together with the cares of their sorrow-full Ladies, they presently sent a Post to *Arcadia* to signifie the news of their safety: but yet there remained the care of dispatching their Armie into their native Countrey *Macedon.* And as they were conferring which way they might compass that matter of such consequence quickly, *Kalodolus* being at the counsel put in his verdict, which was liked very well, and instantly put in practice; for he having a special friend in whom he very much confided, he advised that he might be trusted to be General in *Plangus* room, that they might orderly go home, and after they were payd their due, to dismiss them   1460
and let them go to their own Houses.

When all this was performed: they commanded all conveniences to be prepared for their own accomodation about their return to *Arcadia;* but for curiosities they would not stay for them, but limited a day for their departure. In which time *Erona* imployed her

inventions about a Present for *Pamela* and *Philoclea*, which she was verie ambitious of, they being the mistresses of *Musidorus* and *Pyrocles*, to whom she acknowledged her self infinitely engaged; and without delayance, she set all her Maids to work the Story of their
1470 love, from the fountain to the happy conclusion: which by her busie fancie she shadowed so artificially, that when it was perfected, and she had shewed it to the Princes, they vowed that had they not known by experience those passages to have been gone and past, they should have believed they were then in acting in that piece of workmanship.

Now all the work was ended, their necessaries were in a readiness, fair and temperate weather bespake their fuller happiness. All these so well concurring, enticed the Princes to begin their journey. And Fortune, dealing favourably, conducted them safely and speedily to
1480 the *Arcadian* Court. Where they were received with such joy by their Consorts, and Parents especially, and by all in general, as it would make two large a storie to recount all their discourses with their affectionate expressions that passed between the Royal lovers. Passing by all other, give me leave to tell you, it was a prettie sight to see the four Ladies, *Pamela* and *Philoclea*, with *Helena* and *Erona*, admiring one anothers perfections, all of them having the worst opinions of themselves, and the better of their neighbours. Therefore to decide the controversie, *Philoclea* entreated her *Pyrocles*, to make a motion to *Musidoru's*, *Plangus*, and *Amphialus* to spend their
1490 judgements upon them. *Pyrocles* immediately obeyed her; but esteemed best of their own mistresses.

Pyrocles liked *Philoclea* best, became her sparkling eyes, pure complection, and sweet features were crowned with such modest courtesie, that she ravished all her Beholders, and perswaded them they were in Paradise, when they were in her heavenly Angel-like companie, Earth not affording her fellow.

Musidorus avouched, his fair *Pamela* was always clad with such a Majestie, as bespake her a Queen in spite of the Destines; yet that

Majestie was so well composed with Humility, that it seemed but an out case to a more excellent inward virtue. 1500

Then came *Plangu's* turn, who said that in his judgement, *Erona* deserved to be extolled in the highest measure, for though her splendor was something darkened by her sadness and sufferings, yet under that veil her brightness did appear to shoot forth beams of goodness to every one that did approch her Presence.

Amphialus was last, who protested there could not be a lovelier creature than *Helena* was, so adorned with all gifts of Nature, that he verily believed if she had tempted *Adonis*, as *Venus* did, he could not in the least have denied her. And he assured himself, that by the determination of the Gods, they being in love with her themselves, 1510 *Cupid* had strook him blind, that in the mean time they might pursue their love; but seeing she was resolved to accept of no other but him, they for pitie sake opened his eyes: and now he was amazed at his former perverseness. This conceipt of *Amphialus* made the Ladies exceeding merrie. Till *Evarchus* came to them and spake thus:

Young Princes, I came now to remember you how often you have been by several accidents, frustrated of your desired Felicity: you see a little blast alters your happiness into a world of sorrows. Therefore harken to my counsel, whose gray hairs witness my better experience of the world than your green years. Do not linger away the time in 1520 Courtship: that is as bad as to be carelesly rash. Finish therefore the knot, that no crosses or calamities can unfinish, without further deferrings.

This command of *Evarchus*, did not at all displease the four Bridegrooms. Nothing hindered now but their agreeing about the day; and that made no long disputation neither, for two days following happened to be *Pamela's* Birth-day, and that they concluded should be the Bridal-day.

Now the night before these happy Nuptials, *Erona* presented *Pamela* and *Phyloclea* with her rare piece of work, which they received 1530 with thanks and admiration; and for the honour of *Erona* (she being the inventor of it) they caused it to be hung up by the Image of *Cupid* in the Temple, and after passed the night in quietness.

Early in the morning the Sun shot forth his glorious beams, and awakened the lovers. But when they were up, he hid himself a while within the waterie clouds, weeping that they were brighter Suns than he: yet when they were gaurded with their nuptial Robes, he dispersed the clouds again, and cleared his eyes, that he might with envie gaze upon their lustre; and the Brides without disdain yielded their beauties to his perusal. When the Middle-day had almost run his course to the After-noon, the four Bride-grooms imitating one another in their Apparel, were all in gray cloth embroydered with gold, richly clad, yet not fantastick; in their left hands they held their swords, but in their right their Brides.

First went *Musidorus* leading his fair Princess *Pamela*, whose comely behaviour and sweet sympathie, manifested her joy, that then *Musidorus* and she should be so united to live and die together. Upon her head she bare an imperial Diadem, which agreed comparatively to her stately mind. Her Garments were cloth of Tissue, that in a careless fashion hanged loose about her. And round her Neck she wore a Chain of Orient Pearl. Upon her Alabaster shoulders a blue Scarf was cast, that being whirled sometimes with the wind, did seem to blow her to *Hymens* Temple. Six virgin Nimphs attired in White attended on her. The two foremost perfumed the ayr as they went with their odiferous sweets; but that was superfluous, for *Pamela's* breath left a far more fragrant scent than the artificial curiosities could do; next to them followed two other Virgins with Holie-water in their hands, which they sprinkled as they went, to purifie all sinfull vapors; but that also was needless, for no harm durst come near the Virtuous *Pamela*, whose looks could charm even wicked Fiends: then the two last followed *Pamela*, bearing up her train. Thus was she guarded to the Temple with her beloved *Musidorus;* and after them went *Pyrocles* and *Philoclea*, *Plangus* and his *Erona*, and *Amphialus* with his *Helena*, all in the same order as *Musidorus* and *Pamela:* then the Priest united their hands, and as their hands, so their hearts together; and the former crueltie of *Fortune* was ever after turned into pitie.

The Temple where these Nuptial Rites were thus celebrated, was scituate in a garden, or rather a Paradise for its delightfulness; the murmuring of the waters that flowed from a Fountain at first entrance dividing, themselves into four streams, seeming to threaten, and yet enticing the comers to venter further; the Fountains bedecked with the Images of *Diana* and her Maids, the Goddess figured with an austere countenance, pointing to the lust-full *Venus*, whose Statue at a little distance stood, as she with lacivious actions endeavoured to entrap the modest Boy *Adonis*, but *Hymen* on the other side disputes, those whom his Priests unite, cannot be stiled *Venu's*, but *Diana's*. The perfumed flowers grew so thick in the direct way to the Temple, that they served for Carpets to consecrate the Mortals feet before they approched into it: the Temple was built of Marble; the out-sides adorned with Portratures of the Gods. *Fortune* was seated at the frontier of it, which at the least motion of the beholder, represented a several gesture. And all the Gods, in their degrees, sat presidents to the observers.

The inside was not so uniform as artificial, it winding into several circles in the passage to the sacred place: and all the way were emblems in Marble, of the calamities of Lovers before they can be set in *Hymens* Temple; many of them representing the Princes sufferings. The middle of the Temple is not so gorgeous as decent, where there met with the Princes, some of *Hymens* Officers attired in white robes trailing on the ground. These presented the Bride-grooms with Swords and Ballances, and their Brides with Lawrel; & when they had here sounded a sweet harmonie to *Hymen*, they went back from the Temple to the Court.

Where you may conjecture with what joy they were received by *Evarchus*, *Basilius*, and *Genecia*, they all pouring out their blessings upon them. Then passed they away the remainder of the day with all sorts of Musick, Dancing, and other varieties of mirth.

1570

1580

1590

Whilst a famous Mask was presenting in the greatest glorie to the view of the Princes, and an innumerable companie of noble Person- ages: *Mopsa*, sole heir to *Damatas*, who was by *Basilius* favour, the Princess *Pamela's* Governour, when she resided in the Lodge, went to *Philoclea*, and wrying her neck one way and her mouth another, she squeazed out these ensuing words. Fair Princess, I intend not to for- get the promise you made me, when I told you a part of a curious tale, how you assured me your Wedding Gown, if I would afford to finish my Storie on that welcom day: but now the greatest part of the day is run away, and you are raised so high on your tip-toes, that you do not vouchsafe me to be in your books, but choose rather to gaze upon these strange sights, than to remember me, or your Gown. The sweet *Philoclea* could not forbear blushing to hear *Mopsa* reprove her so sharply; but to make her silent for the present, she renewed her promise, and *Mopsa* very impatiently stayed out the vanishing of their Scenes; which when *Philoclea* perceived, she smilingly led *Mopsa* by her hand into the middest of the Royal companie, where she left her to exercise her discretion; and withdrawing at a distance from her, she discovered to her Paramour *Pyrocles*, *Mopsa's* ambition, who immediately caused all noises to be hushed, that he might with the greater attention hearken to *Mopsa*, and observe all her actions though never so absurd. But *Mopsa* vallued not the laughter of her beholders, her little apprehension had alreadie seized on *Philoclea's* glittering Gown, and she imagined it hung upon her mothie Karkass; and in that firm perswasion she stood looking upon her self like a Peacock, untill *Pyrocles* called to her, which made her skip, and rub her eyes before she could discern her self to be yet in her rustie Feathers. Yet afterwards, playing with her hands, for the more grace; she brake forth into these ensuing words.

It seemeth best to my liking to rehearse the first part of my Storie in brief, that so ye may the better relish the Latter. There was a King, (the chiefest man in all his Countrey) who had a prettie Daughter, who as she was sitting at a window, a sprightlie Knight came to her, and with his dilly Phrases won her to be his own, and stealing out of her Fathers Castle, with many honey kisses, he conjured her not to enquire after his name, for that the water-Nimphs would then snatch him from her: howbeit one time, in a darksom wood, her teeth were set so on edge, that she asked, and he presently with a piteous howling vanished away. Then she, after she had endured such hardship as she never had endured in all her lifetime, went back to one of her Ants, who gave her a Nutt, charging her not to open it before she fell into extremitie; from her, she went to another Ant, and she gave her another Nut, counselling her (said *Mopsa*) in the same words that her first Ant had done before her, and so sent her packing: But she one day being as wearie as my fathers black horse is, when he hath rode a good journey on him, sat her down upon a Mole-hil, and making huge complaints for her mishaps, a grisly old woman came to her, commanding her to open one of the Nuts; and she considering, that of a little medling cometh great ease, broke it open, for nothing venter, nothing have, which Proverb she found wondrous true; for within the shell she found a paper, which discovered that her Knight was chained in an ugly hole under ground in the same wood where she lost him. But one Swallow makes no summer; wherefore she cracked her other Nut, from whence there flew out gold and silver in such abundance, that the old Woman falling down upon her stumps, scrambled up her lap full, and yet left the joyfull maid her load: Need makes the old wife trot; nay, it made both the old and young to trot, and to lug away their bags of money: and when they came to a lane with twentie several paths, the old Woman took her leave of the Kings dainty Daughter, bidding her lay down the money, and it should guid her to her Knight: with that she laid it down, and the money tumbled the direct way before her.

At this passage *Mopsa* conceiting that she saw Mammons treasure so near her, opened her mouth, which was of a sufficient wideness, and wadled along as if she had been practizing to catch flies there: which if she had, the prisoners might have recreated their wings

1640

1650

1660

within their prison walls, they were so large. The princely Societie could not forbear simparing at *Mopsa's* ravishment, and had burst out into a publick mirth, had they not been surprized with a better object.

Which at first view appeared to be the Goddess *Flora* and her Nymphs, their addorning imitating hers, but when they drew near, they discerned their errors, it being *Urania,* a fair Shepherdess, who might be very well taken for *Flora;* for although it was impossible for her to excel the Goddess in beautie, yet without controlement, in *Pamela's* and *Philoclea's* absence she might paralel the most transcendent: on either side of this *Urania,* there walked the two Shepherds, *Strephon* and *Claius,* with their eyes fixed on her in celestial admiration: their countenances resembled despair more than hope, and earnestness more than confidence: these addressed themselves unto the Princess, leaving the prettie Sheperdess at a short distance with her companions, who in Troops attended her; and prostrating themselves at their feet, they burst out into bitter tears.

Musidorus, who was then raised to the height of temporal blessings, disdained not to acknowledge them to have been the Founders of his happiness, repeating in publick, how they had preserved him from the dangers of the Seas: but *Claius* and *Strephon* could not suborn their weepings, but continued weltring in their tears, which astonished and strook a sadness into the least relenting spirits; all being ignorant of the Accident, except *Musidorus,* who surmized the truth.

Now whilst they expected the issue, *Mopsa* laid hold on *Philoclea,* and with many a vineger look, besought her to hear out her Tale: and for fear she should be deprived of her Gown, without depending on a replie, she pursued her Storie in these her accustomed expressions. Leading her, said *Mopsa,* to the very Caves mouth, where her Knight vented a thousand grievous groans, then in her hearing, she might then joyfully sing, fast bind, fast find, for there the Witches bound him, and there his Sweet-heart found him, where they pleasured one another with their sugar-kisses; and after a good while, she unchained him and then they lovingly set them down and slept all night in the Cave, because haste maketh waste; but the next morning, she shewed him her monstrous vast sums of money, which so affrighted him, that he clinging his eyes fast together, was not able to say, Boh to a Goose hardlie: yet at last she perswaded him, and he peeped up, and waxed the merriest man upon earth when he had got himself free, and his Mistress again with such store of Riches: for then the old woman, that had advised the Kings Daughter to open her nuts, and to lay down the money, appeared to him, and released him of his Bondage by Witchcraft, for ever after: wherefore the Knight, and his own sweet darling went back to the Kings Court, as jocundly as could be, and with some of their money they bought them a brave Coach and Horses, just such as are in my fathers stable at home, and in such pomp they went to the King their Father, who entertained them bravelie, pleasing them with delicate sights, as Puppet-plaies, and stately Fairs; and their riches encreased daily, and they lived gallantly, as long as they had a jot of breath in their bodies.

Thus finished *Mopsa* her tedious Tale, which though it was very ridiculous, yet wanted it not applauses from all the Auditors: and *Philoclea* in requital, presented her with her Bridal Roabs, telling her, she deserved larger incouragements to elevate her wit; and more speeches she used in *Mopsà*s commendation, whose partial senses were subject to believe all such rare realities; in which blind opinion I will leave her;

To return to the disconsolate Shepherds *Claius* and *Strephon*, who when they had wept their passionate Fountains drie, they looked about with adoration upon the prettie *Urania*, as the reviver of their languishing hopes, and *Strephon* yielding to *Claius* the preheminence by reason of his years, he with great reverence to *Basilius* with the Bride-grooms and Brides,

1700

1710

1720

Thus spake; Dread Soveraign, and most Illustrious Princes, we beseech you not to reckon it among the number of misdemeanors, 1730 that we shadow the brightness of this Nuptial day with our clowdie Fortunes, since our aim is to disperse our envious mists, and to make it the more glorious by celebrating a Feast; and though our triumph cannot amount to such splendor as the four great Monarchs doth, whose flourishing Dominions can onely satisfie their gladness by their Princes pomp; yet harbour the belief (pardon me if I say amiss) that our Bride may equal yours in Beautie, though not in rich attire, and in noble virtues, though not in Courtly accoutrements; her Soul, the Impartial Diadem of her delicate Bodie, is certainly incomparable to all other of her sex, though heavenly. This Mistress of per-1740 fections is *Urania* the Shepherdess, she it is that causes my eyes to ebb and flow, my joynts to tremble at her looks, and my self to perish at her frowns; but I will not insist too much (upon your Highness patience) on this Subject, her self is an evident witness of all, and more than I have Charactered: and Gracious Sirs, as I am bound by all dutie and Allegiance to live under the servitude of my Lord *Basilius*, as well as under his protection: so am I not confin'd from gratefulness to such as will obliege me in this my prostrate condition, or in any extremitie; for the Destinies have allotted such cruel Fates to my Friend *Claius* and me, whose entire affections are never 1750 to be severed, that we both are slaves to *Urania's* pierceing Eyes! Oh we both are vassals to her devoted graces; yet so much do we esteem of our unfeigned Friendship that we will rather abandon all happiness, than to cause a discontent, or suspition of our real wishes of one anothers prosperitie; out of which intention, we submit to be ruled by the judgement of you, renowned Bridegrooms, whose prudence and justice is not to be swayed by any partialitie; to you it is that we do humbly petition, to distinguish which of us two may best deserve to be admitted into *Urania's* spotless thoughts, as her lawfull Husband.

Claius had not ceased his suit so suddenly, but that *Strephon* inter- 1760
rupted him thus abruptly:

Good *Claius*, bar the passage of thy tongue, and grant me libertie
to speak and ease my fierce torment: the reverence I bear to your
age, and my sinceritie to your person, permitted you to disburden
your fancie first, but not to deprive me of the same priviledge.
Know then, most excellent Princes, that this incomparable *Urania*,
(O her virtues cannot be expressed by humane creatures! for at the
very mentioning of her name my tongue faltered, and my self condemns my self for being too presumptuous, but yet this once we
strive against her powers that thus possesses me, and will not be per- 1770
swaded from telling you that) she is compounded so artificially, as
she cannot be paralleld nor described; for believe it, she is above the
capacitie of the most studious Philosopher: and do not harbour, I
beseech you, a prejudicial opinion of her, under the notion of her
entertaining two lovers at one instant, since it hath been always contrarie to her chast disposition, to accept of the least motion concerning a married life; and for Platonick Courtiers, her heavenly
modestie is a palpable witness of her innocencie. Besides the many
dolorous hours that my friend *Claius* and I have passed away, our
onely recreation we enjoyed being in recounting the careless actions 1780
she used when we declared our passions, and commending our
choice though she was cruel. But when this your happie day was
prefixed, she shot forth beams of goodness on us, and in charitie she
concluded, that her intentions were far from our destructions; and
since now she perceived our lives were in jeopardie, and we
depended onely upon her reply, she would no longer keep us in sus-
pence, but was resolved her Nuptials should be solemnized on this
day, following the example of the two Royal Sisters whom she ever
adored. And because she would not be an instrument to disturb that
knot of Friendship between *Claius* and me, she referred her choice 1790
to your wisdoms, worthie Sirs, the excellent Sisters Bride-grooms,

you it is whom she desires to pronounce either my felicitie, or my overthrow.

Then *Strephon*, closing his speech with an innumerable companie of long-fetcht sighs, departed to his Goddess *Urania*, who was environed by her fellow Shepherdesses, which in admiration, love, or envie stood gazing on her; but he pressed through the thickest of them to do homage to her sweet self, she looking on him carelesly, without either respecting or disdaining him.

1800   But aged *Claius* had cast himself at the Princes feet, where he pleaded for his own felicitie on this manner;

Consider my ancient years, and in compassion think how easily grief may cut off the term of my life; when youthfull *Strephon* may baffle with Love, and Court some other Dame, Ile finde him one who shal be as pleasing to his eyes, as *Urania* is in mine; unless the fates have raised him to be my victorious Rival. But alas, O tell me *Strephon!* did I ever injure thee, that thou seekest my untimely death? hast not thou ever been in my sight as a jewel of an unvalued rate? why dost thou then recompense me so unkindly? I know thou
1810   wilt argue, that the passion of Love with a Woman, and with such an one as *Urania* is, cannot be contradicted by the nearest relations. But I pray thee *Strephon*, cannot the importunities of me, thy Foster friend, regulate, nay asswage thy passions, to keep me from perishing? Now *Strephon*, when he had revived his drooping heart, with perusing the delicate *Urania*, and fearing that *Claius* was supplicating to *Pyrocles* and *Musidorus* for her, he returned back, happening to come at the minute when *Claius* questioned him; to whom he thus replied: What the Gods have appointed, cannot be prevented, nor quenched by the powerfullest perswasions of any Mortal: and let
1820   that suffice. *Claius* being so fully answered to his conjecture, rested silent to hear his sentence. *Strephon*, who was of a more sprightly constitution, recreated himself sometimes with glosing upon *Urania*, and then to observe the looks of the Princes as they were confer-

ring together, about what to determin on concerning them. Besides his Pastoral songs that he sounded in *Uranids* praise.

But the Princes, who were then in serious consultation, listened to *Basilius*, who advised them in this manner:

Despise not *Claius* his complaints, though he be afflicted with the infirmities of old age; youthfull *Strephon* may seem more real and pleasing to the eye, yet *Claius* his heart, I am confident, is the firmest settled; Youth is wavering, Age is constant; Youth admires Novelties, Age Antiquities. *Claius* hath learned experience by age to delight *Urania* with such fancies as may be suitable to her disposition; *Strephon's* tender years cannot attain to any knowledge, but as his own Genius leads him. Wherefore consider before you denounce your Sentence, whether *Urania* may not be *Claius's* Spouse better than *Strephon's*.

Pyrocles knowing that *Basilius's* aim was to plead in defence of Dotage, refrained to make any other reply than, What you command Sir, we must and will obey. For as he was both by Birth and Education a Prince, so had he not neglected to be instructed in the dutie of a Subject. Not that he was forced to acknowledge it to *Basilius's* as his due, any otherwise then as his goodness enduced him to; that he might be a pattern to draw the *Arcadians* to follow his example, they wholly determining to be ruled that day by *Pyrocles* and *Musidorus*, who after *Basilius's* decease was to be their successive King. And they were not ignorant of the intimacie between his Cosen *Pyrocles* and him; wherefore they reverenced and observed both their actions. But the Princes *Musidorus* and *Pyrocles*, to avoid the rumours of the People that thronged about them, to over-hear their resolution concerning the Shepherds, retired to an Arbour-walk, where none but the sweet societie of Birds attented them: there *Pyrocles* ripped open his supposition to *Musidorus*, which was to this effect.

My dear Cosen, said he, for of that honoured Title my memorie shall never be frustrated, dost thou not imagin *Basilius* guiltiness,

1830

1840

1850

when he pleads for dotage so extreamly? he hath not unburdened his conscience yet of his amorousness of me in my Amazons Metamorphosis: I know it stings him by the Arguments he supports. However he may cease his fears of my discovering his courtship, for I have always persevered in Allegiance and dutie to my Father, my King; nor do I doubt my failing now in those Principles, since I have you my worthie Cosen so near me. *Musidorus* embracing his Cosen, protested that he harboured the same fancie, and said he, the stammering of his words declared the certainty: but did you not admire the heavenly behaviour of my *Pamela* to day, when she ascended into the Temple, how her soul seemed to flie with her body to that sanctified place, as transported with entering into so holy an Habitation which was too sacred for any other but her self. And replyed *Pyrocles*, *Philoclea* might be admitted with her, whose Humility did seem to guard her, or else sure she had stumbled; so lightly did she set her feet upon the Pavement, lest she should profane it. And sometimes dropping Agonies did so surprize her, that she seemed to contemplate with divine mysterie; and then to look down upon her own unworthiness with such humbleness as made her most into tears, as it were for soaring above her elements. Whilst the Princes were discoursing in commendations of their Brides.

 Claius in the presence of *Basilius* and the remaining Princes, fell down and fainted. *Strephon* stood thumping his breast, and crying, O *Musidorus!* think upon us who succoured you, and let not a third Rival deprive us of the incomparable *Urania*. This unexpected passion of the Shepherd's, astonished the senses of all the beholders: yet none were so stupid as to neglect their serviceable care: yea *Urania* her self, though just before when *Pamela* and *Philoclea* sent and entreated her company, she had returned a modest refusal; yet now perceiving *Strephon's* and *Claius's* distress, she tarried not to hear the news by Harbingers, but went the foremost to relieve them: upon distracted *Strephon* she smiled, saying, Is *Fortune* thine enemie *Strephon?* but her voice sounded so harmoniously in his ears, that he disclaimed all sadness, promising himself the victorie. She then absented from him, that she might work as effectual and sudden a cure upon aged *Claius*, who gastfully lay foaming on the ground, yet that terrible sight was not so obnoxious to her as to oversway her compassion, she pinched and pulled him, endeavouring to restore his life again; but nothing would recover him, until she breathed on him with stooping near him, and pronouncing these words:

Unhappie *Claius*, whose life depends upon a woman! this once look up, & speak me blameless. Have not I ever abhord the thought of *Strephon* or your ruins? yes sure, I have, & have dallied with you both, apprehending eithers danger, if I should forsake one, and resign my self up to the others disposal; neither have I regarded the piping of the Shepherds, nor the songs of the Shepherdesses: and on Festival days, when they have elected me Queen of their Triumphs, I have excused my self, and retired into solitarie Groves, where I have spent the day in musing upon my Lovers desperate conditions, and studying for the probablest Antidotes that might cure their distempers, without blemishing mine own reputation. But that was so hard a task, that I could never accomplish it. *Claius* age could not endure such a penaltie as my denial without miscarriage: and *Strephon*'s working brain would not receive it without practicing a Tragedie upon himself. Wherefore I made patience my friend, and coyness my favourite, neither slighting, nor esteeming their large allusions of my Beautie and their Passion, which they oft repeated, until the reports of the consummating of the Princesses Nuptials were confirmed. And then I resolved, that as I abhorred murder, so I would no longer admit them into my companie, before the Priest of *Pan* hath united me to one of them, that then I might without derogating from my honour, by censorious suspitions, enjoy the societie of him whom the Princes shall select to be my wedded Husband. So indifferent is my choice of these two constant Friends, and unmoveable Servants.

Before *Urania* had finished these words, *Claius* in a rapture of joy, roused up his drowned spirits. And then *Urania* retired back to her fellow Sheperdesses; but the Princes were so inquisitive to know what accident had brought *Claius* and *Strephon* into such despairing Agonies, that they would not permit them to tender their service to *Urania* at her present departure, for desire of questioning them. *Strephon* made this quick replie; that a stranger presumed to gaze upon *Urania;* and his feet going as nimblie as his tongue, he tripped after her, not asking leave of the concours of People that thronged about him.

1930   But aged *Claius*, whose tongue was livelier than his feet, spake after this manner:

My greedie eyes, said he, being dazled with looking too long upon *Urania*, who is adorned with as glorious beams as *Phœbus* can boast in his brightest day; I yielded them respite, giving them leave to take a view of mortals, clearing their dimness with their equal light; but there I did espie an hautie Youth, who scoffingly stared upon me, seeming to call me insolent, for striving to purchace *Urania*, and conceiting himself to be worthier of her, he did so amorously seal his eyes upon her, that sundry times he made her paint her cheeks with
1940   harmless blushes: and my jealous fancie comprehending no other reason, than that as he obtained free access with his eyes, so he might with his person; I rendring my self into the hands of cruel death.

The Princess could no longer tollerate *Claius* in his ungrounded mistrusts, but interrupted him, by enforming him that *Basilius* had sent for *Musidorus* and *Pyrocles;* the Messenger happening to come at the immediate time when they were extolling their Mistresses; but then they left off that subject till a more convenient hour, and applied their Answer to the Intelligencer, promising to follow speedilie: yet contrarie to their resolutions, they lingred in the way, a doal-
1950   full voice perswading them to stand and hearken, which sounded out these words.

Faire *Titan*, why dost thou deride me with thy smiles, when I do homage to thy resplendent beams! and you pleasant Bells, why do ye not compel your notes to ring me to my Funeral? for since she is tyr-

annous, why should I live to endure her torments? my Superiors triumph in their Loves: my Fellow shepherds can boast of theirs: it is
wretched *Philisides*, oh it is I that am singularlie miserable, made so
by a beautifull, yet cruel Mistriss; the Princess knew him to be *Philisides* the despairing Shepherd by his sorowfull subject; and he rising
from under an hedge, discovered himself to be the same: there the
Princess leaving him in a forlorn posture, hastened to their other
companie, to execute their Office, which they had agreed upon as
they went: *Claius* and *Strephon* were amazed at their sight, their fear
commanding them to give way to sorrow, but their hopes bad them
both to burie sadness in the lake of Oblivion: in this unsetled condition they continued not long, the division of their thoughts being
suppressed by the Sentence which *Musidorus* uttered thus.

An Oration might be acceptable to the ears of these Auditors, but
that the Evening desires me not to be tedious, especiallie to these
expecting Lovers: in compassion to you both, oh *Claius* and *Strephon*, I doe heartily wish there were two *Uranià*s, and should be
exceeding well content, if some others were to decide this business,
than my Cosen *Pyrocles* and my self, he for my sake being equallie
oblieged with me to you for your unspeakable courtesie to me when
I was a distressed stranger, and incompassed by the frowns of Fortune; our affections to you both may be evenly ballanced, but your
activitie cannot be justlie summoned together: *Claiu's* age manifests
a dulness, and *Strephon's* youth his lightsomness; or else your worthiest exploits, without disputing, might conquer *Urania*. At this
Claius, as if he had been revived, ventured to jump, but his heels
served him a trick, teaching him to kiss his mother Earth, as more
suitable to his ancient years than a young Shepherdess was: but he
vexing at so publick a disaster, fell in a rage upon *Strephon*, who
esteemed it more Nobleness to hold his hands, than to recompence
his blows, *Claius* holding in disdain his backwardness, left his eagerness, and turning to the Princess with tears in his eyes, he beseeched
them, if it should be his unhappiness to be deprived of *Urania*, to

1960

1970

1980

grant him the priviledge of her presence, though at as great a distance as possibly he could discern her, *Strephon* not knowing the
1990 subtiltie of Fortune, and doubting the worst, desisted not from craving the like favour: the Princess mercifully yielded to their requests,
and *Musidorus* proceeded in his sentence.

    Urania deserves to possess the first lodgings of the wisest hearts,
she is too pure to be a second; out of which consideration, we have
resolv'd that you shall both swear by the sacred Name of *Pan*,
whether you have ever been defiled with another object, or have
been afflicted with *Cupids* dart, though in a virtuous way; which if
you both can protest against, we will prohibit this invention, and
determin on some other; and if but one can clear himself, he shall be
2000 acknowledged the fittest Husband for her.

    Strephon without scruple offered to take his Oath; *Claius*, though
he was enticed by the force of Beautie, yet his Conscience withdrew
him from perjuring himself, perswading him to defer the time: the
Princess perceiving his slowness, guessed the matter, and lest he
should be surprized with the vanities of this world, they commanded
him and *Strephon* to convey *Urania* to the Temple: *Musidorus* and
Pyrocles, with *Pamela* and *Philoclea*, and the other Royal Bride-
gromes and Brides, besides the resort of shepherds and shepherdesses
attending on them: where being come, *Claius* and *Strephon* ascended
2010 to the Altar, and with great reverence *Strephon* professed his Innocence from Female Creatures, and withall his chaste affection, which
he constantlie bare to *Urania:* and *Claius* with jealous devotion
affirmed that *Urania* was a precious Jewel, locked up in the Treasurie
of his heart, which none could bereave him of, unless they murdered
him, neither spared he room for any other to abide there, but her
Divine self: yet he could not denie, but that in his younger days his
indulgent Phantasie had seized upon a Shepherdess, though not
with anie other entire affection than as her prettie songs enveigled
him; and since he had wholie abandoned her, and cleaved to *Urania*,
2020 the severest Justice could not make that a sufficient pretence to give
away his elected Spouse.

Thus *Claius* advocated for himself; but *Pyrocles* and *Musidorus* caused silence to be made, and then *Musidorus* said;

For as much as you have referred your selves, before evident Witness, to the judgement of Prince *Pyrocles* and my self; who without any expulsion to your side, have sincerelie bestowed it upon you; we will admit of no addresses to recal our judgements, for that were to accuse our selves of Infidelitie; but we will not see it put in execution: and *Strephon* shall enjoy his first Love, the Shepherdess *Urania*, and *Claius* may dwell in the view of her, to save him from perishing.   2030

Strephon, as a man who newly embraced a life ransomed from the power of hatefull death, to inhabit a glorious Paradice, snatched *Urania* from out of the hands of amazed *Claius*, and in a ravishment ran for the Priest of *Pan*, who in the mid'st of the throng, consumated their Union. This last Couple wanted not aplauses, though they were inferior to the other in dignitie; for *Straphons* comeliness, and *Uranias* gracefulness seemed to adorn their harmless roabs: their becomming Modestie enthral'd the hearts of their observers, their courtesie conquered the eyes of their profession, that beheld in what estimation they were with the Princes, and their happiness equalled   2040 the greatest Personages.

But alas, in *Strephons* felicity consists *Claius* miserie, his grief being so infinite, that his passages of tears was stopped, and a frantick Brain possessed him more than a Womanish sorrow, against this life he exclaimed, *Strephon* and himself he abhorred, and endeavouring to set a Period to his afflictions, he brake out into these words: Proud love, who gloriest in tormenting mortals, this once moderate thy rage by dispatching me quickly from under thy Tyrannie; for in what have I displeased thee, you cannot signifie, I have so faithfully served to your crueltie. But now to gratifie me, you   2050 plunder me of my onely blessing, and yet in derision you make me to live. But O *Cupid!* if any pitie or remorse dares harbour in thee, as thou hast deeply wounded me, so directly slay me, and I shall entitle thee mercifull. But if thou fliest from such a compassionate act, then Prince *Musidorus* and *Pyrocles*, whose fame is enriched with

goodness, replenish it more by my speedy destruction and make me breathless. And Shepherds and Shepherdesses, let not the dreadfull Name of Tragedy affright you, my Death will be the obsequies of a Comedy; therefore if any spleen reign victor in you, revenge your
2060 self upon me that am the most contemptible wretch.

This Speech he uttered with such distracted actions, that terrified the women and afflicted the men. But at appointment of the Princes they conveyed him to some private habitation, where he had attendants, who oftentimes prevented him from mischieving himself. But for *Strephon* and *Urania*, the Princes solemnly invited them to their societie for that evening, where at *Pamela's* and *Philocleds* entreaties, they retiring to a pleasant summer House, *Strephon* rehearsed these passages concerning *Urania*, *Claius*, and himself, on this manner:

To recollect *Uranids* virtues, or what surpassing beautie engaged
2070 *Claius* and me to be her servants, would be superfluous, since her divine self is present to merit divine praises from the dullest spectators. Onely first her prettie innocence withdrew our eyes from gazing on the stars, to salute her heavenly spheres that reflected upon us as she passed by. For *Claius* and I having separated our Flocks from our neighbouring shepherds into a fresh and sweet pasture, where none frequented or trode the pleasant grass, but savage Satyrs, and dancing Fairies, we espied a Tree, whose flourishing branches seemed to fortifie themselves against the heat of the sun, and we enticed by the shadow, repaired to it: there we lay down, purposing to trie our
2080 skill in describing the pitifull decorums of the shepherds that were inchanted by *Cupids* quiver, to adore the fair beautie of Mortals: but the wonderfull Justice of the highest Powers, taught us to acknowledge our frailtie, by inflicting the like punishment upon us: for as we were reproching their lovesick infirmities, fair *Urania*, enduced by a Sparrow that flew from her when she had courteously bred it up, pursued after it, to take it prisoner, her course bending towards us: but when she had surprized it, she confined it to a Paradise, putting it between the pillows of her Breast, and checking it no otherwise

than with her harmless kisses, she went away, leaving *Claius* and my carkass behind her, but our souls cleaved immoveably unto her, and fixing our eyes upon one another, as ashamed of our prodigious censoriousness of our Neighbours, we suffered not our lips to open, till we were acquainted with the subject that did triumph over us; but sounding our Bell, we secured our Flocks, and hastened to repose our selves upon our beds, but our memorie of the most Divine *Urania* taught us a more watchfull lesson than drousiness: her Image, which was engraven in our fancie, disdained to be blurred by our forgetfulness, wherefore the restless night we passed over with sighs, reviling the Fates for burying our felicitie in the depth of adversitie, so hard and explete did we account it ever to obtain *Urania;* and though *Claius* and I were one anothers Rivalls, both aiming at one, yet did it not any way mittigate our friendship, I applauding *Claius* choice, and he mine; neither did we ignorantly admire our judgements, but did enquire, and receive the approbation of a multitude of Swains, who with abundant devotion extolled *Urania's* worth: yet Fortune, that favours not the purest souls, knit her brows, frowning upon our Goddess *Urania*, who mildly strived to wash them away with her Christal tears: the occasion I heard her whisper out one time, when she imagined little, and I resided so near her, in these sweetly expressed, yet dollorous words.

Too great a burden for me to bear oppresses me, *Antaxius* is too officious in his love, I wish he were more calm; my Parents rigor is too too intollerable, unless my disobedience had been palpable; I have never offended them wilfully, no not in this their desired Match, except they interpret my silence for a refusal, that being the onely symptom of my discontent, nor do I reveal my affection to any but to thee my Sparrow, who canst not discover it with thy chirping, and that note of thine is to me condoling, and chearfull; my disconsolate Heart not knowing how to value any other melodious sounds: but alass my incredulitie of the divine Providence may justlie reprove and punish me; yet since I do humbly acknowledge

2090

2100

2110

2120

thy alsufficiencie, let thy Mercie chastise me, and deliver me from the thraldom of *Antaxius*.

Then wiping her bedewed eyes, she arose, as confident her devout Prayers had conjured the Gods to pitie her distress, and beseeching the Deities to make me their instrument; call'd after her. Fair Creature, pardon me if I profane your sacred Title with a feeble one, since your humilitie vouchsafes earthly troubles to perplex you; and believe me, the Fabrick of this world is built upon divers motions, it can boast of no firm foundation; the rarest Beauties in their age seldom escape advers Billows, and boysterous winds, and without relying on a Rock, their perishing is sure: wherefore, sweet Nimph, accept of me to be your Rock, and questionless you shall be preserved from all tempestuous weathers.

Urania trusting in no other Power, than what was celestial, looked up to the Element, where seeing no heavenlie Object, she cast her eyes down, fixing them upon me with such blessedness, as strook me to the ground, not being capable of assisting my self; however I fed upon her voice, which she displayed in this language.

What a presumptuous mortal art thou to frame thy self to be a God, that by such a pretence thou mayst insult over me? For better Powers cannot support me from furious storms. This spoken, she went away, as loathing the sight of such a blasphemous serpent, as she thought me to be. Which I perceiving, and rowsing my self from out of a transe, I began to crie, O stay, stay, stay, but she deaf to my perswasions, hastened beyond the limits of mine eyes; but the rebounding of my words sounded in the ears of the Pastor *Claius*, who was with his and my Flock at a little distance from me. He harkening to my voice, and discerning me to wander out of the close, his jealous brain supposed the reason, & walking as swiftly as his aged leggs would suffer him, he found me out, his inquisitiveness enforcing me not to be niggardly in my answers, which were so tedious, that the Sun vanished from our Horizon, as tired with our unnecessary speeches, and took his farewel, highing him to his Eastern home. But at length *Claius* and I yielding our selves to silence though not to rest, experience had taught us to despair of sleeping, until *Cupids* wounds wear curable. And early in the morning when the Sheperdesses had driven their Flocks into the Pastures, we lingering with ours, that we might see the place made happie with *Uranids* abiding there, her Enimie *Antaxius* the wealthy Heardsman, driven by a flattering current of his success, approched near us, not scrupulous in asking *Uranids* harbour: we making much of our opportunitie directed him the contrary way from her, to the Island of *Citherea*, her Parents dwelling there, onely they had trusted her with the Flock on this side the River, to feed them with a livelier pasture. But we protested to him, that in the morning we saw the Grass to weep for her departure, and the seas dance with joy that she relyed on their mildness. *Antaxius* easily believed our intilligence, and thanking us for it, he hastened to overtake her: and we pleased with our prosperous subtletie, drove our Flocks to a Pasture adjoyning to *Urania's*, and entreating *Pan* to be their Guardian, we left them to trie Fortunes courtesie.

Urania blushing at our presence, at mine especially, who had before abruptly assaulted her, seemed to rebuke me with it, as in earnest so it did, my trembling witnessed my guiltiness, and my tears and sighs my repentance: my slowness to utterance allowed *Claius* a convenient time to discover his passion to *Urania*, the policie used to *Antaxius*, he forbore to repeat, until my repentance had obtained a pardon, and then he related in what expedition we sent away her undesired suitor; which at first vanished the red from her face, her fears usurping in her tender breast, lest her Parents should doubt her safetie at *Antaxius* report. Yet when she remembred her absence might extinguish *Antaxius* lust, her vermilion came back to mixture, and adorned her, as detesting to be deprived of such an Alabaster shelter.

Claius made Poesies in her praise to please her, dedicating to her service all his studies. My art in framing of Garlands, shewing the

2160
2170
2180

flowers natural curiositie in their varietie of shades, a device that sets them forth most perfectly I did teach her; oftentimes presenting her with the choisest of my Flock, when she would accept of them; and if Wolves or other ravenous beasts had happened to lurk that way, I never left hunting them till their hands evidenced me their Conqueror, which I used to lay at *Urania* s feet; other tricks I invented to be admitted into her societie.

Here *Strephon* stopt: but the Princes entreated him to go on. Which happiness of mine, saith he, continued not long without interruption. *Antaxius* learning that *Claius* and I pretended affection to *Urania*, he proudly landed at our haven, rudely carrying her away without resistance. Her commands, that could not be disobeyed, ordained the contrary. Then it was, most gracious Prince *Musidorus* that you escaped the seas, O then it was that *Urania* floted on them, and we bitterly bemoaned our loss. Certainly by the appointment of the Gods the Ocean waxed so calm, yet about where she was embarqued, the waters murmured, and the winds sweetly whistled, combining their voices so harmoniously, that she might really believe, they conspired to crown her with some unexpected blessing; as indeed so they had: for when we had conducted you to my Lord *Kalenders* house, we received a Letter from our adored Goddess. We might have been justly taxed of incredulitie at the first view of it, our rememberance of her uncivil Carrier demollishing all hopefull thoughts; but when we had more believingly read over and saluted those heavenly lines, we taking a short farewel of your Highnes, conformed our pace to our eagerest disposition, and came to the Sands against the Island of *Citherea;* where not caring for any other passage but *Charon's* Boat, we committed our selves to heavens protection, and fixed our eyes upon *Urania's* Island, leaping into the sea, there we had like to have participated of *Leander's* entertainment, but our luckie Stars preserved us to better fortune. The waves growing turbulent, the winds roared, the skies thickened, and all tempestuous weather threatened to combine against us. My Friend *Claiu's* faint

limbs I was glad to support with my tired ones, and we both had perished and resigned our breaths to the Giver, but that the storm
forced a Bark to cast Anchor, and harbour in our Coast, from
whence we had not swom far, though the Billows had thrown us up
and down, as contemning us for our presumption in pursuing our
loves to *Urania*, but the companie in the Bark, weighing our calamities, and their own too, should they neglect so charitable an act as
endeavouring to help us, imagining the Gods would be deaf to their
prayers, if they were careless of ours: they let their sails flie towards
us, & lengthening the cord of their Cock-boat, they sent it to us; we   2230
skilled in their meaning laid hold on it, and by degrees we purchased
the in-sides for our security, they pulling us to the Bark, helped us in.

Where we were gazed on with astonishment by all; neither were
our eyes indebted to theirs, so manie of *Urania's* Associats did we
espie in the Bark to look upon; and amongst the rest there was
Antaxius: Oh *Claius*, hadst thou been here, thou wouldst have justified thy paleness, and my cholerick flushes, that with zeal strove for
Victorie over our haughtie Rival; who being vexed at the sight of us,
and minding nothing so much as our fatal ruine, stretched his voice,
which was most hideous, to condemn us. What monsters are these,   2240
said he, that you have had pitie upon? their Physiognomies resemble
ours, but the shape is different; therefore hurl them overboard, lest
they do drown us with their Inchantment. The gulph of salt-Water
that flew out of our mouths, and our wett garments that hung confusedly, with his aggravations pierced into the stupid senses of the
Companie, who doubted whether we were very *Claius* and *Strephon*
or no, yet dreaded to question us: my anger for *Antaxius* unworthie
affronting us, could not be moderated, but acting the fierceness of a
Tygar, I fell upon him, and flung him into the sea, where he deserv-
edlie tasted of such pleasures, as he had allotted for us: such is the   2250
wisdom of the higher Powers to recompence what is due.

The affrighted People fled into their Cabins, the Pilot and Sailors
forsaking their imployments, hid themselves under the Decks: but

all this time I never ceased to pray for *Urania's* safeguard, being ignorant of the chance that brought *Antaxius* thither, or where she
resided; her letters signifying onely how much she wished to see us,
our vowed friendship obliging her in all virtuous ways to honor us:
but having quelled the courage of the Sailors, the storm asswaging,
we shewed our authoritie, commanding them to strike their sail to
2260 the Island of *Citherea:* and giving a visit to our Prisoners in the Cabins, we intreated them to suppress all prejudicial conceit of us, who
never intended to injure them, though we had revenged our selves
upon *Antaxius* for scandalizing us, and perswading them barbarously
to murder us, under the pretence of Sea-Monsters: nor did we
neglect to tell them how infinitly they would favor us, in relating
what accident had inticed *Antaxius* to that Bark, without his Mistress *Urania,* who was reported to be his onely delight.

    The young Shepherd *Lalus,* being present, interrupted me thus:
Urania disdains to be the Mistress of so base a fellow, though his
2270 importunitie both to her nearest relations, and to her divine self,
forced her to grant him the priviledge of Charactering her perfections in Poetrie, amongst which he had declared his Lust, shadowing
it with the title of Love, when he might as well transform a Dove to
a Kite, or a Wolf to a Lamb, as lust to Love; *Urania* abhorring him
for it, charged me, who am bound to obey her charge, to be urgent
with *Antaxius* to come this voyage with me. I assaulted him with the
question; he thought it no ways requisit for his proceedings, but at
her perswasions he ceased to argue: This Voyage we intended for a
chearfull one, but it hath proved a fatal one to him, though a fortu-
2280 nate one to *Urania;* for she as far excels *Antaxius* in deserts, as our
Princess *Pamela* does *Mopsa,* Master *Dameta's* daughter.

    At this passage the Princess smiled, and *Strephon* blushed at his
true, yet blunt expression: but longing to be freed from Tautalogizing, his modestie not suffering him to Court *Urania* there, he persisted in his rehearsal.

It afflicted me to reckon; O I could not reckon the number of Rivals that waited to frustrate me of my felicitie, all that ever beheld her, commended her, few they were that did not Court her, but most lived in hopes to enjoy her; however I dissembled my grief, and congratulated with *Lalus* for his courteous relation, telling him, I had seen that Paragon, and did as much admire her, as I could any of her sex, though my delight consisted chiefly in other recreations, than to extoll a woman. This drift of mine enticed him earnestly to better my opinion, and in his highest Rhetorick, he laboured to inform me concerning the Passion of Love, that though it were mixed with bitterness, in consideration of some griefs that follow it, yet seldom it is, but that the conclusion is happie. I making as though I listened not to his discourse, sung a song, the subject whereof tended against Love and Women: he encreasing in his desires to work my conversion, determined to bring me to *Urania*. I willingly seemed to yield to his request, *Claius* wondred at my disguised heart, yet held his peace, trusting to my poor discretion.

Now the Sea-men, bringing us news of our safe arrival in the Ports of *Citherea*, we landed, releasing the Bark; I could hardly confine my joy within so small a compass as my heart, when I went upon the ground where she had trode, and not reveal it; but I restrained it as much as possibly I could, slighting his description of *Urania*'s worth. But alas my hopes of the success, my designment might have, was frustrated; upon so tottering a climat do we Mortals restless live, that when we think we have escaped the dangerousest storms, our feet stand upon the brims, ready to be blown down at evry flirt of wind, to the depth of miserie.

For *Urania*, my secret Jewel, and *Lalus* that reveiled me, was missing, not to publick Pastorals, nor yet solitarie Retirements, but by the foul practises of a Knight named *Lacemon*, who violently carried her away from her sheep, whilst she was complaining of *Claius* and my tedious absence; the reporter of this dolefull News lay hid under a hedge, the glistering of rude *Lacemon*'s Armour advising him to conceal himself; such was the cowardliness of the simple Swain.

2320 *Lalus* would have murdered him, had not we by force withheld him; yet I made him feel the stroak of my Cudgel, to make him repent his folly, a poor revenge for so hainous a trespass, yet that disburdened me of a greater, so subject are we in affliction to double our error with a crime more odious: *Urania* was lost, yet the memorie of her Name, Virtue or Beautie could never be expired: neither did we linger in pursuance of *Lacemon*, nor in her search, whose heavenly soul, as we imagined, must needs perfume and leave a scent where it had breathed, which was the signe that we besought the Sacred Powers to grant, might be our convoy to her. Then *Lalus*
2330 departed from us, choosing his path; *Claius* and I would not be separated, if possibly we could avoid it. I know not whether this unwillingness to part with me proceeded from a jealous humour, his nature being always inclinable to it; but I am sure, mine was real, doubting not, but what the Divine Providence had agreed on, should be accomplished what ere it were.

The byest ways, as we conceived, might be the likeliest to find *Urania*, *Lacemon* having many: his felicitie, since he had deprived the Land of its Goddess, and we as deeply ingaged against him, our presumptuous Rival, as any other, searched the most suspitious Cor-
2340 ners; but no tidings could be heard of *Urania* up the Island, where we had wandered, except profane ones; for ask the Swains that sluggishly sate nodding by some of their scattered sheep, whose fellows had been devoured by Wolves, through the carelesness of their Shepherds, when we examined them concerning *Urania*, whom we described by her Praiers and tears made to a Knight accoutred in a Martial habit; their reply would be so absurd, nay between sleeping and waking, divers did affirm they saw her, directing us to unseemly Mortals, who indeed had usurped *Urania*'s Name, though they came short of her perfections. I cannot judge which was victor in me of

Rage and Sorrow; furious I was at the counterfeit *Urania's*, and des-   2350
perate, despairing of ever finding the real one.

At this passage *Strephon* burst out into floods of tears, which he
endeavoured to conceal, excusing his too large rehearsal, & desired
to break off; but the Princess earnestness to hear *Urania* rescued
from the power of *Lacemon*, induced him to proceed on this manner: My chollerick Passion I vented upon the stupid men, instructing them to entitle their Dames with some meaner Name than
Urania, under penaltie of their lives, which they dearly valued: and
then *Claius* and I renewed our languishing travels.

When we had passed through the publick and remote places of   2360
the Island, meeting with no obstacles in the way, either by Freinds or
Enemies, we crossed the Ocean, landing at the sands over against the
Island, we continued not there, though we could not determin
where we had best continue, but a Pilgrims life we resolved on,
unless *Urania's* unexpected securitie should forbid it; when therefore
we had traced about the Confines of *Arcadia*, without any comfortable reports of her, we rose with the Sun, to take a longer journey,
but the tiredness of our legs prolonged the time, and so proved faithfull instruments to further our felicitie, by delaying our haste: Upon
a bank we sate down, chafing at the grass for looking fresh and green   2370
in *Urania's* absence; and *Claius* folding his arms, and casting his eyes
on the ground, as a fit object for him to view, especially when he
pitched on such a subject as deserved opposition, as he then did;
uttering these words:

Seldom it is, but the fairest Physiognomies harbour the foulest
souls, all reason proves it so; nay the Gods abhor partialitie; why
then should they adorn a Creature so richly surpassing above the rest
visibly, and yet give her a soul answerable? *Urania!* O *Urania!* I will
not, no I durst not say unchaste, though the Summers mourn not
for her exilement, nor the Birds cease from their various notes,   2380
which comfort we heretofore apprehended they made to invite

Urania to reside altogether in the Woods; nor yet the Shepherds refrain from their pleasant sports; nor do the Shepherdesses neglect their care of medicining their tender Lambs, to celebrate a Day in their bewailings.

Age we reckon stands at the gate of Death: yet *Claius* years was a Target to defend him from it, otherwise I should not have thought a replie a sufficient revenge, which I did in these terms. A suspitious head is as great a torment as I could wish to light upon *Lacemon*, besides the unjustness of it, your uncharitable censures may too soon redound upon you, when repentance hath lost its opportunitie to crave and receive a pardon: expose not your self to that crime, which never can be purged away, should it dammage the reputation of those that imitate *Diana's* qualities in as great a measure as her Beautie; for if the Gods have bestowed on them reasonable souls, why should we pine at their industrie to make them admirable: You argue, that the Summer keeps its natural course, though *Urania* is missing, which is a manifest testimonie of her virtues, boisterous and cold weather being a foe to Travelers, but the warm Sun is delightfull; and the birds proudly chant their Tunes, for I am confident, they ravish her far above the loftie expressions of *Lacemon:* neither wonder at the mirth and imployments of the Shepherds and Shepherdesses, for the Virgins are glad to exercise their inventions, to charm back the belief of *Urania's* loss, so darksom and odious is it to them, the Shepherds their Paramours fostering (though with sadness) their busie fancies.

Claius fixing his eyes on the ground, as convinced of his error, sought not to frame an excuse, yet to shew that Age had not deprived him of his senses; he thus spake: An odoriferous scent seems to command me to rest silent, and to bear the blame without controulment, and dreadfulness mixed with hope possess me. O *Strephon, Strephon*, faithfully conceal my follie, I beseech thee.

At this suddain Allarm, I gazed about me, an happie sight, though an amazed one approaching near me, *Urania* it was, with her arms spread, and cryes in her mouth, which mentioned murder, her hair contemptibly hung about her, though delicate; and patience and anger seemed to combat in her rosie cheeks for the Victorie; but at the last, abundance of Christal tears became the Arbiter, which when she had vented; she distributed to us these words:

Never was I yet in the Turret of felicitie, but I have stumbled, and 2420 fell to the pit of adversitie: *Antaxius*, in the Island of *Citherea* lustfully expects me; and here, if I continue, the Furie *Lacemon* will overtake me; O whither shall I flie for safetie? my pitie would not suffer me to retain her in ignorance, wherefore I related *Antaxius* death: her silence seemed to condemn me of rashness, for granting him no time of repentance; but my excuse was prevented by the ragefull coming of *Lacemon*, who with eyes sparkling, and Armour stained with bloud, an Emblem of the Tragedie he had committed, holding in his right hand a spear, and a shield in his left, he mustered up to us; we nothing dreading, but *Urania*'s trembleing, with our staves, weak 2430 instruments (as he imagined) to resist him, made towards him: he disdaining *Claius* age, and my youth, exercised neither vigilance to withstand our blows, nor strength to repay them: I vexed at his so slight regard of my valour, and perswading *Claius* to retire to *Urania*, who willingly yielded to my counsel; I renewed the incounter, and with such fierceness, that *Lacemon* was forced to stand on his own defence; his want of experience might be the cause of his overthrow; for I am certain I can boast but of little that caused it, though the fortune of my blows proved fatal to him, thrusting him off his horse, and beating out his brains: his life was so hatefull, that his death was 2440 welcomed by most, and commiserated of none: *Urania* highly commended my action, too large a recompence for so poor a desert, yet I thanked the Gods for giving me such success as she thought worthie of her acceptance; and waiting upon her to the Island of *Citherea*, by the way she yielded to our request, gracefully delivering these words.

The motions of this world I cannot comprehend, but with confusion, so unexpectedly do they surprize me, *Antaxius* by *Lalus* instigations, trusted to the Seas fidelitie, your compulsion forcing them to deceive him, in whose banishment I sent a Letter to you, wherein I acknowledged your sincere affection, and by all the ties of virtuous friendship, conjured you not to denie me your Counsel or Companie in my extremitie; and happening to repose my self upon the Clifts, my harmless Sparrow I set down at a little distance from me, learning it to come at my inducement, the prettie fool, with shivering wings aspired to mount towards me; but the Tyger *Lacemon*, or Monster, for his disposition could never pretend to humanitie, being prepared in a readiness to commit such a treacherous act, came from a darksom hole, suitable to his practises, and seized on me and my Sparrow for Prisoners, and conveying us to his provided Boat, we were sailed over, and by him conducted to this Countrey of *Arcadia*, where in a Cave he hath enclosed me: and perceiving, that I consorted with my Bird, and delighted in its Innocencie, a virtue which he mortally detested, he unmercifully murdered it, lingeringly tormenting it to death, whilst my Sparrow with its dying looks, seemed to check me, for enduring its sufferance without resistance: thus he endeavoured to terrifie me with his crueltie, but if it were possible, it made me more enflamed to withstand his assaults; neither threats, nor intreaties were wanting to tempt me to his base desires, but I absolutely refused him, till necessitie perswaded me to trie the effect of Policie.

His own reports signifying *Phalantus Helena*, the Queen of *Corinths* Brothers defiance to the *Arcadian* Knights, his Lance willing to defend his Mistress *Sortesid's* beautie against other Champions; I counterfeited earnestness to *Lacemon*, in exercising his skill to purchase my glorie: he puffed up with hopes of future success, considering it was the first time that I had imployed him, and so publicklie, with all expedition, hasted to the lodge with my Picture where by a thrust from off his horse, he was made to leave my Picture, to reverence *Sortasid's* surpassing one; with a cloudie soul, he returned to me, I being compassed to stay within his bounds, so

manie bars and bolts frustrating my escape; but by his muttering I discerned his discontent, an humour that best suited his condition: I strictly examined concerning my Pictures triumph, and his Fortune, he studying to delude me, replied, That business of importance had enforced *Bisilius* to defer the challenge for awhile, out of which regard, he, by the example of other Noble Personages, resigned up my Picture to the custodie of the Governor of *Basilius* lodge, and should be extremelie well pleased, if I would vouchsafe him my companie into the fresh aire; few perswasions served to remove me from that stifling cave, besides the hopes that I relied upon of your   2490
encountering *Lacemon;* but little imagined the Shepherd *Lalus* would be the first; kind *Lalus!* it was the least of my thoughts of thy so chearfullie loosing thy life for the preservation of mine; for when *Lacemon* had with boastings, for not being overcome by any of his subjected Rivalls, brought me near the confines of *Arcadia,* swelling with pride, his rough Arms rudely striving with me: then it was that *Lalus* succoured me with his own fatal ruine: for though I was by *Lacemon* desguised, by his suggestion, I knowing no other signe, he discovered me to be *Urania:* his desire to rescue me from *Lacemon,* extinguished the reprehension of his own eminent danger, his cour-   2500
age, though exceeding *Lacemons,* yet his strength and shield was far inferior to him, in the heat of the blows, before conquest, was decided on either side; I fled from dreadfull *Lacemon,*

His speedie pursuance after me, might be a means to preserve *Lalus* life, yet I doubt it, *Lacemons* bloudie Armour prenominating his wicked action. But I protest, that I had rather my skin should imitate *Pan's,* and my complexion *Vulcan's,* than that any one Trage-die should be committed in its defence.

Fountains running from *Urania's* sparkling eyes, stopped the remainder of her speech. *Lalus* being my assured Rival, mitigated   2510
very much my sorrow for him. However, lest I should forfeit *Ura-nia's* favour, I seemed sad, yet strived with it, that I might be a more acceptable instrument to moderate hers. Neither was *Claius*

negligent in his love, but with Rhetorical speeches he sought to win on her affections; and the Island of *Citharea* in awhile flourished with her adored Goddess. Her Parents in heavenly raptures welcomed home their dearest Daughter, keeping her watchfully under their eyes, and jealous of our depriving them of her the second time, though we had safely delivered her into their hands. And *Urania* her self suspecting our often resorting to her, might redound to her prejudice, made excuses to abandon our companie. But death in a short time appeared in his visage to *Urania's* Parents, carrying them to the Elizian fields: she then having the libertie to dispose of her self, which she with confinement did, not delighting in the Pastorals, nor yet in our societie, until this happie Day was nominated. And now great Princes, I humbly beseech you to pardon this my tedious Relation.

The Princes courteously declared *Strephon* to be worthiest of *Urania*, the particulars of his exploits witnesing it. *Basilius* on that day preferring him in his Court, honouring him with Knighthood, and both he and his Ladie *Urania* lived in great reputation with all, obtaining love and esteem from the stateliest Cedar to lowest shrub.

But when *Cynthia* drew her curtains, commanding the Princes to hide themselves within their Pavilions, and they retiring to obey her; just then an unusual voice sounded to them, and close behind it rushed in *Lalus* the Shepherd: anger composed with reverence beset him, both being so officious, that reverence environed Passion within the compasse of civilitie, and Passion allowed Reverence to shew a prettie decent behaviour, though not affected; both dying cheeks with ruddiness, whilest he applying his speech to *Pyrocles* and *Musidorus* spake to this purpose:

Great Princes, I will not presume to question your Justice, but your knowledge. It was I that gave *Lacemon* his deaths wound. *Strephon* did but lessen his torments by quick dispatching him when he fled from me, pretending *Urania* was his onely happiness that he desired to enjoy, and not my bloud

The Princes certifying *Lalus*, that other arguments enjoyned them to bestow *Urania* on *Strephon*, they left him, but not so disconsolate for *Uranid*'s loss, as to keep his eloquence from courting other Shepherdesses, in as high a degree as ever he did her. But aged *Claius*, 2550 having wrestled with death all the night, not that he desired to live, but unwilling to leave off calling on *Urania*, blessed *Urania!* yet in the morning he was overcome, resigning up his breath with her name in his mouth. *Basilius* had him sumptuously buried, and *Musidorus* caused a famous Monument to be built in his memorie. On the top of it, before the Sun had fully dried it, there was found *Philisides* the despairing Shepherd dead, yet not by other practices than a deep melancholly that over-pressed his heart: these lines were engraven on a stone that lay by him. *Judge not uncharitably; but believe the expression of a dying man; No poysonous draught have I* 2560 *tasted of, nor any self-murdering instruments have I used to shorten my miserable life: for by the authoritie of the Gods, the time of my end was concealed from all but my self. I am sure it came not unwished for, for why should I live to be despised of her, whom above all the world I honoured? I will forbear to name her, because my Rival shall not triumph in my death, nor yet condemn me for coveting so rare a Person. My ambition is to have the tears of the* Arcadian *Beauties shed at my Funeral, & sprinkled on my Hearss; and when my bodie is so magnificently embalmed, let it be interred with* Claius *two Lovers, both finishing their lives for their Mistresses sakes, his is publickly known to be* 2570 Urania, *my Breast is the Cabinet where mine is fixed, and if you rip that open, you will find it; though perhaps not so perfect as I could wish it were, the Cabinet melting into tears for its unkindness. And now farewel all the world; and I beseech the Divine Powers to bind* Cupids *hands from wounding, unless he have a certain salve to cure them.*

Thus died *Philisides;* his Will being faithfully performed by the Princes and the beauteous Princesses, with *Urania* and other prettie Shepherdesses, needing no imprecations faithfully bemoan his death, burying him with plentie of tears.

2580   Thus were there Nuptials finished with sadness. But before the solemnities were quite over, there came more Princes that had partaken of the benefit of *Musidorus* and *Pyrocle's* valour, with Presents of gratitude for their Brides, *Pamela* and *Philoclea*. Then after all Ceremonies accomplished, they retired severally to their flourishing Kingdoms of *Thessalia* and *Macedon*, and *Armenia*, with *Corrinth*, where they increased in riches, and were fruitfull in their renowned Families. And when they had sufficiently participated of the pleasures of this world, they resigned their Crowns to their lawfull Successours, and ended their days in Peace and Quietness.

FINIS.

SYNOPSIS OF THE MAIN ACTION OF THE 1593 ARCADIA OF SIR PHILIP SIDNEY

[Sidney's 1593 *Arcadia* is the *Arcadia* Weamys knew and used. (See Introduction, page xxxvi). The 1593 *Arcadia* attempts to complete the narratives of the *New Arcadia* of 1590 by appending the last two-and-a-half books of the *Old Arcadia*.]

New Arcadia

King Basilius of Arcadia has received from the oracle at Delphos a dire prophecy of his and his family's fate:

> Thy elder care shall from thy careful face
>> By princely mean be stolen, and yet not lost.
> Thy younger shall with Nature's bliss embrace
>> An uncouth love, which Nature hateth most.
> Both they themselves unto such two shall wed,
>> Who at thy bier, as at a bar, shall plead
>> Why thee (a living man) they had made dead.
> In thine own seat a foreign state shall sit.
> And ere that all these blows thy head do hit,
> Thou, with thy wife adultery shall commit. (II.28)

To escape this destiny, he has retired to the Arcadian countryside with his wife (Gynecia) and his two daughters (Pamela and the younger Philoclea), leaving his country in the charge of Philanax. The princes Pyrocles and Musidorus arrive in Arcadia and fall in love with the princesses. Basilius has forbidden courtship of his daughters, and so Pyrocles courts Philoclea in the guise of an Amazon (Zelmane), and Musidorus courts Pamela in the guise of a shepherd (Dorus). The daughters are won over by their disguised suitors, but both parents are also romantically attracted to Zelmane.

The two daughters and Zelmane are abducted by Basilius's sister-in-law, Cecropia, who is angry that his marriage late in life to Gynecia has produced heirs supplanting her son, Amphialus, in succession to the Arcadian throne. Civil war results as Basilius's forces combat Amphialus's. Cecropia tries, through cajolery and threats of torture and death, to persuade one of the sisters to marry her son. Amphialus, after being rebuked by Pamela and Philoclea (with whom he has fallen in love), extracts the truth of his mother's behavior from one of her women. Intent on killing himself in front of his mother, he approaches her with sword drawn; she, mistaking his meaning, backs away and falls to her death. Amphialus, now stricken with remorse for his complicity in so much suffering, attempts suicide. He lies near death when Helen of Corinth arrives and persuades Amphialus's ally, Anaxius, to help her take Amphialus to Corinth to be cured. Anaxius, upon his return, sees Zelmane (who has been assaulted by one of his brothers) kill his two brothers; whereupon he attacks her, and the *New Arcadia* ends (in mid-sentence) with the two in mortal combat.

Old Arcadia

After the civil wars, Pamela, Philoclea, Zelmane/Pyrocles and Dorus/Musidorus return to Basilius's Arcadian lodgings. Musidorus has persuaded Pamela to elope with him to Thessalia.

Meanwhile, Pyrocles is trying to press his case with Philoclea, but Gynecia has seen through his disguise and insists on his loving her; Pyrocles tries to appease her by agreeing to an assignation in a few days. Philoclea becomes jealous of her mother. Pyrocles lodges himself in a cave to be close to Philoclea. Unable to resist Basilius's and Gynecia's pressings any longer, s/he consents to an evening assignation in the cave with each of them, hoping that in the dark they will enjoy one another. He persuades Gynecia to dress as himself (Zelmane). Gynecia's own scheme is to take a love potion to her assignation with Pyrocles. When Basilius arrives in the cave, Gynecia recognizes him, but he thinks her Zelmane. While Philoclea's father is making love to her mother, thinking her Zelmane, Pyrocles arrives in Philoclea's chamber, reassures her of his love, and sleeps beside her.

Dametas, whom Basilius has made Pamela's guardian, searches for her in Basilius's lodging and discovers Pyrocles (now undisguised) sleeping beside Philoclea. He goes off to inform Basilius of the betrayal.

In the cave, Gynecia, angered by her husband's praise of Zelmane in their love-making, reveals herself, and she reproaches him for his betraying her. Basilius drinks the love potion that (unknown to him) Gynecia had brought for Pyrocles, and he falls to the ground, apparently dead.

Philanax, Basilius's regent, puts Gynecia, Pyrocles, and Philoclea under restraint as apparent accomplices in treason. Philanax's soldiers catch up with Pamela and Musidorus, and they too are placed under restraint. Fortuitously, Euarchus, king of Macedon, arrives in Arcadia on a visit to his old friend Basilius, and he agrees to act as judge.

In the trial scene that concludes the *Arcadia*, Euarchus, not recognizing his son and nephew, condemns them to death, and he refuses to change his verdict even after he learns their identities. Fortunately, Basilius awakens from having taken what was in fact a sleeping potion. All are forgiven, and Gynecia's reputation left untarnished. Basilius reflects on how the oracle's prophecy has come true.

APPENDIX 2

LIST OF CHARACTERS IN SIDNEY'S AND WEAMYS'S ARCADIAS

[The List of Characters gives the Sidneian background for Weamys's characters; hence Sidney's spelling of the characters appears first, followed by Weamys's spelling (when it differs) in parentheses. All material is taken, unless otherwise specified, from the 1593 *Arcadia.* The book and chapter divisions, supplied in the 1590 *New Arcadia* but not in the 1593 *Arcadia,* follow those of Maurice Evans in his edition of the 1593 *Arcadia* (Penguin, 1977). All quotations are from this edition.]

AMPHIALUS ("between two seas"), nephew to Basilius and unrequited lover of Philoclea. He is an accomplice after the fact in the abduction by his mother, Cecropia, of his cousins Philoclea and Pamela in an effort to put him on the Arcadian throne (III.2). He attempts suicide after realizing the full extent of his mother's, and his own, cruelty, and is last seen being carried off on a litter by Helen of Corinth for medical help in Corinth (III.24–25). (See HELEN and Appendix 1.)

ANAXIUS, a supporter of Amphialus's insurrection against Basilius, noted for his arrogance and cruelty.

ANTAXIUS, the choice of Urania's parents for her hand, and rival of Strephon and Claius; described by Lamon in the First Eclogues (1593 *Arcadia*) as "a herdman rich, [who] of much account was, / In whom no evil did reign, nor good appear."

ANTIPHILUS (ANTIFALUS) ("anti-love"), the base-born and unscrupulous husband of Erona.

ARTAXIA, Queen of Armenia upon the death of her brother, Tiridates; cousin of Plangus. She has a deep hatred of Erona, Pyrocles, Musidorus, and Antiphilus, because of their involvement in her brother's death. (See ERONA, PLANGUS, and Appendix 3A.)

ARTESIA (SORTESIA), pursued by Phalantus, but indifferent to him. "Thinking she did wrong to her beauty if she were not proud of it," she orders Phalantus to go through Greece defending her beauty against all challengers (I.15). In I.16, there is a triumphal procession in which are displayed the pictures of women whose champions have unsuccessfully challenged Phalantus; and in I.17, there is a tournament in which Phalantus is challenged and finally overcome by Zelmane/Pyrocles.

BASILIUS ("king"), King of Arcadia, husband of Gynecia, and father of Pamela and Philoclea; described by Kalander as "a prince of sufficient skill to govern so quiet a country.…Though he exceed not in the virtues which get admiration…, yet he is notable in those which stir affection" (I.3). (See Appendix 1.)

CECROPIA, sister-in-law of Basilius, mother of Amphialus. (See AMPHIALUS and Appendix 1.)

CLAIUS, shepherd, close friend of the younger shepherd Strephon and (with him) languishing lover of the shepherdess Urania. Described by Lamon (First Eclogues): "Claius for skill of herbs and shepherd's art / Among the wisest was accounted wise, / Yet not so wise as of unstained heart: / Strephon was young, yet marked with humble eyes / How elder rul'd their flocks and cur'd their smart, / So that the grave did not his words despise." (See Appendix 3D.)

CLITIPHON (CLYTIFON), son of Kalander and Basilius's sister (hence Basilius's nephew). Clitiphon is the (losing) defender of Helen of Corinth's beauty in Phalantus's tournament defending the beauty of his mistress, Artesia, over all challengers (I.17).

DAMETAS, husband of Miso, father of Mopsa, described by Kalander as "the most arrant, doltish clown [rustic] that I think there ever was," whom Basilius has given "the office of principal herdman" and "hath in a manner put the life of himself and his children into his hands—which authority…doth oversway poor Dametas that…he might be allowed it now in a comedy" (I.3).

ERONA, queen of Lycia (in the *New Arcadia*) or Lydia (in the *Old Arcadia*). Upon repudiating the display of Cupid's naked images, Erona falls hopelessly in love with the base-born Antiphilus and refuses the husband her father chose for her, King Tiridates of Armenia. After Erona attempts suicide, her father dies. Erona, now Queen of Lycia, continues to resist Tiridates, who now declares war on her. In order to prevent a long war, he challenges Musidorus, Pyrocles, and Antiphilus to fight him and two knights. Tiridates is killed, causing his sister, Artaxia (now queen of Armenia), to hate all three challengers. Erona marries Antiphilus (II.13), who abuses both her and their subjects; he also makes a law allowing polygamy in an effort to become the husband of Queen Artaxia. Artaxia feigns interest in order to capture the two of them; her plan is to kill them on her brother's tomb. Prince Plangus of Iberia falls in love with the captured Erona, and tries to assist her by helping Antiphilus escape; but the cowardly Antiphilus (unbeknownst to Erona) betrays his own rescuers, only to have Artaxia reward him by forcing him to throw himself from a pyramid. To save Erona, Plangus raises forces against Artaxia, abducts Artaxia's nephew, and threatens him with whatever harm she imposes on Erona. [Here A.W.'s narrative begins.] Armenian nobles intervene and forge an agreement that all prisoners should be freed—except Erona, who would be put into the hands of an Armenian nobleman; and if within two years of the date of Tiridates's death, Pyrocles and Musidorus have not overcome two knights of Artaxia's choosing, Erona will be burnt to death (II.29). (See PLANGUS, ARTAXIA, PLEXIRTUS, and Appendix 3A.)

EUARCHUS (EVARCHUS) ("good ruler"), King of Macedon, father of Pyrocles and uncle of Musidorus. (See Appendix 1.)

GYNECIA (GENECEA), wife of Basilius, mother of Pamela and Philoclea; described by Kalander as "a woman of great wit, and in truth of more princely virtues than her husband, of most unspotted chastity, but of so working a mind and so vehement spirits as a man may say it was happy she took a good course, for otherwise it would have been terrible" (I.3). She married Basilius when he was "already well stricken in years." (See Appendix 1.)

HELEN (HELENA), Queen of Corinth. Helen became deeply enamored of Amphialus when he wooed her for his friend Philoxenus, but imprudently she revealed her love of Amphialus to Philoxenus. Philoxenus challenged Amphialus and was killed, whereupon his father died. Amphialus blames Helen for these deaths and will not speak to her (I.10–11). She pursues him through Greece and western Asia, and at the end of the *New Arcadia* (after Amphialus has almost mortally wounded himself in a suicide attempt) she enlists Anaxius's aid to carry him off to Corinth, where her surgeons are noted for their great powers of cure (III.25). (See Amphialus.)

Kalander (Kaleander), Arcadian nobleman to whose house Claius and Strephon took Musidorus upon rescuing him (I.2).

Kalodoulus (Kalodolus), described by Musidorus as his "trusty servant." He reveals to Euarchus at the trial of Pyrocles and Musidorus that he is judging his son and nephew. He is raised to second place in Thessalia by Basilius (V.8).

Lacemon, "a rich knight…, far in love with [Urania], [who] had unluckily defended" (I.16) her picture; he is mentioned only in the context of Artesia's triumphal procession. (See Artesia.)

Lalus, "a shepherd stripling…the fine shepherd Lalus" (I.17), who (subsequent to Lacemon's defeat) offers to defend Urania's beauty with his club against Phalantus. (See Lacemon.)

Miso. (See Dametas.)

Mopsa, daughter of the "doltish" herdsman Dametas's "ill-favored" wife Miso; described by Kalander as "a fit woman to participate of both their [her parents'] perfections" (I.3); "a very unlikely envy she hath stumbled upon against the princess' [Pamela's] unspeakable beauty" (II.2). (See Dametas and Appendix 3c.)

Musidorus ("gift of the Muses"), Prince of Thessalia, nephew of Euarchus, cousin and friend of Pyrocles; perceived by Kalander as having "(besides his bodily gifts beyond the degree of admiration)…a mind of most excellent composition…an eloquence as sweet in the uttering, as slow to come to the uttering, a behavior so noble as gave a majesty to adversity: and all in a man whose age could not be above one and twenty years" (I.2). (See Appendix 1.)

Pamela ("all sweetness") and Philoclea ("lover of glory"), older and younger daughters of Basilius, courted by Musidorus and Pyrocles, respectively; described by Kalander as "so beyond measure excellent in all the gifts allotted to reasonable creatures that we may think they were born to show that nature is no stepmother to that sex…[M]ethought there was…more sweetness in Philoclea but more majesty in Pamela" (I.3). (See Appendix 1.)

Phalantus. (See Artesia.)

Philisides ("star lover"=Astrophil=Philip Sidney), Philip Sidney's pseudonym and persona as a languishing lover (II.21 and Third Eclogues).

Philoclea. (See Pamela.)

Plangus ("lamentation"), Prince of Iberia, in love with Erona; described by Basilius as "one of the properest and best-graced men that ever I saw, being of middle age and of a mean stature" (II.12). In exile from Iberia because his stepmother has turned his father against him, Plangus takes refuge in Armenia (II.15) and is involved in his cousin the King of Armenia's, Tiridates's, besieging of Erona and Antiphilus of Lycia. Tiridates is killed, and Artaxia tries to revenge his death against Erona and Antiphilus, has them ambushed and prepares to have them killed. Plangus sees Erona and falls in love with her, and tries to save both her and her husband (II.29). (See Erona.)

Plexirtus (Plaxirtus), the bastard son of the King of Paphlagonia, who turned his father against his other son Leonatus (II.10 and 22). (This narrative is the basis of the subplot of *King Lear*.) Plexirtus pursues Artaxia, once she becomes Queen of Armenia. An enemy of his forges a letter from Artaxia to Plexirtus saying she would never marry "but some such prince who would give sure proof that by his means [Pyrocles and Musidorus] were destroyed" (II.23). Plexirtus gives orders that Pyrocles and Musidorus be killed on a ship he furnished for them; during the fight on board, the ship catches fire and the two are separated, and are by some (including Artaxia and Plangus) thought to be dead (II.24). (See Artaxia, Erona, Plangus.)

Pyrocles ("fire and glory"), described as "a young man...of about eighteen years of age" (I.1); younger and more impetuous (fiery) than Musidorus, but of greater physical and martial prowess. (See Appendix 1.)

Sortesia. (See Artesia.)

Strephon. (See Claius.)

Urania, shepherdess beloved of Strephon and Claius, as well as Antaxius, Lacemon, and Lalus (I.1–2 and First Eclogues). (See Appendix 3D.)

APPENDIX 3

NARRATIVE SOURCES

[The following entries provide the narrative background in Sidney's 1593 *Arcadia* of Weamys's four main narratives: A, Erona and Plangus; B, Helen and Amphialus; C, Mopsa's Tale; D, Urania, Strephon, and Claius. The material in block quotations is the material from Sidney that Weamys summarizes or paraphrases. All quotations, as well as book and chapter numbers, are from Maurice Evans's edition of the complete 1593 *Arcadia* (Penguin, 1977).]

3A: Erona and Plangus

[See entries in Appendix 2 for Erona, Plangus, Artaxia, and Plexirtus.] Most of the Sidneian material Weamys summarizes and rewrites is from Basilius's account to Zelmane/Pyrocles of Plangus's love for Erona in the *New Arcadia* section of the 1593 *Arcadia* (II.29). Basilius learned this history when he earlier met Plangus, weeping his and Erona's fate under a tree; Plangus was passing through Arcadia on his way to Macedon to inform Euarchus of the apparent death of Pyrocles and Musidorus and to request military assistance for the rescue of Erona (II.12).

Basilius's tale of Plangus assumes a knowledge of Philoclea's tale of Erona, which she told earlier to Zelmane/Pyrocles (II.13): in Philoclea's tale, Erona, having persuaded her father to have all naked images of Cupid eliminated from his kingdom (Lycia), falls in love with a young man of "mean parentage," Antiphilus. After her father dies, the man her father had wanted her to marry, King Tiridates of Armenia, makes war on Lycia in an effort to force her to marry him. Tiridates is killed through the "wonderful valour" of Pyrocles and Musidorus, and Erona and Antiphilus are married. Artaxia, Tiridates's sister, becomes queen of Armenia and vows revenge on all four of them.

In II.18–24, Pyrocles continues Philoclea's tale of Erona by his relation to her of the adventures that befell him and Musidorus after Erona and Antiphilus were wed: after Pyrocles and Musidorus leave Armenia, the duplicitous Plexirtus courts Artaxia, now that she is queen. An old enemy of his, learning of his courtship, forges a letter to him from Artaxia, saying she will never marry any one but a prince who will arrange the death of Pyrocles and Musidorus (II.23). Pyrocles and Musidorus board a ship furnished by Plexirtus, who gives orders to the crew to kill them. Just off the coast of Arcadia, there is a fight on board and a fire. In the melee, Pyrocles and Musidorus are separated and are by many presumed dead.

In II.29, Basilius continues the narrative Philoclea had begun, and Pyrocles continued: Antiphilus proves to be a bad king and husband, though Erona continues to adore him. Artaxia, intent on her revenge, has Antiphilus and Erona captured, and at this point Plangus (who has been in exile in his cousin's kingdom) finds Erona's beauty increased in her affliction, and he falls in love with her. To show his love for her, he plots to aid Antiphilus's escape. The cowardly Antiphilus betrays his would-be rescuers, but Artaxia has him killed. In order to protect Erona from being burned alive, Plangus takes one of Artaxia's nephews hostage. Armenia is on the verge of civil war.

Weamys intercepts Sidney at this point, and her own narrative begins by summarizing and rewriting the following passage, which is the last part of the tale of Plangus that Basilius has been telling Zelmane/Pyrocles:

> "But now (some principal noblemen of that country interposing themselves) it was agreed that all persons else fully pardoned, and all prisoners, except Erona, delivered, she should be put into the hands of a principal nobleman who had a castle of great strength, upon oath, if by the day two years from Tiridates' death, Pyrocles and Musidorus did not in person combat and overcome two knights, whom she appointed to maintain her quarrel against Erona and them of having by treason destroyed her brother, that Erona should be that same day burned to ashes: but if they came, and had the victory, she should be delivered; but upon no occasion neither freed nor executed till that day. And hereto of both sides, all took solemn oath, and so the peace was concluded.... But Artaxia was more, and upon better ground, pleased [than was Plangus] with this action; for she had even newly received news from Plexirtus that upon the sea he had caused them both to perish, and therefore she held herself sure of the match.

"But poor Plangus knew not so much, and therefore seeing his party...hungry of any conditions of peace, accepted them: and then obtained leave of the lord that indifferently [impartially] kept her to visit Erona, whom he found full of desperate sorrow, suffering neither his [Antiphilus's] unworthiness, nor his wrongs, nor his death...either to cover with forgetfulness or diminish with consideration the affection she had borne him. So that when Plangus came to her, she fell in deadly trances, as if in him she had seen the death of Antiphilus because he had not succoured him: and yet (her virtue striving) she did at one time acknowledge herself bound and profess herself injured; instead of allowing the conclusion they had made, or writing to the princes as he wished her to do, craving nothing but some speedy death to follow her (in spite of just hate) beloved Antiphilus.

"So that Plangus, having nothing but a ravished kiss from her hand at their parting, went away towards Greece whitherward he understood the princes were embarked. But by the way it was his fortune to intercept letters written by Artaxia to Plexirtus, wherein she signified her accepting him to [as] her husband, whom she had ever favoured, so much the rather as he had performed the conditions of her marriage in bringing to their deserved end her greatest enemies...Whereupon, to make more diligent search, [Plangus] took ship himself and came into Laconia enquiring and by his enquiry finding, that such a ship was indeed with fight and fire perished, none, almost, escaping. But for Pyrocles and Musidorus, it was assuredly determined that they were cast away....

"...a new advertisement from Armenia overtook him which multiplied the force of his anguish. It was a message from the nobleman who had Erona in ward, giving him to understand that since his departure, Artaxia, using the benefit of time, had beseiged him in his castle, demanding present delivery of her whom yet for his faith given he would not before the day appointed, if possibly he could resist—which he foresaw long he should not do for want of victual...: and therefore willed him to haste to his succour, and come with no small forces, for all they that were of his side in Armenia were consumed, and Artaxia had increased her might by marriage of Plexirtus....

"Plangus...determined to go to the mighty and good king Euarchus.... Therefore with diligence he went to him, and by the way (passing through my country) it was my hap to find him, the most overthrown man with grief that ever I hope to see again.... I was moved not to let him pass till he had made a full declaration, which by pieces my daughters and I have delivered unto you. Fain he would have had succour of myself, but the course of my life being otherwise bent, I only accompanied him with some that might safely guide him to the great Euarchus...."

Plangus's next and final appearance is a brief one in V.2: "The woeful Prince Plangus receiving of Basilius no other succours" goes to Euarchus in Macedon and relays the "lamentable narration of his children's [i.e., his son and nephew's] death." Euarchus, "receiving of Plangus perfect instruction of all things concerning Plexirtus and Artaxia, with promise not only to aid him in delivering Erona, but also with vehement protestation never to return into Macedon till he had pursued the murderers to death," furnishes Plangus with a ship, and Plangus departs for Armenia.

3B: Helen and Amphialus

[See entries in Appendix 2 for Helen, Amphialus, and Anaxius.] Towards the end of the *New Arcadia* section of the 1593 *Arcadia,* Amphialus stabs himself out of remorse, especially for his complicity in his mother's (Cecropia's) imprisonment of Philoclea and Pamela in his castle. (Cecropia had hoped to force Philoclea to marry her son so that he might become Basilius's heir, and Amphialus was deeply in love with Philoclea.) Helen of Corinth, unrelenting in her pursuit of Amphialus's love and despite his contempt for her, arrives "to carry away Amphialus with her to the excellentest surgeon then known, whom she had in her country." Admitted into his chamber, she bursts into tears over his body:

> "Often, alas, often hast thou disdained my tears: but now, my dear Amphialus, receive them: these eyes can serve for nothing else but to weep for thee.... Yet, O Philoclea, wheresoever you are?—pardon me if I speak in the bitterness of my soul—excellent may you be in all other things (and excellent sure you are since he loved you) your want of pity, where the fault only was infiniteness of desert, cannot be excused. I would, O God, I would that you had granted his deserved suit of marrying you, and that I had been your serving-maid, to have made my estate the foil of your felicity, so he had lived. How many weary steps have I trodden after thee, while my only complaint was that thou were unkind? Alas, I would now thou wert [i.e. alive], to be unkind. Alas, why wouldst thou not command my service, in persuading Philoclea to love thee...?"

With that the body moving somewhat, and giving a groan full of death's music, she fell upon his face and kissed him…, and then would she have returned to a fresh career of complaints, when an aged and wise gentleman came to her, and besought her to remember what was fit for her greatness, wisdom, and honour: and withal, that it was fitter to show her love in carrying the body to her excellent surgeon.

Helen, not entirely trusting Basilius's promise of safe passage, persuades Anaxius to escort her to Corinth; and the Helen-Amphialus narrative ends with Helen causing "the body to be easily conveyed into the litter," as Amphialus's people "do honour to him: some throwing themselves upon the ground, some tearing their clothes and casting dust upon their heads, and some even wounding themselves, and sprinkling their own blood in the air" (III.25).

3C: Mopsa's Tale

[See entry for Mopsa in Appendix 2.] Mopsa's tale (a parody in part of Cupid and Psyche) follows Philoclea's tale of Cupid's revenge (Erona's love for Antiphilus) and her mother Miso's tale against Cupid. Zelmane beseeches Pamela to continue her sister's story. Pamela reminds her that, under Miso's government, they are all to draw lots to determine the order of tellers: "Mopsa (though at first for squeamishness going up and down with her head like a boat in a storm) put to her golden gols among them [i.e., she put her golden paws among the hands of the other women], and blind fortune (that saw not the color of them) gave her the pre-eminence; and so being her time to speak (wiping her mouth, as there was good cause) she thus tumbled into her matter":

"In time past," said she, "there was a king, the mightiest man in all his country, that had by his wife the fairest daughter that ever did eat pap. Now this king did keep a great house, that everybody might come and take their meat freely. So one day, as his daughter was sitting in her window, playing upon a harp, as sweet as any rose, and combing her head with a comb all of precious stones, there came in a knight into the court upon a goodly horse, one hair of gold, and the other of silver; and so the knight casting up his eyes to the window did fall into such love with her that he grew not worth the bread he eat; till many a sorry day going over his head, with Daily Diligence and Grisly Groans he won her affection, so that they agreed to run away together. And so in May, when all true hearts rejoice, they stale out of the castle without staying so much as for their breakfast. Now forsooth, as they went together, often all to-kissing one another, the knight told her he was brought up among the water-nymphs, who had so bewitched him that if he were ever ask'd his name, he must presently vanish away; and therefore charged her upon his blessing, that she never ask him what he was nor whither he would. And so a great while she kept his commandment; till once, passing through a cruel wilderness as dark as pitch, her mouth so watered that she could not choose but ask him the question. And then he, making the grievousest complaints that would have melted a tree to have heard them, vanish'd quite away, and she lay down, casting forth as pitiful cries as any screech-owl. But having lain so, wet by the rain and burnt by the sun, five days and five nights, she gat up and went over many a high hill and many a deep river, till she came to an aunt's house of hers, and came and cried to her for help; and she for pity gave her a nut, and bade her never upon her nut till she was come to the extremest misery that ever tongue could speak of. And so she went, and she went, and ever rested the evening where she went in the morning, till she came to a second aunt, and she gave her another nut."

"Now good Mopsa," said the sweet Philoclea, "I pray thee at my request keep this tale till my marriage-day, and I promise thee that the best gown I wear that day shall be thine." Mopsa was very glad of the bargain, especially that it should grow a festival tale…"(II.14).

3D: Urania, Strephon, and Claius

[See entries in Appendix 2 for Urania, Strephon, Claius, Antaxius, Lacemon, and Lalus.] The *New Arcadia* (1590) and the 1593 *Arcadia* open with the shepherds Strephon and Claius on the Grecian shore looking out towards the island of Cithera, where Urania has gone. They console themselves by reflecting on the Platonic transformation their love has wrought on them: "Hath not the only love of her made us, being silly ignorant shepherds, raise up our thoughts above the ordinary level of the world, so as great clerks do not disdain our conference?" (I.1) They then discover Musidorus shipwrecked on the shore and take him to Lord Kalander's house. They have barely arrived there when a letter arrives from Urania, and upon reading it, the two shepherds leave at once. That, for all intents and purposes, is where their narrative breaks off in the *New Arcadia,* though Strephon and Claius later appear and lament the absent Urania ("Ye goat-herd gods" and "I joy in grief" [in the First and Second Eclogues, respectively, in the 1590 *New Arcadia;* in the Second Eclogues in 1593]).

The account of the origins of Strephon and Claius's love for Urania is delayed until the First Eclogues (of the 1593 *Arcadia;* the account does not appear in the 1590 *New Arcadia*), when Lamon tells "a shepherd's tale" of "a pair of friends":

> He, that the other in some years did pass,
>> And in those gifts that years distribute do,
>>> Was Claius call'd (ah, Claius, woeful wight!)
>
> . . . .
> Claius for skill of herbs and shepherd's art
>> Among the wisest was accounted wise,
> Yet not so wise as of unstained heart:
>> Strephon was young, yet marked with humble eyes
> How elder rul'd their flocks and cur'd their smart,
>> So that the grave did not his words despise.
>>> Both free of mind, both did clear dealing love,
>>> And both had skill in verse their choice to move.
>
> . . . .
>> While thus they liv'd (this was indeed a life)
> With nature pleas'd, content with present case,
>> Free of proud fears, brave begg'ry, smiling strife
> Of climb-fall court, the envy hatching place[,]
>
> . . . .
> One day (O day, that shin'd to make them dark!)
>
> . . . .
> They saw a maid who thitherward did run
>> To catch her Sparrow which from her did swerve,
> As she a black-silk cap on him begun
>> To set the foil of his milk-white to serve.

Urania captures her sparrow and binds him in the "ivory cage" of her breasts. Sighing and troubled, she sits down on the grass:

> She troubled was (alas that it might be!)
>> With tedious brawlings of her parents dear,
> Who would have her in will and word agree

To wed Antaxius their neighbour near.
A herdman rich, of much account was he,
   In whom no evil did reign, nor good appear.
      In some such one she lik'd not his desire,
      Fain would be free, but dreadeth parents' ire.
Kindly, sweet soul, she did unkindness take
   That bagged baggage of a miser's mud
Should price of her, as in a market make.

Gazing on the weeping Urania, Cupid aims at Claius and Strephon:

Claius straight felt, and groaned at the blow,
   And call'd, now wounded, purpose to his aid:
Strephon, fond boy, delighted, did not know
   That it was love that shin'd in shining maid.

Urania leaves, and Strephon quickly learns her name and haunt. His attentiveness pleases her parents "for simple goodness shined in his eyes," and he did not know himself to be in love—until one evening he and Claius, with Urania and other shepherds, play a rustic lover's game (allegorizing the lovers' dilemma), and then their "woe began." The elder Claius accepts the painful yoke of love, but does not realize that Strephon, too, bears this yoke until (while behind a bush) he overhears his love-complaint.

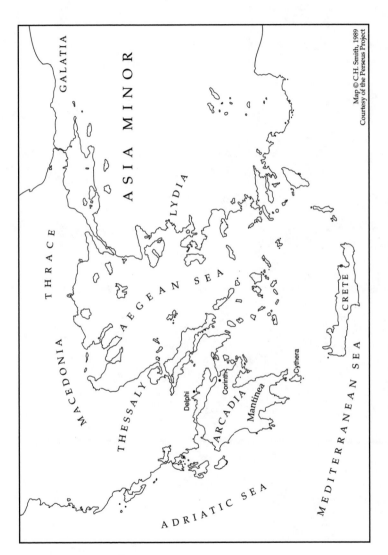

GALATIA

ASIA MINOR

THRACE

LYDIA

MACEDONIA

AEGEAN SEA

THESSALY

ARCADIA

Delphi

Corinth

Mantinea

Cythera

CRETE

ADRIATIC SEA

MEDITERRANEAN SEA

Map © C.H. Smith, 1989
Courtesy of the Perseus Project

MAP OF GREECE AND THE ANCIENT WORLD